THE SKILLS
OF SELLING

THE Skills OF Selling

ROGER W. SENG

A division of American Management Associations

Library of Congress Cataloging in Publication Data

Seng, Roger W
  Skills of selling.

  Bibliography: p.
  Includes index.
  1. Selling. I. Title.
  HF5438.25.S46   658.85   77-12040
  ISBN 0-8144-5458-5

Third Printing

TO MY MENTORS

Dorothy, Carolyn, and Beverly

PREFACE

Countless books and courses on selling are available, and more appear regularly. Moreover, trade and professional journals publish a steady stream of discerning articles on salesmanship. And nowadays most marketers of goods or services provide some formalized training for their sales people. With such an abundance of advice on how to sell already at hand, can there be justification for offering more?

Sales managers and trainers generally agree that sustained training in the skills of selling that is closely integrated with on-the-job practice produces the best results. Yet many companies that conduct intensive, if brief, sales training programs provide little follow-up training on the job. Why this inconsistency, in the face of general agreement that a skilled sales force exerts notably positive impact on an enterprise's success? And why do some companies assume that their sales people will learn how to sell well without any special training? The most commonly given reasons include:

Training budgets and staff are limited.
Customized sales training programs are expensive.
Sales force down time during training is costly.

The common denominator of all reasons for not training is usually cost, or cost effectiveness. There are situations, of course, in which cost objections are entirely justified and less expensive training alternatives are needed. Often overlooked, however, is the negative impact that hidden costs of *not* training can exert on a company's prosperity. A factor in these costs is the high turnover rate among sales people induced by lack of adequate training. The most promising young sales people won't wait around long today when their training needs aren't being met.

Nevertheless, few sales managers discount the desirability of deploying competent, well-trained sales people. And most field sales managers are delegated primary responsibility for training their own sales people. But many receive little assistance in handling this task for which they often feel ill prepared. As a result, countless thousands of potentially skillful sales people must rely largely on their own ingenuity in learning how to sell. Inevitably, many adopt inept techniques that limit their sales effectiveness.

During many years as a sales manager and sales training manager, I searched for practical, insightful books that could help sales people acquire the skills of selling through self-study, books that first-level sales managers could also use for training their own sales people. I found few books that can fill this need.

There is much literature on salesmanship that provides profound psychological insights valuable to skilled sales people and to sales trainers but that offers too rich a diet for those still learning the basics. And many books contain very interesting collections of inspiring anecdotes about sales successes chalked up by outstanding sales people in unique selling situations. But such books, while helpful, also bypass the more fundamental needs of those learning the basics — often mostly by trial and error. The primary objective of this book is to provide a systematic discourse that new sales people can follow as a guide for mastering the skills of selling, largely while on the job.

Paradoxically, selling is both simple and highly complex. It is simple in that the fundamental principles of good salesmanship are surprisingly few, virtually unchanging, and easy to understand when not fragmented into ambiguity. It is complex in that the real task of every sales person is to make those basic principles work *for him* in the context of the widely differing markets and customers with which he deals. Every sales person is also a unique individual having a broad range of personal attributes and abilities. The resulting interaction among infinitely variable selling situations and personalities provides both the challenge and the fascination of sales work.

Even highly skilled sales people can find it difficult at times to translate accepted principles of selling into positive results. This is even more difficult for the inexperienced who are still learning the inner workings of a business that is new to them. Typically, they have neither the time nor the patience for studying how to apply the finer points of theory to the problem of landing the next order from an important customer, particularly when the boss is pressing for results *now*.

Most sales people are outgoing by nature. They like working with other people; they're instinctively doers rather than analysts. And sales people welcome help in upgrading their selling abilities. But they want help that is clear and forthright, help they can apply readily with manifest effectiveness. Few sales people are innately dedicated students of the psychology of selling; most are kept too busy by their daily sales problems for in-depth study of the "reasons why." However, those who do resolutely delve into the complexities of this uniquely people-oriented skill can usually teach themselves to sell quite well.

This book strives to meld many of the already well-documented principles of good salesmanship into concepts that any sales person can readily apply. The approach used is orderly explanation with examples, analogies and questions intended to stimulate creative thought or discussion. For those most eager to sharpen their selling skills, learning exercises are provided for trying out some of the techniques. This kind of personal involvement helps turn new ideas into skills. And when study and practice can be reinforced by periodic exchange of ideas and experiences with peers, new sales people become productive still more quickly.

Experienced sales people usually don't need to be taught so much as they need to be reminded, but they too can find renewed motivation in these ideas. Personal satisfaction as well as skill reinforcement can result from reading a book like this and being able to say, "That's what I've been doing all along; but now I understand better why it works."

This book is prepared for use in three related, progressive ways:

1. It can be read primarily for its "how to" content about the skills of selling.
2. It can be studied by new sales people, who will benefit by carrying out the learning exercises.
3. It can be used as the basis for sales training courses conducted by line sales managers for their own sales people.

Guidelines for the second and third applications are provided in the section entitled "How to Use This Book."

This book concentrates on the functions of the "outside" sales person, although most of the principles examined apply to retail sales people as well. But the differences in customer relationships and selling environment in retail sales warrant separate treatment. Women and men both have full access to the exhilarating opportunities for personal success and satisfaction afforded by a career in selling. Wherever possible I have used terminology applying equally to women and to men, such as sales person and sales representative. Because of language limitations, however, the third-person singular pronoun "he" is sometimes the best word for the context.

I sincerely hope this book will help you sell better and enjoy it more.

Roger Seng

CONTENTS

HOW TO USE THIS BOOK   **1**

For a Self-Development Course in Selling / For a
Group Participation Sales Training Program

1   THE NATURE OF SELLING   **5**

The Changing Image of Selling / Selling: A Key
Social and Economic Function / Selling: Trigger for
Economic Growth / Impact of Our Market
Economy on Selling / Rewards of the Career Sales
Person / Basic Concepts of Professional Selling /
Creative Selling / How This Book Can Help You

**2   PRODUCT KNOWLEDGE – THE PRIME
SOURCE OF SELLING SKILL**   **21**

Product Knowledge / Features and Benefits /
Learning the Right Things About Products / Fea-
ture-Benefits Inventory / Knowledge About
Competitive Products / Information Supportive to
Product Knowledge / Summary Perspective on
Product Knowledge

**3   COMMUNICATING WELL – A CRITICAL SKILL
IN SELLING**   **47**

The Nature of Communication / The
Communication Process / Barriers to Communication / Summary on Sales Communication

4   PERSUASION — THE CORE OF THE SELLING PROCESS   **65**

The Selling Process / Selling a Problem-Solving Idea / Customer Buying Motives / The Selling– Buying Process / Origins of Idea Selling / Specifics of Idea Selling / Summary on Persuasive Selling

5   COPING WITH CUSTOMER RESISTANCE, OBJECTIONS, AND COMPLAINTS   **94**

Coping with Sales Resistance / Coping with Objections / Coping with Complaints and Claims

6   REINFORCING THE APPEAL OF SALES PRESENTATIONS   **129**

Display and Explain / Visual Props for Sales Talks / Demonstrations / Showmanship

7   COPING WITH COMPETITION   **147**

Competition: Genesis of the Selling Function / Strategy and Tactics of Competitive Selling / Coping with Price Competition / A Brief Anatomy of Pricing / Some Legal Aspects / The Unethical Buyer

8   PROBLEM SOLVING AS A SELLING SKILL   **169**

The Sales Person as a Manager / The Nature of Sales Problems / Problem Solving Starts with Sales Objectives / Developing Sales Objectives / Specifics of Problem Solving

9   TERRITORY MANAGEMENT AND PERSONAL DEVELOPMENT   **195**

Freedom to Succeed — or Fail / Territory Management / Prospecting for New Customers / Credit Considerations / Plan Your Work, Work Your Plan / Time Management / Continuing Self-Development

APPENDIX: THIRTY LEARNING EXERCISES   **215**

BIBLIOGRAPHY   **246**

INDEX   **247**

HOW TO USE
THIS BOOK

For a Self-development Course in Selling

This book focuses especially on those who are relatively new to selling who want to learn to sell more effectively and cope better with the complexities of their work. It includes suggestions for personal involvement that can contribute to converting ideas into practical skills. The Appendix provides a series of learning exercises to help learners absorb the meaning of selling ideas or acquire simulated experience in selling skills. In the text, there is a reference to each learning exercise immediately following the subject to which it relates.

Each learning exercise is presented in two parts. Part A is addressed to the individual sales person studying this book on his own or as guided by his supervisor. Part B contains suggestions for adapting the exercise for use in a group participation training session. This organization enables use of this book as a self-development sales training course, if desired. This provides unique advantages for sales representatives located far from headquarters and for those with few opportunities for meeting with sales managers and fellow sales people.

The format thus provides means for decentralized training of individual sales people. Sales managers using this method should provide their sales people with imaginative support. This means demonstrating willingness to help learners improve their skills, showing interest in their problems, offering suggestions for solving them, and commending learners for the progress they make. The best results are achieved when the manager helps each learner adapt the learning exercises to fit his own particular skill needs and the products or services he sells. Or each sales person can devise simple adaptations himself.

The manager reviews progress with the learner whenever suitable opportunity can be arranged. The manager should also personally amplify the selling ideas as presented to relate them more closely to the particular product or business involved. Personal coaching on how to improve sales call effectiveness can also be very instructive. When objectively sustained, this one-on-one training/learning relationship can be highly effective.

For a Group Participation Sales Training Program

Learning to sell—or how to sell better—is always more fruitful when the experience is shared with other learners. Seminar participants tend to help one another reach their common objectives. They exchange ideas, share experiences, help each other overcome difficulties, and applaud shared successes. A subtle spirit of competition also keeps each participant alert. And those who are more experienced gain satisfaction as well as reinforcement from being able to help others who are less advanced. This kind of friendly "forum on salesmanship" becomes a highly productive means of sales training, particularly when guided by an able, empathetic sales manager. His function is to contribute his own ideas and experiences, moderate and stimulate discussion of selling theory and practice, and conduct role-playing exercises designed to develop selling skills.

This book can be the vehicle for such a program. The seminar moderator—either sales manager or sales trainer—can make study and preparation assignments from the book, moving through the topics consecutively or selectively according to evidence of learner needs. The moderator can schedule training seminars as often as practical—covering during each session only as much material as can be dealt with successfully. Intervals between sessions should provide ample opportunity for homework as well as for on-the-job practice of the skills being learned. Additional reading from other books on selling can enrich the learning process.

The moderator should take pains to relate the *generic* message of the book to the *specific* sales problems of the learning group. For example, variations of the following question can launch constructive discussion of any critical topic: "How can we best apply this idea or skill to selling X product or service within our markets?" The moderator can modify Part B of each learning exercise to relate it more closely to selling situations actually faced. Other exercises fitting special needs can also be devised and conducted. In this way, the moderator can customize the book's content by showing how the ideas and skills examined can be transformed into practical results by members of the learner group.

No book can adequately treat *all* the specific selling functions of any one business. These can be explained only by insiders intimately familiar with that business. However, this book provides a framework for filling in those specifics. The sales manager or seminar moderator can introduce any topic needing amplification with words like these: "That subject as covered in the book relates closely to techniques we can use in selling X product or service. Let me first explain what I mean; then we'll open it up for discussion of your ideas."

The seminar moderator's preparation can be as simple or as elaborate as desired. A brief, penciled outline can suffice. And the moderator need not be an experienced sales trainer to lead an effective seminar on selling skills. The prime requirement for good results is that all involved have a sincere desire to learn—including the moderator.

Here are several suggestions for the moderator that may be helpful:

- Announce the "ground rules" at the outset: what you expect to accomplish, group involvement plans, time schedules, breaks permitted, etc.
- Read thoroughly beforehand the subject matter to be covered; plan how to lead discussion of those topics particularly relevant to the selling problems of your group.
- Early during each session, ask volunteers to comment on their experiences in applying the ideas examined during the last session. Stimulate discussion of the results re-

ported as well as of how the skills being learned can be polished.

— When introducing selling ideas related specifically to your business, present them positively and explain how they apply; then encourage discussion to ensure understanding.

— When a participant asks a question, direct it to others for response. Inject your own ideas only when the answers offered are inaccurate, inadequate, or misleading.

— Try to maintain balanced involvement. Some participants tend to monopolize the discussion; curtail their comments tactfully. Some are reluctant to contribute; ask for their ideas.

— Rotate role-playing assignments among participants so that all become involved.

— Stay on the track. Enthusiastic participants may overwork one topic or digress to others, thus wasting time. Bring the group back to your meeting plan whenever necessary.

— Summarize the selling ideas and skills covered during a session; schedule the next meeting at a time when all can attend.

To the sales manager who has never held sales training sessions like these, you'll find that they're not that difficult to conduct. Your sales people will like them and learn from them. And you'll enjoy the experience and learn from it too.

CHAPTER 1

THE NATURE
OF SELLING

All sales people should walk tall and straight because of their vocation. Selling – the action arm of marketing – has been one of the catalysts of the tremendous upsurge in living standards of the free Western world during the past century. Moreover, selling is now helping to increase the physical prosperity and to enlarge the cultural base of the developing nations as well. Sales work, at its best, is an agent for positive change in the quality of life. This is the prime fulfillment of selling as a function that both initiates and sustains service. Sales people are proclaimers of creative ideas that herald the good news of improved means being marketed for satisfying human needs. Conversely, sales people are also sources of ideas for the innovators constantly at work developing ways to relieve other human wants and needs. Startling concepts? Perhaps. But they are justified, as we'll demonstrate.

The growth of our American economy has been phenomenal beyond meaningful measure by any standards most of us can comprehend. Our creativity, productivity, personal conveniences, and cultural advantages coalesce into a way of life that is the envy of the rest of the world. Other nations try to emulate our growth as well as participate in our prosperity.

Although most of us are well aware of our fortunate condition, we seldom pause to consider *why* we happen to be so privileged. There are many underlying reasons. But paramount among them is the freedom of choice that prevails in our land as a key causative factor in the ongoing American Dream. For freedom of choice has created and sustains the social climate in which selling has become a powerful force. The work of sales people contributes significantly to America's economic vitality and cultural leadership.

Freedom of choice characterizes all aspects of American life and is safeguarded by our form of government. But our particular interest lies in the impact that freedom exerts on patterns of productivity and trade. Each of us is free to choose what to buy — or not buy — according to how we evaluate our needs and our resources. This creates competition for consumer favor among all who offer goods or services for sale. Competition generates effort to develop improved means of meeting consumer needs and preferences. Freedom of choice also creates opportunity for innovation in goods or services by those with visionary ideas. Those visionaries are motivated, in part, by the substantial rewards that historically have been in store for successful entrepreneurs. Competition also stimulates suppliers to offer their wares attractively and persuasively in order to favorably influence consumer choice. And the incentive of besting the competition contributes to the challenge of selling.

Challenge it is, indeed, because it is human nature to resist change. We are seldom eager to accept new things and new ways or to discard the old, even when doing so can be much to our advantage. We doubt; we question; we're comfortable with the old and suspicious of the new. Thus selling is always an uphill effort.

This was true even in the early days of our country when people had so little and needed so much. Developers of our railroads had a hard time selling the merits of the steam locomotive to a doubtful citizenry who didn't want to risk giving up the old ways of transportation for the uncertainties of the new "iron horse." The same was true for McCormick and his reaper, for Westinghouse and his air brakes, Edison and his electricity, Bell and his telephone, Howe and his sewing machine, Ford and his "horseless carriage," and many, many others. That same characteristic human resistance to change still obstructs progress today, and it is still being overcome by visionary people who are also masters of persuasion.

During our earlier periods of growth, the entrepreneurs often had to personally demonstrate and sell their revolutionary ideas in order to gain grudging public acceptance. They often employed schemes that utilized showmanship to bring attention to the possibilities of their new devices. For example, Peter Cooper raced his tiny locomotive "Tom Thumb" against a horse to dramatize the potential of railroad cars drawn by steam engines. Besides the drag of suspicion, doubt, and inertia, the resistance to new ideas often has an economic origin—the substantial investment at stake in established methods. So the values and advantages represented by new methods have to be sold over and over again. This is as true today as when our country was new.

Obviously, those early entrepreneurs possessed many talents. Fortunately, their modern-day counterparts are still creating and heralding new ideas. But as our country and its economy developed and as our productive organizations became larger, selling became a separate function providing opportunity for people with special abilities. However, the broad social sway of selling remains unchanged—proclaiming how people's wants and needs can be satisfied with means at hand today as well as helping uncover new ways to realize still more dreams tomorrow. And the energizing force behind it all is that ever potent freedom of choice.

The Changing Image of Selling

Sales people occasionally suffer needlessly from poor self-image. Here and there a few reflect feelings that their chosen vocation is somehow not quite worthy. When asked what they do for a living, some reply, "Oh, I'm just a salesman," in a faintly apologetic way. Others imply somewhat uneasily that they settled on a career in selling because no "better" options were open to them. What a negative reason for undertaking an occupation so inherently positive in orientation.

Whenever this vaguely defensive attitude about selling appears, it usually isn't difficult to identify some of the false notions that have fostered it. We've all heard legends about the colorful "drummers" of days long gone by whose sales tactics weren't always honorable by today's standards and who were sometimes personally objectionable as well. Then there were the "Yankee peddlers" who traveled about by horse and wagon purveying miscellaneous necessities to rural America. Barter was often the basis of their trade, because people had little money. Many peddlers became shrewd bargainers and sometimes outsmarted their unsuspecting customers. But they did perform a much-needed service. They were even a welcome source of news and entertainment on their overnight stops. Unpalatable characteristics as well as unethical practices still persist today in some sales people — as they do in some people in every other occupation.

In the main, however, selling has matured into a vital business function with strong overtones of social benefit. Past images no longer prevail. The vast majority of today's sales people exhibit a high degree of professionalism, and the transformation continues apace. Some who remain only dimly aware of the service implications of their vocation are nonetheless motivated by other creditable challenges into steadily upgrading their selling skills. As they come to perceive and practice more fully the privilege that is theirs for contributing to the well-being of others, the success and satisfaction they gain from selling will steadily increase.

The lingering doubts about personal image still harbored by some sales people probably reflect blind spots in their perspective of the true stature of selling in our twentieth-century world. For others, they may reflect feelings of inferiority fostered by repeated rejection by customers who choose not to buy. For new sales people, this rejection can be a very real occupational hazard. But it is surmountable and can even be turned to advantage, as we'll explore later. First, let's review some of the contributions sales work makes to the well-being of mankind.

Selling: A Key Social and Economic Function

Surprisingly, many sales people are not adequately aware of the fundamental position of sales work within the framework of productive enterprise in the free world. As a result, they sometimes don't fully understand and value their own "reason for being." This inhibits the ego satisfaction that, when nourished, can contribute so much to personal productivity and success. Given moderate external support, the self-esteem of sales people becomes self-generating because of the nature of their work. But some employers tend to ignore the motivating power of making sure that their sales people understand the major part they play in the success of the enterprise and that this contribution is valued. A strong sense of personal pride in being identified with a worthy, people-oriented organization that supplies utilities needed and valued by many is far more effective in generating enthusiastic sales effort than any number of sales pep talks.

THE PRIMARY FUNCTIONS OF PRIVATE ENTERPRISE

Every profit-oriented enterprise must embrace three primary, interdependent functions. It must (1) create a product or service, (2) sell that product or service to those who need it, and (3) finance the entire operation successfully.

This three-part foundation is characteristic of all productive ventures in our free enterprise system. It also prevails among most privately supported institutions that provide services to the public. Furthermore, these three basic functions must be maintained in good balance for any given undertaking to succeed. Diminished effectiveness of any one of the functions can bring about collapse of the entire business or service organization.

It is an interesting exercise to examine whether this organizational triad exists in every enterprise that markets a product or service. On cursory review, this pattern may not always seem to fit. But it is virtually impossible to find any business or private agency serving people to which this analogy doesn't apply. Try it. For a manufacturer, the application is readily apparent: a factory makes a product; sales people sell it; financing for the whole operation is generated by selling stock and perhaps by borrowing funds as well. The parallel is scarcely less obvious for a bank. Here the "products" created are loans and other types of financial services. The loans are "sold" (negotiated) by loan officers; financing is obtained from stock sold, funds on deposit, interest received on outstanding loans and from other resources.

For variation, apply this reasoning to an educational institution — a private college. Here the marketable utility created consists of knowledge or learning — an education. These "products" are "sold" through the functioning of admissions officers and field agents, through course catalogs and other literature, and even by the president of the college through public speeches and other community activities. Financing is derived from tuition payments, endowment income, fund drives, grants, and other sources.

Can you imagine any of the foregoing types of enterprise surviving for long *without* the input of an effective sales function no matter what it is called? Furthermore, each enterprise must also be managed profitably in order to generate the continuing flow of funds needed to pay costs of operation, of innovation to meet new needs, of expansion when justified, and of taxes as well as to pay "rent" for the funds invested in the business. But the need for profit is another story that we'll return to later.

Apply this analogy to other types of business. If you're involved in a sales-related function, can you identify this pattern within your own organization? This test proves valid for every profit-oriented productive enterprise. Removing any one of the three basic functions cripples its reason for being. It can no longer create or perform a service that provides people with needed benefits.

SELLING: THE SUSTAINING FORCE OF PRIVATE ENTERPRISE

It is apparent that in sales work you are in the forefront of a vital function of whatever productive venture you represent. You are the venture's agent in its interaction with the sector of society that it serves. The success of your selling effort is indispensable to the health and growth of your organization — sometimes even to its survival. In turn, its prosperity is a requisite for realizing its social purposes. All this responsibility is seldom settled on one person alone; it is usually shared by a great many people, each carrying out his or her own special phase of the overall marketing function. But your individual performance is no less important to accomplishing the objectives of the enterprise.

This view of the marketing/selling function detracts not one iota from the major contributions of those whose ingenuity and skills combine to develop and produce needed goods and services in such abundance. Nor does it diminish the importance of maintaining a sound financial structure and good business controls in order to assure continuity and growth. Sales people, however, create justification and outlet for the productivity of an enterprise by persuading the consumers to try, to buy, and to use. Without the sustaining contribution of sales work, the expertise of those whose functions are to produce and to finance would be fruitless.

Turn to Learning Exercise No. 1 in Appendix.

Selling: Trigger for Economic Growth

An astute sales manager once said, "Nothing happens until somebody sells something"—an expression so meaningful it is repeated over and over again. Consider the rippling effect of the forces set in motion whenever you make a sale. The people in the chain between you and the source of the product or service you have sold are put to work. So are those who create and deliver the product or perform the service. Those involved in financing and accounting carry out their contingent functions. Suppliers of component materials or contributory services are also activated, thus setting off still more waves of productive energy.

The stimulus as well as the focal point of all this creativity is the act of supplying something of utility and value needed by the customer to whom you made the sale. Multiplied infinitely, selling initiates the employment, productivity, and earnings that bring about economic growth and prosperity for us all. This process in turn supports and stimulates the cultural development of our society as well. Quite a payoff from that freedom of choice we value so highly but sometimes take for granted.

BUSINESS ENTERPRISE MUST SERVE TO SURVIVE

The socioeconomic order of our free world nurtures continued existence only for those enterprises able to supply the types of goods and services that keep pace with the burgeoning needs of society. This is another truth about selling that is often overlooked. Businesses thrive and survive as social and economic institutions only so long as they serve our society constructively. Those that cannot meet this test by adjusting to ever changing demands do not long endure. Witness the decline or demise of many businesses that were thriving half a century ago or even more recently; note also the recurring eclipse of some enterprises and launching of new ones. Those buggy whip makers who didn't convert to producing automobile sparkplugs or other products are a fast-fading memory.

As a sales person, your primary function is to seek out and supply *current customer needs* for the products or services you sell. But it is also your function to be ever watchful for *changes in their needs* or in their customers' needs—changes that can bring about mutations among the utilities they'll be seeking in the future. How well you foresee and interpret future customer needs to your employer will not only have an impact on your personal success but can be a critical factor in your employer's continuing prosperity as well.

The following quotation from *The Royal Bank of Canada Monthly Letter* may help bring this concept into clearer focus:

> An opportunity in business consists of certain conditions which, if detected and handled properly by the right person, may be made to yield a profit or win a promotion.
>
> Business exists to supply people's wants, and these wants are insatiable. Every one gratified gives birth to two more wants, thus new opportunities are endless. New trends and new goods come into being; unusual happenings offer unexpected opportunities.
>
> Consider Thomas A. Edison's coup. In 1862 he was a Detroit newsboy of 15. A report of a battle appeared in a newspaper. Edison bought a thousand copies on credit, hopped on a train, sold the papers at railroad stops for 25¢ a copy, and finished the day with $250 in his pocket, representing several hundred percent profit. He detected a

public want, he determined to satisfy it, he invested capital, and he went to work.*

Reflected in this fascinating episode are all the functions essential for a viable business. Edison first identified a human want—in this case up-to-the-minute battlefield news of the Civil War. To satisfy that want, he:

Financed his "business"—on credit.
Implemented a service satisfying that want.
Sold that service—profitably.

This interesting account also characterizes the vision, creativity, and initiative that are needed to become a good sales person—qualities possessed by many noted inventors and industrialists as well, as exemplified by Edison.

Impact of Our Market Economy on Selling

Selling has matured only gradually into the stature it enjoys today in response to demands of markets that have become progressively more selective. A century ago the basic wants of people in the Western world were still so widely unmet that primary emphasis in business and industry was on production and distribution. Little genuine selling was necessary after initial customer resistance to novel but sorely needed goods had been overcome. Buyers then clamored to be supplied, and this sometimes led to abuses.

However, the basic needs of today's affluent society have been largely satisfied. And technology continues to create an amazing array of competing goods and services that have become abundantly available. Society employs and enjoys the utilities and benefits of all the countless wares now available. But society has also quite properly become highly selective. Having such a wide range of choice, buyers now insist on learning *which* goods and services are *most* beneficial in order to make intelligent buying decisions.

* "A Wise Person's Opportunities," *The Royal Bank of Canada Monthly Letter*, September 1975.

Thus the "market economy" has evolved, in which the discriminating dictates of customer need and satisfaction determine what will be produced and used as well as what will be discarded. This has engendered need for a high order of salesmanship capable of discerning customers' true needs and recommending the most constructive means of satisfying them. Such sales people must understand fully both the functions and advantages of their products or services and their limitations. In such a market climate, accomplished, professional sales people are much esteemed and much in demand. Not only do customers' doors open for them more readily, but doors of opportunity open upward for them within their own organizations, if they choose that route to self-realization.

Accompanying the steady shift from a production economy to today's more characteristic market economy has been a corresponding shift in the career backgrounds of those who reach high levels in business management. More and more market-oriented managers are reaching the top. Why? Because skill in discerning the most pressing wants and needs of people, as well as in devising the most suitable means of supplying them, often outweighs know-how in production or finance in terms of critical importance to viability of the enterprise. And managers skilled in marketing are likely to have started their careers as sales people.

Rewards of the Career Sales Person

Fortunately, not every sales person wants to become an upper-echelon business manager, because there wouldn't be enough openings to go around. There are many dedicated career sales people who simply love to sell and feel that selling is their niche in life. They obtain a great deal of satisfaction from daily interaction with the customers they serve and the close personal friendships they develop with many of them. Capable career sales people are also usually quite well rewarded. Depending on their relative personal abilities and the industries in which they sell, the most accomplished often find they can earn almost as much as those who reach upper management levels — sometimes even more — and certainly with many fewer headaches. Surveys have shown that the average sales person earns more than the average employee of like education in other sectors of private enterprise.

One of the attractions of sales work for many is the opportunity it provides for "being one's own boss." A sales career is made to order for people with initiative who thrive on setting their own goals and then working to achieve them. This is the nearest situation to being in business for oneself—but with the advantage that others supply the products or services to be sold and finance the selling effort. That's a fine arrangement for the energetic and ambitious; for the lazy, it's disaster. Those do best who learn early to manage their sales activities as they would a business of their own. Indeed, for some the experience gained from selling provides the confidence and impetus needed for starting enterprises of their own. Many are the entrepreneurs in business and industry who rise from the ranks of successful sales people.

Basic Concepts of Professional Selling

It has long been debated—quite inconclusively—whether selling classifies as a profession. The outcome is largely a matter of definition and isn't very important to us. What is scarcely debatable is that there are a great many sales people who qualify as professionals. A dictionary definition of a professional is "one having great skill or experience in a particular field or activity." And that's what this book is intended to help you learn as well as practice: the arts and skills of professional selling.

We have been stressing the theme that there are certain basic concepts that should be absorbed into the very marrow of one's bones in order to sell well and enjoy it too. The arts and skills of selling begin to unfold and become easier to master for those who have come to understand and accept those concepts. Many authorities recommend breaking down the selling process into a series of sequential steps that lead to landing an order. Unquestionably there are specific techniques that contribute to making a sale. We'll study and practice some of them, because they do help. Selected how-to formulas for selling effectively have considerable merit when kept in perspective. But learning certain routines for customer prospecting or for selling by the rules isn't nearly as important as assimilating the fundamental concepts of good selling into your personal philosophy.

You are then prepared to develop *your own* selling techniques based on your perception of each selling situation and evaluation of the needs of each customer involved. You can then absorb into your selling style selective adaptations of sales strategies and tactics that others have demonstrated can work well. Following are previews of some of the fundamental concepts; they are explored in more depth in succeeding chapters.

SERVICE

Of prime importance is the concept that selling is a service-oriented vocation. This has already been emphasized, but we'll be exploring it much more because good customer service is an indispensable standard of good selling. The scope of sales-related service encompasses helping customers uncover their wants and needs realistically and supplying those needs fairly and satisfactorily after obtaining adequate assurance of their ability to pay. This concept precludes any perversion of the selling function that involves deception or fraud. Such deviations have no place in the kind of sales activities and customer relationships advocated in this book.

PRODUCT KNOWLEDGE

In order to serve their customers well, sales people must possess thorough knowledge of the products or services they sell so as to relate them readily and accurately to the wants and needs of customers. This calls for a particular kind of product knowledge that focuses more on *why* the product is made available than on how it is made. We shall discover that this distinction is quite important. Also, those sales people who acquire an almost proprietary feeling of pride in their products or services — their quality, unique characteristics, superior performance — have a distinct advantage in selling. This attitude often emerges as an infectious enthusiasm for their wares, which is sensed by wavering prospects and customers and tends to encourage them to buy.

FEATURES AND BENEFITS

The importance of possessing the right kind of product knowledge comes into focus quickly in the light of the features and benefits concept of selling. This holds that customers buy a product not so much for what it *is* as for what they become convinced it *can do for them*. Thus the features of a product or service must be translated into the benefits it affords customers in order to persuade them to buy. The features are those special characteristics that make the product desirable for reasons meaningful to buyers or users. Customers want to know, in effect, "What's in it for me if I buy it?"

GOOD COMMUNICATION

The right kind of product knowledge — the creative ideas substantiating how customers can use a product or service to their best advantage — must be conveyed to customers in convincing terms that they can readily understand and accept. This calls for articulate *explanation* and *persuasion* so structured that all ideas are expressed at the right time, in the right order, and with the right emphasis. This involves study and practice of the techniques of effective two-way communication as they relate to each individual prospect's capacity to comprehend.

A FAIR EXCHANGE

Another critical concept is that every sale should constitute a fair exchange between buyer and seller. This means an exchange of values that are well balanced; in other words, the transaction results in benefits and advantages for both. If the scales are tipped unduly in either direction, one of the parties is very likely not getting a fair deal, and the concept of service as a factor in selling no longer prevails. The sale/purchase transaction can thus be viewed as a matter of negotiating to arrive at a fair balance between the utilities, services, and values that are exchanged between buyer and seller, This is worlds removed from the superficial attitude of some that selling consists of talking people into buying something they may neither want nor need.

Turn to Learning Exercise No. 2 in Appendix.

Creative Selling

Sales people who apply these fundamental concepts most constructively and consistently practice creative selling. They strive to help their customers solve their problems. This requires them to study and understand their customers, their objectives, aspirations, frustrations, special interests, and even their deficiencies in order to accurately identify their real needs. Their ultimate purpose is to satisfy customer needs through appropriate use of their products or services in a sincere spirit of service.

Every sales person can readily uncover ample opportunity for being creative — from the route man making seemingly routine sale-delivery calls to the account executive negotiating sale and installation of complex equipment or services. This is the most personally satisfying form of selling, and it tends to be the most rewarding monetarily. Service has a way of benefiting both server and served. At the highest levels — such as selling complex computer systems — creative sales people become virtual consultants to their customers. Customers learn to rely on their expertise, their judgment, and their honesty to help them evaluate their needs and devise optimal solutions for their problems involving use of the sophisticated equipment or software systems the sales people sell. Consummation of the sale — the closing — is often anticlimactic in such enlightened selling/buying relationships.

Professional, creative sales people become skilled in all facets of the selling process. They engage in activities such as prospecting for customers, sales planning, sales solicitation, efficient territory management, and good control of their time. They become masters of good communication, which includes the arts of persuasion. They realize that every sale they make constitutes a purchase for the customer. So they study not only the steps to a sale but also the steps involved in the purchasing process. This enables them to time the successive phases of their selling efforts for maximum effectiveness when the customer is most receptive.

No one can teach you to do all these things well; but you can learn how to do them well if you know why and how to try and are willing to work at it. This book provides guidelines for the why and the how, but you must provide the personal motivation.

ACQUIRING CREATIVE SELLING SKILLS

This brings us to another highly important concept — that is, creative selling skills can be learned. In fact, that's the only way they can be acquired. The old saw that "salesmen are born and not made" does not apply at the levels of professionalism we're considering here. Naturally, it helps to have a built-in liking for people and a knack for getting along with them. But don't those characteristics apply in the main to most people you know — including yourself? And most of us also have a sense of reserve where human relationships are concerned. This can be an asset in selling — not a liability.

People relate best to other people who seem to be much like themselves. That seldom includes the expansive, overvoluble sales person who tries to sell by bluff and bluster rather than by knowledge and skill. This person usually doesn't wear very well for very long and seldom makes it to the top. Ability to sell creatively and with professional skill can be acquired by any average, well-motivated person by study and practice — the same as ability is acquired in any other field.

How This Book Can Help You Sell Better

It has been pointed out that the primary purpose of this book is to help you learn principles rather than procedures. The fundamentals of persuasion are well-nigh universal and unchanging. They were discovered and formulated by the ancients, and they're applicable to whatever you sell. The methods and techniques involved vary infinitely, however: by product or service, by business or industry, by customer classification, by trade practice, even by legislative requirements, and by numerous other bases of comparison. Accordingly, we'll concentrate on explaining the fundamentals as clearly as possible. But we'll also suggest guidelines for procedures and techniques you can adapt to selling your own particular product or service.

There is no provision within this framework for a collection of tales about how *other* sales people have used unique techniques with notable success in selling various products or services in difficult situations. Such examples are always interesting and impressive, but they're also always difficult for most sales people to relate meaningfully to their own very different products that they sell under altogether different circumstances. Instead, we'll encourage you to study and absorb the fundamentals. At the same time, we'll provide guidelines and learning exercises designed to help you develop *your own* techniques for applying the fundamentals with your own products or services within your own selling situations.

The performances of skilled professional sales people are often so smooth that even knowledgeable observers find it difficult to identify the specific principles and techniques they employ. And such sales people are themselves often hard pressed to explain precisely how they do it. They subtly blend use of one principle or technique into another, often returning to reinforce a prior point or step as they sense the need for strengthening some phase of progress toward landing an order. No two selling performances are ever quite the same; nor is there ever just one right way to make a sale.

To help you sell better, however, we do have to take the process apart somewhat clinically for study and practice. The principles and techniques examined separately in the chapters that follow are not necessarily in order of importance. However, we do give early attention and emphasis to those selling skills considered to be most critical. Your challenge is to synthesize them into a practical selling pattern that works effectively for you. And that pattern is likely to vary somewhat with every customer you sell and with every sale you make. But then that's what makes a career in selling so fascinating.

PRODUCT KNOWLEDGE – THE PRIME SOURCE OF SELLING SKILL

CHAPTER 2

The essence of the task of all sales people is finding prospects to whom they can sell goods or services that satisfy identifiable customer needs. This capsulizes the planning/action/results sequence of the selling process, each phase of which contributes to a mutually advantageous outcome. Success of the process is contingent on the result it produces for the customer. Consummation of a sale *must* satisfy some want or need the customer regards as important or desirable. Otherwise, any desirable aspects of the sale from the seller's point of view are likely to prove deceptive and transitory.

Thus the starting point for planning and carrying out any selling effort consists of formulating the results and satisfactions that the sale can create for the customer. This involves discerning what the product or service *can do for the customer.* From this emerges the unifying theme of every phase of selling: establishing precisely how a product or service can benefit any given customer and then communicating this to him persuasively enough to induce him to buy. So it is logical to begin study of the selling process by examining the kinds of things a sales person needs to know about a product in order to sell it.

Let's pause briefly to define one item of terminology. Vendible products or services can be infinitely variable, very simple or highly complex. They can be tangible or intangible. They can consist of merchandise, commodities, manufactured goods or equipment, real estate, investments, services – to mention a few of the more obvious categories. Or they can be concepts that – when "sold" – generate sales of goods or services actually closed by others. The critical criteria in every case are the utilities and values that the wares or ideas sold represent to buyers. The selling process involves essentially the same basic concepts and techniques regardless of what one sells. So, for the sake of simplicity and consistency, please accept the term "product," whenever used alone, as being synonymous with whatever your particular stock-in-trade happens to be.

Product Knowledge

Good product knowledge is an indispensable asset in sales work. Skill in communication and persuasion, self-assurance, and all the other attributes usually associated with superior selling skill prove ineffectual unless you can explain your product and its function in terms meaningful to potential customers. Even inexperienced or inept sales people are likely to land some orders if they are well informed about their products and their uses. But superb selling skills—although valuable to top performers—cannot compensate for lack of adequate product knowledge.

WHAT KIND OF PRODUCT KNOWLEDGE?

Some authorities on selling maintain that it is impossible for sales people to know too much about the products they sell. This can be quite true, but only with respect to knowledge of those things about a product that are important to customers. This critical qualification brings into focus the *features and benefits* concept of selling. What this means is that to sell a product, a sales person needs to know well *only* those particulars about how a product is made, its composition or components, finishes, functions, clauses, provisions, and so on, that have some bearing on how it performs—*what it does for a customer*. All else about that product may be nice to know or useful for other purposes, but is of little value for selling the product effectively.

It follows that it is shortsighted for sales people to devote much time and effort to learning a mass of particulars about a product, its functions, and how it is manufactured or created, unless they also learn how each of those particulars affects product performance. You must always answer your customers' key question: *"What will this do for me?"* even though it may not be verbalized openly. Thus the measure of relevance of any product feature is how it benefits the customer. Absorbing this concept thoroughly and learning how to apply it fruitfully are vital to selling successfully. So we'll explore this skill in some depth to establish a good foundation for examining other aspects of selling—including the persuasive skills.

Features and Benefits

Sales people sometimes confuse product features with their corresponding customer benefits. Or they're inclined to think it's not very important to distinguish between the two. Some say, in effect, "Why not just tell a prospective customer all you can remember about *either* product features *or* benefits?" Let's zero in on what these terms mean and why the way you interpret and apply this concept in selling makes a difference.

A *feature* is a desirable characteristic that is inherent in the product or in its performance; often a feature is "built in" because of the specific value it represents to customers. Features may be described in terms of size, weight, composition, color, finish, texture, durability, function, performance, yield, or any combination of these and other distinctive properties. A product is likely to possess many features, which, taken together, comprise its characteristics. In short, the features of a product distinguish what the product *is*.

Some examples: One *feature* of a *pencil* may be that it contains a strong, fine-grained lead that is unusually free of abrasive impurities. One *feature* of an *office copier* may be that it can print on both sides of the same sheet of paper. Or, less tangible, a principal *feature* of a *truck leasing service* may be a provision for buying a customer's present fleet of trucks and then leasing new ones back to him for a monthly charge.

All of these features may appear to be good selling points, and indeed they are. So you may ask, "Then aren't the features of my product just what I need to know in order to sell it?" The answer can be only a qualified yes, because communicating only this much product knowledge is seldom enough to make a sale. This is because in an absolute sense *people don't buy a product for its features.* They buy what the features of a product will do for them. They buy to solve problems or fill needs. A product and its features are only means to those ends. What people seek when they buy are solutions and satisfactions. These can be translated as benefits.

A *benefit* is a definable advantage, improvement, or satisfaction customers acquire or experience that derives from a feature of the product they buy. Benefits may be described in terms of gain, profit, savings of time or money, convenience, performance, pride, safety, satisfaction, or any combination of these and a host of other advantages that are important to customers. These are terms that are useful for describing what a product *does* — what it accomplishes for buyer or user. It merits repeating that, in the main, features describe *what a product is,* while benefits describe *what a product does* — the results it produces. And the results are the most meaningful to a customer. Occasionally a feature is virtually indistinguishable from its benefits, but this fortunate circumstance is usually an exception. Also, such a feature generally offers other potential benefits that are not so readily apparent.

The wisdom of crystallizing for a customer the benefits a product represents was expressed very succinctly in an issue of *The Royal Bank of Canada Monthly Letter:*

> Knowing how to appeal to customers through their particular wants is the secret of successful selling. People buy things, not for the things themselves but for the service those things perform. . . . There is a bonus value if you can send the customer away with a lively anticipation of enjoying what he has purchased. The customer has not bought a suit, but his appearance in it; he has not bought a vehicle, but a car of prestige; he has not bought professional service, but freedom from trouble. An advertising agency advised shoe stores: "To women, don't sell shoes — sell lovely feet!"*

Now let's reconsider the examples given above. This time

* "Finding and Keeping Customers," *The Royal Bank of Canada Monthly Letter,* July 1976.

we'll state the feature first and follow it with some of the corresponding benefits a customer might experience in each case.

The pencil

Feature: This pencil contains a strong, fine-grained lead that is unusually free of abrasive impurities.

Benefit: This pencil writes more smoothly, making distinct lines that are easy to read, and it doesn't snag the surface of the paper. Because it doesn't need sharpening so often, it lasts longer.

Office copier

Feature: One advantage of this office copier is that it can print on both sides of the same sheet of paper.

Benefit: This can cut your copy paper costs in half. It also saves handling and mailing expense. It can even reduce filing space requirements. Considering your present volume of one-side copy work, this new copier can save you at least $___ per month for copy paper alone. This amount will increase when other related savings possibilities are factored in.

Truck leasing service

Feature: An important feature of our truck leasing plan is that we buy your present fleet of trucks and then lease new ones back to you for a flat monthly charge.

Benefit: This can release for other uses the capital you now have invested in trucks. It eliminates your truck maintenance problems and costs because we take care of maintenance for you. And we keep you supplied with operable equipment at all times; this means no down time for repairs and no idle drivers on your payroll. Considering the number of trucks now in your fleet, this plan could free as much as $___ of capital for other purposes. The plan should also save you at least $___ in operating costs each month. To this you can add the profit potential represented by the capital freed for other investment.

Keep in mind that there may be a number of applicable benefits generated by the impact of a single product feature on any given customer's particular problem or need. Additional benefits could result from *each* feature cited in the examples above. And only one feature was given for each of the example products although more could be readily identified.

FEATURES – ADVANTAGES – BENEFITS

Some eminent authorities on selling insert an intermediate step in this process — *advantages*. That is, features generate advantages, which result in benefits. Advantages is used here to denote the potential improvement in customers' circumstances brought about by buying or using the product — in relation to their prior status or perhaps in comparison with performance obtainable from a competitive product. Advantages lead to customer benefits. This refinement in reasoning does have merit. When it can be used appropriately, it is well worth adopting by sales people seeking to polish their selling techniques. In most usage, however, advantages constitute a subdivision of benefits. For our present purpose, it seems more instructive to concentrate on clarifying the simpler and more universal concept of feature-benefits selling.

FEATURES DO NOT SELL THEMSELVES

Perhaps you can see better now why merely describing the product and its characteristics is not enough. If you relate only product features, you're shortchanging your prospective customer as well as yourself on the most persuasive part of your selling message. It's tempting to concentrate on all the unique features of a product. Often, that's what a sales person knows best about it — its dazzling beauty, its amazing intricacy, its fabulous functions, its providential provisions and so on. It is also tempting for the seller to dwell with pride and enthusiasm on all the marvels of what the product *is*. Those wondrous particulars can even be memorized for ready playback in a sales talk.

But prospective customers may be turned off by such a recital — especially if it stops with the features. Their attitude is likely to be, "So what? Why should I be impressed by all these meaningless superlatives?" If you want to sell these customers, you'd better include the benefits: customize what the product *does* specifically *for them*. That's what it takes to motivate them into thinking seriously about buying.

BUT AREN'T THE BENEFITS OBVIOUS?

Sales people sometimes take it for granted that their prospects just naturally understand and appreciate all the benefits of a product. After all, aren't benefits the self-evident results of all those outstanding features? The answer is no. As a sales person, you can be expected to know all about your product; it's part of your job to be well informed. But your customers don't have this advantage; they haven't had your training; they need you to explain and translate for them the results they can expect from all those notable product properties. Product features are also most likely to be tangible; they can be observed, felt, or experienced. Benefits, on the other hand, are often intangible; they require explanation or interpretation to bring into proper perspective their merit and value to your customers.

At best, it's risky to assume your customers will draw the right conclusions unaided; they may overlook entirely the points most beneficial to them. At worst, they may misinterpret the features completely. Results: no sale made; no service performed; no commission, bonus, or sales credit for you.

CUSTOMER WANTS AND NEEDS

Another major consideration is that customer wants and needs vary. Your product may be largely uniform even though offered in several models or with special modifications available to broaden its utility and appeal. Your prospective customers, however, are anything but uniform. Their problems, wants, needs, and special interests are likely to be quite diverse. It follows that not every feature of a product appeals equally to every customer. Some features are much more attractive than others in relation to the situation of each customer. Thus a random recitation of *all* product features is not apt to be overwhelmingly effective. This might be likened to hunting with buckshot when rifle accuracy is needed.

Targeted selling calls for selecting the unique product features and their corresponding benefits that zero in on the special needs of one prospective customer. This adds another dimension to the feature-benefits concept of selling. Intelligent sales people who are well informed about a product can usually narrate its features fairly fluently. But if they haven't done any preliminary probing of their prospect's needs, they may be hard pressed to tailor product benefits on the spot to fit the distinctive requirements of that particular prospect. Doing that well requires creative forethought and sales planning. This is the sort of preparation that distinguishes a notably successful sales person from one who's merely mediocre. This is also perhaps the most telling reason why "canned" sales talks are usually only moderately effective. Standardized sales pitches are focused on the "average" customer — one who never really exists.

TRANSLATING FEATURES INTO BENEFITS

We've seen that product features and benefits are inextricably linked in a cause-and-effect relationship. We've also observed that benefits don't speak for themselves and that they're not equally meaningful to every customer. It is your function to study each customer and translate *selected* product features into the benefits that can fill *his* needs or solve *his* problems.

There are two relatively direct ways of making this translation so that the cause-and-effect relationship becomes manifest to your prospective customer. One way is to employ expressions like *"this means for you"* as a transition clause. To do this you first describe the feature, follow with a transition phrase, and then go on to state the benefit. Here are some uncomplicated examples:

> Mr. Manufacturer, this new reinforced plastic sheet is as strong as the metal sheet you're now using for your appliance casings. It can be shaped with your present dies, yet it weighs only half as much as the sheet metal and costs a third less. *This means for you* a substantial savings in raw material costs plus the economies of easier handling. Besides, you won't need all new tooling to make the changeover to that improved model mixer you'd like to get on the market quickly. And these advantages will be attractive to *your* customers as well — especially if the savings might make it possible to effect some reduction in selling prices. This will help both you and your customers to be more competitive.

Another example:

> Mr. Warehouse Manager, our new line of perforated steel shelving enables rapid adjustment of the spacing between shelves by using only simple tools. *This means for you* handy flexibility for stocking multisized, odd-shaped packages of merchandise without wasting space. You can readily enlarge or contract space needs for special-size items as inventory requirements change. And the perforated steel shelves reduce dead load on your building structure as well. This can help you adhere to that stringent new building code requirement without sacrificing warehouse capacity. Also, because of their special design, our lighter-weight steel shelves can support heavier loads than other types of shelves.

Note in each example that some benefits focus on a specific problem for which the sales person has learned the prospect is seeking a solution.

Another way to make this translation reverses the pattern by using words like *"that's because"* as a connecting phrase. When using this method, you state the customer benefit first, follow with "that's because," and then go on to describe the product feature that makes the benefit possible. Here are two simple examples of this technique:

> Mr. Architect, by including this new mineral fiber insulation blanket in your design you'll save your client as much as 40 percent on fuel bills and 15 percent on air conditioning costs. This will help reduce that building operating budget your client says is getting out of hand. *That's because* this product has a very high insulating value against heat loss as demonstrated by laboratory tests, which I can document. Also, this adds to the fire safety of the building; *that's because* mineral fibers will not burn – a plus factor that helps reduce insurance costs as well.

Another example:

> Mr. Executive, establishing your own private air transport service will help you achieve that increase you're seeking in the effectiveness of your management team. At the same time it will

conserve their energies and reduce overall travel expenditures. *That's because* our fast new business jets will enable your key managers to make one-day round trips to many of your hard-to-reach operating locations that now require several days of tiring, expensive travel.

Again, note that certain benefits described in the examples are customized to apply to already-known, specific needs of the particular prospects.

Many variations of these techniques are possible. With experience, you will develop your own more subtle and sophisticated ways of interweaving product features with their corresponding benefits into your sales messages — always focusing on each customer's particular situation. The critical consideration is making your presentation so that this cause-and-effect relationship comes through clearly. The conclusion you want the prospect to reach in every case is that the benefits — the potential improvements in his circumstances and/or the services and satisfactions he will enjoy — will all *result* from the unique features of your product that seem almost made to order for him.

As a perceptive sales person, you will realize that you have already learned much about one basic skill of selling — the technique for explaining clearly to your customers just how your products or services can serve them. With study and practice, effective application of this feature-benefits selling concept can become almost second nature to you. By using this technique consistently, you'll find it easier to land more orders. Many more skills are examined in the chapters that follow. But as additional techniques unfold, you'll discover that each serves mainly to refine further this basic process of communicating the feature-benefit message persuasively to your customers.

Turn to Learning Exercise No. 3 in Appendix.

Learning the Right Things about Products

Perhaps you're ready to concede that sales people must have a penetrating knowledge of their products. Let's assume you also agree that they should be well versed in a particular kind of product information—knowledge of product features and their corresponding customer benefits. Your question at this point may be, "Where and how can I possibly acquire this degree of selective understanding of the things I sell and their uses?"

The answers to this question can vary widely according to what you sell and for whom. But most sales people find it necessary to research and assemble much of this product know-how on their own. This requires a lot of objective, tedious work; it's a sort of solo market research task. One can contend—with justification—that this kind of critical information about products and their performance should be carefully worked out by marketing specialists and supplied to sales people for their use. Sometimes it is. But seldom do the data supplied reflect the degree of objective, sensitive insight needed for maximum selling effectiveness. That's because the needs of individual customers vary so widely. Therefore, all well-motivated sales people must learn to do for themselves the kind of incisive, creating thinking about their products and their optimal uses that it takes to do their selling jobs well.

Many well-established producers or marketers of goods or services do supply their sales people with excellent support for acquiring the right kind of product knowledge. Where provided, it is usually in the form of well-developed training programs, product manuals, and sales literature. But lack of such information about products or services is not necessarily a discredit to the organizations marketing them. Some may be small or new enterprises; some may still be struggling to become established in their markets—perhaps with revolutionary products or services possessing great potential. And it takes time, talent, and money to develop good marketing data and sales aids. For these and a host of other valid reasons, some companies may have little choice but to hire only experienced sales representatives considered capable of "making it" with a minimum of training and supervision.

But the outlook for sales careers in such organizations may still be outstanding—in part because they afford the opportunity to help develop and refine selling data, strategies, and tactics whose effectiveness you can demonstrate personally. The important career criteria are soundness of the company, evidence of ability of its managers, the merit of its products, and your personal commitment to devising effective techniques for selling them. So let's examine some ways of learning the things you need to know about your products in order to sell them outstandingly well.

SOURCES OF PRODUCT KNOWLEDGE

It's not unusual for new sales employees to be given temporary assignments in a factory to learn all about how products are made as a part of their training. Or they may be attached for a time to various staff departments to "learn the business inside out." This is effective for training only when the prospective sales people receive careful guidance on *what* it is important for them to learn and *why*. Unfortunately, such guidance is sometimes deficient or even totally lacking. The trainers may be technical staff people who teach the new sales representatives with loving care and pride many facets of product manufacture or business processes that, although quite important for other reasons, contribute little or nothing to solving customers' problems.

Unless you know what to look for, you can be handicapped in a quest for the right kind of product knowledge during a random experience in a plant or staff department. But such assignments can be very fruitful if carried out with an inquiring mind that asks, "Why is this important to a customer?" as each new aspect of product information unfolds.

Time spent with customers can be even more enlightening for sales training if ample opportunity is provided to observe and question how your products actually function or to witness what happens if they are processed into other end products. In this way, you can learn quickly — sometimes dramatically — how your products are used and what their principal performance features are from a customer's point of view. And you're likely to learn firsthand about product limitations as well — information that is also very valuable in selling.

The principal sources generally relied on for product information are company sales promotional literature, manuals, bulletins, samples. However, these can present problems not unlike those encountered in a tour of training duty in a factory unless the data are well organized for objective study and are explained intelligently. Unfortunately, sales literature is often long on impressive, colorful description of what the product *is*, but short on the type of performance and results data that spell out clearly what the product *does* for a customer. Most conventional sources of data are likely to require much study and probing in order to bring product features and benefits into clear perspective with respect to the interests of various types of customers.

If you've about concluded that uncovering and accumulating the kind of product information you need for selling is mostly up to you, you're right. No matter how much or how little training and sales help data you receive, it remains for you to analyze and organize the material into facts and ideas that you can use for selling your particular customers.

Feature-Benefits Inventory

One good way to identify, organize, and assimilate the right kind of product knowledge is to prepare a feature-benefits inventory form for every product you sell. Putting such an inventory together will do much to fix in your mind *why* a customer should buy your products; it also creates a ready-reminder file for convenient reference before making sales calls on problem prospects.

The inventory can take the form of one or more cards or sheets for every product. Each card is divided into two columns. The left-hand column is headed "Product features" and the right-hand column, "Customer benefits." For each entry made in the "features" column, make as many entries in the "benefits" column as have influential meaning for your customers. Figure 1 shows what a feature-benefits inventory form might look like. This technique and format help you uncover and accumulate the kinds of information adaptable to your own particular selling needs. By establishing such a system, you accomplish several important purposes. For example, you:

Figure 1. Feature-benefits inventory form.

Product: _____

Product features	Customer benefits
1.	1a.
	1b.
	1c.
2.	2a.
	2b.
	2c.

1. Establish an orderly basis for learning about your products — whether in the factory that makes them, during a training program, or from on-your-own study of product literature, manuals, and other sources.
2. Organize and record data in a form that tends to clarify and fix them in mind.
3. Apply the feature-benefits test, which helps identify information worth recording by answering the question, "What does this *do* for my customer?"
4. Create a file of very useful data for reference when making plans to capitalize on unusual selling opportunities.
5. Establish a pattern for accumulating and refining additional feature-benefits data as acquired from experience.

Obviously a separate inventory is needed for each product. In addition, variations in a product or its applications that alter its performance or utility may warrant special treatment in your feature-benefits summary. This is good reason for maintaining such data in a card file or loose-leaf notebook; it is then easier to augment each inventory entry as needed.

CODING BENEFITS ACCORDING TO CUSTOMER APPEAL

A useful variation is noting those benefits that relate specifically to particular customer categories. Some benefits are meaningful to certain types of customers but not to others. For example, the lower premiums of term life insurance relative to face value can be highly important to a young head of household who is primarily seeking maximum family protection at minimum cost. On the other hand, a middle-aged business person more interested in building an estate may find the benefits of other types of policies more attractive.

Where a wide variation exists in benefits appeal by customer category, it's a good idea to add a third column in the inventory format as a means of signifying such diversity. A suitable coding system can utilize letters, numbers, colors, or other devices. The coding process itself helps fix in mind significant variations in benefits appeal. Figure 2 shows a feature-benefits inventory form with a column for coding customer categories.

Figure 2. Feature-benefits inventory form.

Product: _____		
Product features	Customer benefits	Customer coding
1.	1a.	M
	1b.	X
	1c.	L
2.	2a.	X

FEATURE-BENEFITS CONCEPT APPLIED TO COMMODITIES

The feature-benefits inventory form should be adaptable to every product or service you sell. But perhaps your product is a commodity that seems to differ little in ultimate customer utility from like products sold by competitors. Can a feature-benefits inventory make any worthwhile contribution to selling commodities?

It is likely that there are *some* features of the particular commodities you sell that distinguish them from those marketed by others. Such variations may derive from origin, processing, grading, sizing, or other characteristics that can create preferences by certain customers if the variations are singled out and brought to their attention. Furthermore, jobbing, wholesaling, and similar marketing enterprises often rely quite heavily on services to build and maintain customer establishment. If this is your situation, augment your inventory to include the unique services that your company offers — or that you are prepared to provide personally — with the potential *advantages* each affords your customers.

With a little thought, you're likely to come up with a surprisingly impressive compilation. These service advantages constitute the stock-in-trade you have to sell with your commodity-type products — that is, the special benefits of doing business with your particular company and with you. This exemplifies the oft-repeated truism about selling: "When all else is equal, the sales person can make the difference."

FEATURES DISTINGUISHED FROM BENEFITS

When working out an inventory of features and their corresponding benefits, it's very important to distinguish clearly between the two. This calls for careful delineation of the cause-and-effect relationship. Otherwise you may come up with parallel tabulations of rather vague, loosely related product properties instead of clear-cut features and the customer benefits they create. The convincing ideas that generate sales involve these well-defined combinations of product characteristics and what they do for the customer. And the studying and recording of such cause-and-effect combinations are highly effective means of learning what you need to know about products for creative selling. All this helps speed the day when the contents of your feature-benefits inventory have become indelibly imprinted on your mind so that they're ready for instant recall during the most sensitive selling situation.

Turn to Learning Exercise No. 4 in Appendix.

Knowledge about Competitive Products

Unfortunately, a sales person can seldom pursue an unobstructed course to landing a customer order. Not infrequently competitors get in the way with claims for their products that must be reckoned with. This immediately multiplies your burden. In order to counter competitors' claims successfully, you must become almost as familiar with their products as with your own.

This is a much tougher and touchier task than gaining adequate knowledge about your own product. Generally, you get much less help from your associates, and you must do even more of the work on your own. And there's always the risk of picking up misinformation about a competitor's product, which—if you spread it about—can be to your disadvantage. It's never wise to detract from a competitive product unless you have supportable reasons for believing your information is right. Even then, it's a tricky tack to take. It's far better to sell on the strengths of your product than on your competitor's weaknesses.

The difficulties and risks notwithstanding, you do need to become well enough acquainted with competitive products and their performance characteristics to counter them fairly and effectively. How do you approach such a formidable task? One way—when feasible—is to examine the competitive product personally and observe how it performs. Another less direct but quite productive method is to accumulate and study the competitor's sales literature and space advertising. And *always* analyze objectively all competitive product claims reported by your customers, who are usually quite willing to relay such

Figure 3. Product comparison form.

Competitive product:		My product:
Competitor characteristic	Competitor disadvantage	Offsetting feature-benefits of my product
1.	1a.	1a.
	1b.	1b.
	1c.	1c.
2.	2a.	2a.
	2b.	2b.

claims to you. In effect, they are challenging you to prove your point when you're representing yours as the better product.

To meet that challenge, you need to be able to compare the competitor's product with your own on specific points. Professional sales people are prepared to neutralize competitive claims tactfully with facts they can document or demonstrate. This is never an easy task. In our free choice economy, competitors market good products and services. Unfounded statements detracting from a competitor's product won't sell your product and can destroy your reputation as a sales person with integrity.

Whatever your sources of information on competitive products, it's wise to analyze the products' characteristics systematically and to record your findings. This helps you think out how you can counter competitive claims constructively. And this provides you with a ready reference source when needed. Your record can be similar in format to the features and benefits inventory covering your own products. Your purpose now, however, is to catalog confirmable disadvantages of the competitive products with offsetting benefits of your product. There is usually little need to record the advantages your competitors claim; their literature and advertising as well as your customers will keep you well informed about them.

Figure 3 shows a sample format that the cards or reference sheets in your catalog might follow.

Turn to Learning Exercise No. 5 in Appendix.

Information Supportive to Product Knowledge

We've stressed the need for good product knowledge because if that is deficient, all else in a sales person's repertoire of knowledge and skill is likely to prove ineffective. However, there are several knowledge areas closely identified with products in which the sales person should become well versed in order to employ them in selling when they can contribute. The principal categories involved here include history and stature of the enterprise, background and development of the product, relative competitive position, company sales supportive services, physical characteristics of the product, and product sales policies and prices.

Obviously price and conditions of sale become involved at some point during every sales transaction. The key consideration relative to the other product knowledge categories is *selectivity of use.* They comprise funds of reserve knowledge to be drawn on whenever useful for supporting the primary feature-benefits selling message. Much of this collateral knowledge should be utilized only to the extent that prospects signify they want it. The discussions that follow enlarge on this concept and should clarify the reasoning involved.

HISTORY AND STATURE OF THE ENTERPRISE

Sales people should learn early in their careers the highlights of the history and growth of the company for which they sell. They should also become familiar with the position the enterprise holds within its industry and in relation to the markets it supplies. This knowledge serves mainly to orient sales people realistically within the segment of the economy they serve. This helps give them a sense of identity and reinforces their "reason for being" as sales people. Such knowledge also tends to increase self-confidence and sense of company loyalty.

Use of this knowledge as part of a sales talk, however, should be carefully tempered and highly selective. If you represent a large, well-established organization, an unsolicited recitation of such information is usually redundant and can even be resented as unseemly boasting. But if yours is not a well-known firm, relating this information with suitable restraint can help close a sale; it may even be solicited by a prospect seeking reassurance about the merit of your product or the reliability of your company. As you accumulate experience, you'll gain sensitivity to how much of this kind of collateral information about your organization you can use appropriately in talking with any given sales prospect.

BACKGROUND AND DEVELOPMENT OF THE PRODUCT

This is a close cousin of company history. To provide foundation for good product knowledge, sales people should become familiar with the origins of a product and the various steps in its development together with corresponding advances achieved in its applications, performance, and degree of customer acceptance. The principal utility of these data lies in the self-assurance they generate in the sales people themselves when selling that product. Such self-confidence helps convey to a prospect the impression that you know what you're talking about.

This kind of information is a distinct selling asset when the firm you represent enjoys recognized industry leadership because of its consistent history of innovation in quality and performance characteristics of the product involved. Reminding prospective customers of these happy circumstances can help you sell your product and resist competitive encroachment. But let moderation be your guide. Extolling too persistently all the evidence of entrenched leadership of your product can wear thin and even create sympathy for a competitor whose line may be a close second best.

COMPETITIVE POSITION

Sales people must always be well informed about the competitive position their company holds within its industry and with respect to any given product. This knowledge guides them in evaluating their strength or weakness in specific selling situations when deciding on selling strategy.

For example, if you are selling a superior but little-known product in a market dominated by a well-established name brand, you'll need to develop techniques for emphasizing and exploiting the demonstrable merit of your product as an offset for its lack of market acceptance. And you'll need to employ these tactics consistently and persistently. This is exemplified by the well-known Avis car rental selling theme that stated since Avis was only second, "we try harder." However, if yours is the position of strength, do your best to capitalize on it quietly but positively during every sales call.

SALES SUPPORTIVE SERVICES

This is a category of knowledge that you need to know well – very well – in order to employ it effectively in reinforcing your product selling message. This relates to the services your company supplies or makes available to its customers in conjunction with the products it sells. Some of these services are:

Shipping and delivery	Design services
Installation	Advertising programs
Instructions for use	Sales promotion programs
Employee training	Sales literature and catalogs
Technical and inspection	Merchandising support
Maintenance and repair	Credit provisions
Consultation and evaluation	Financial services
Studies and recommendations	Resale assistance

This list comprises only some of the more typical of a proliferation of customer services offered by modern-day marketers of goods and services. You'll almost certainly find that several of the functions listed above are representative of services performed by your company for your customers.

The critical concept here is that service is a major marketing tool for helping to sell products, ensure their proper use, and create maximum customer satisfaction. Customer service is accordingly one means of landing an order in many critical selling situations. In a broader sense, service is at once both primary objective and result of the selling function in our free enterprise economy. Service, however, has become so commonly accepted by those supplied as well as by their suppliers that it is often taken for granted. This is tacit evidence that our production/marketing system is evolving toward serving ever more people ever more satisfactorily.

Nevertheless, sales people sometimes fail to see the opportunities at hand for selling through objective and imaginative use of service knowledge. When competitive products prove to be virtually equal, the offering of a service valuable to a customer or his awareness that it is available is often a decisive factor in where that customer places his order.

The message in this for you, the sales person, is threefold:

1. Become thoroughly familiar with the sales supportive services provided by or available from your company.
2. Learn how to use those services effectively as selling tools; employ service to "make the difference" in competitive situations.
3. Keep your customers informed about the services your company stands ready to supply; they are part of your stock-in-trade.

The specific nature of services available and guidance for using them are usually provided by your employer's training programs. If not, make it one objective of your personal learning program to discover, identify, and understand the services you can employ to help sell your products. These meaningful benefits of doing business with your company reinforce the benefits your customers derive from your products. Results for you: more sales, more satisfied customers, and more personal satisfaction from selling.

Turn to Learning Exercise No. 6 in Appendix.

PHYSICAL CHARACTERISTICS OF THE PRODUCT

Although the need for being highly conversant with the details of a product's physical nature is obvious, it may merit brief review nonetheless. This knowledge category has to do with such aspects as:

Sizes and weights	Packaging
Colors, textures, and finishes	Guarantees
Types, models, and designs	Clauses and provisions
Composition	Limits of utility
Quality variations	Prices and discounts
Performance variations	Terms of sale
Specification details	Payment details

Sales people should have this information well memorized — or certainly have it at their fingertips for ready reference. This category constitutes the minimum level of knowledge a prospect can rightly expect a sales person to be able to provide readily about the product being offered.

Where do you obtain these data? Very likely they constitute the core of sales training provided by the enterprise you represent; they usually make up the principal content of product descriptive bulletins and manuals prepared for sales use. Study them well and inquire of your superiors and associates until you are confident that your understanding of all particulars is accurate. This is the most elementary form of product knowledge; thus it can be highly embarrassing to be unable to supply it correctly.

PRODUCT PRICES AND SALES POLICIES

Prices and policies are probably the most sensitive of all types of information relating to any product or service offered for sale. And they are also perhaps the most difficult and worrisome aspect of product knowledge a sales person must master. When all the cards are on the table, it is often price that determines which supplier gets the order — price as related to competition, to quality, to performance, to availability, to delivery, to a host of other bases for comparison, including other uses the prospect may be considering for his funds. So the price has to be right. If it is too high, the order is lost. If it is too low, the anticipated profit is lost. And if the latter happens repeatedly, the seller's company may court financial disaster. Not least of all, if prices or pricing policies do not conform with applicable legal restraints, the seller's enterprise may also find itself running afoul of the laws that regulate commerce.

So it is that most sales people find stringent limitations are imposed by their employers on any personal authority accorded them within the entire scope of product pricing and sales policies. Requirements or guidelines are usually carefully delineated relating to particulars such as:

Applicable prices	Zone prices
Pricing policies	F.O.B. prices
Pricing procedures	Guaranteed prices
List prices	Quantity discounts
Net prices	Trade discounts
Distributor prices	Competitive discounts
Dealer prices	Cash discounts
O.E.M. prices	Terms of sale

Experienced marketers can readily point to notable omissions in this list or add more items that bear on pricing in their particular business or industry. This only emphasizes that this subject must be learned thoroughly; and it can be taught only by people who are expert at handling pricing and at administering sales policies in your company. These would generally include your sales manager. As a new sales person, try to ensure that you obtain in-depth instruction in how to price your products in all the varieties of selling situations you are likely to encounter.

Broad guidelines for selling competitively, ethically, and legally are reviewed in Chapter 7. But comprehensive training in all aspects of price and pricing problems should be provided you by qualified individuals designated by the organization for which you sell.

Summary Perspective on Product Knowledge

We've concentrated heavily on the need for thorough product knowledge and collateral data as powerful selling tools and as means of thwarting competition. Although these are sufficient reasons for becoming an expert about your product, competence in this area will also enhance your sales effectiveness by increasing your self-confidence, enthusiasm, prestige, and personal satisfaction.

CONFIDENCE

Sales people are often afflicted with a vague uneasiness about facing customers – especially new prospects. They rationalize all kinds of delaying tactics while working up enough courage to make sales calls they think may be difficult. This hesitation stems mostly from fear of being asked questions they may not be able to answer – a natural reluctance to face embarrassment. Or place yourself in the position of a sales person who finds that his customer knows more about his products than he does. That hardly reinforces the seller's sense of control of the sales situation. The only cure for this malady is to acquire more product expertise. Well-informed sales representatives look forward to opportunities for explaining the merits of their products. Proficiency generates confidence.

However, if you're new at selling, you may ask, "What about me? I have to start selling *now*, before I've had time to become a product expert!" That situation isn't easy. But it's usually best to admit your deficiencies candidly while retaining your dignity and self-respect. Buyers are aware of your shortcomings anyhow and are often disposed to overlook your ineptness – even help you if they can – if they sense that you're really trying. As a beginner, you can scarcely be faulted for not being able to answer all product questions. Your response should go something like this: "I don't know, but I'll find out for you." This usually gets you off the hook temporarily. But you must follow through on that promise. You will be severely faulted if you're unable to answer the same questions repeatedly. If you don't learn and return with the information requested, you only prolong your misery in facing customers. And you don't make many sales either.

ENTHUSIASM

Were you ever approached by a sales person who was noticeably lukewarm about what he had to sell? Chances are your response was just as lukewarm; you weren't much interested in learning whether his product had any merit. On the other hand, genuine enthusiasm expressed by a sales representative who knows his product well gives him considerable selling leverage. His enthusiasm is apparent and contagious. His attitude is a sort of testimonial that the product will perform as represented. His exuberance comes through as a desire to share good fortune with others. This spirit becomes hard to resist.

To be so enthusiastic, it is necessary for you first to *believe* in your product as well as in your company. If you don't, or are unsure, you'd better check out the reasons. It's likely that your doubts will dissipate as you become more fully informed about your product and the company behind it. However, if you find you cannot believe in your product because it doesn't measure up to the claims you're expected to make for it, you may have a basic personal decision to make. You need to feel good about what you sell and the enterprise you sell for.

PRESTIGE AND PERSONAL SATISFACTION

There's an aura of prestige that goes with becoming an expert on the products you sell — prestige among your peers as well as among your customers. This can be a source of much personal satisfaction. Most people like having the distinction of being among the best in whatever vocation they undertake. But besides enhancing personal pride, your reputation for possessing product expertise generates business for you. The high regard in which you are held precedes you — opening doors that might otherwise be difficult to enter. Your recommendations become sought after and highly regarded. Your competitors find it difficult to break into your customer establishment. You have achieved the status of "sales counselor" to your customers — a mark of the creative, professional sales person.

Sales people who know their products well can sell. But they can sell much more if they also possess good persuasive skills. The following chapters explore some of the skills of selling that enable sales people to communicate better to their customers what they and their products can do for them.

COMMUNICATING WELL – A CRITICAL SKILL IN SELLING

Development of good communication skills is an imperative for every sales person. "Elementary," you may say. "Doesn't selling always involve talking customers into buying, and isn't that persuasive communication?" True enough, up to a point. But difficulties develop unless effective sales communication is clearly perceived as a two-way process. Numerous problems can arise when sales people fail to foster an *exchange of ideas* with their prospective customers. Some sales people find themselves being misunderstood frequently and losing orders unaccountably even in highly favorable sales situations. Yet they are fluent conversationalists and seem to be skilled in the arts of selling.

What can be the problem? Surprisingly, perhaps, it often stems from an inadequate grasp of the basic concepts and skills of effective communication. Such sales people become so engrossed in what *they* are saying and trying to accomplish that they fail to see their customers as people with ideas that should be sought out, listened to, and considered respectfully.

For those who play contract bridge, a relevant analogy might be trying to play by Goren's rules while failing to heed the nuances involved in bidding and response. Such disregard can cost a bridge player tricks, sometimes even a game. Similar lack of sensitivity to the subtleties of effective communication can lose a sales person orders, sometimes even a customer.

Sales persuasion relies heavily on well-chosen words and phrases – oral and written – often supported by charts, graphics, demonstrations, and other media. Yet a good sales presentation that is focused on evident customer need under the most favorable circumstances can still fail to sell. Often, it's because the prospect never really receives the sales message intended for him. Paradoxically, what he *thinks he hears* means something different to him than what the sales person *thinks he is saying*. Therein lies the nub of most problems in sales communication.

The Nature of Communication

Communicating is a very complex activity. It involves much more than simply transmitting and receiving information. Good communication comprises the transferring of an idea, a message, an impression, or a feeling from one person to another but with *minimal distortion of meaning* in the process. Ideally, the meaning intended by the originator of a message should be perfectly understood by its receiver.

The principal tool employed in communication between people is language—spoken or written. But besides transmitting information or ideas, we frequently project emotion as well. And to complicate things even more, we often seek to evoke both an intellectual and an emotional response. To augment the spoken word, we make gestures, vary facial expression and tone of voice, use pictures and symbols, sounds, textures, flavors, scents—anything that can help convey our message in full, brilliant intensity. When writing, we choose words and style to arouse emotion as well as to inform; and we often supplement a written message with illustrations or other graphics.

Furthermore, communication is a two-way process. Can you conceive of any need for a message unless someone can be expected to receive *and react* to it? The objective of all communication—though seldom fully achieved—should be to create a message of such clarity and to convey it so completely that the receiver comprehends its meaning *exactly* as conceived by its originator.

In selling, we carry this process one step further. Our purpose is not only to inform but also to induce the prospective customer to respond favorably. This is quite a challenge. Customers are unique individuals. Their attitudes, education, understanding, temperament, social values, personal objectives, and responsibilities are almost certainly unlike those of the sales person. A customer's cultural background and vocational environment are also likely to be different. Yet in selling we are faced with trying to anticipate and accommodate all of these differences in order to communicate effectively with a prospective customer and obtain the response sought. Little wonder we don't always succeed. But knowing something about the causes of communication problems and the methods for overcoming them can help boost our success ratio.

The Communication Process

For even the simplest communication to take place, five basic factors become involved:

The originator or sender of a message.
The message.
The receiver of the message.
Transfer of meaning.
The situation in which communication occurs.

Also, there are ordinarily *barriers to communication* that must be penetrated or neutralized—barriers that can frustrate or complicate any of the five basic factors. Figure 4 shows a linear model of the communication process that may help clarify its nature by depicting how the various factors and barriers interact.

Figure 4. Model of the communication process.

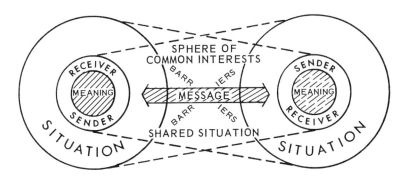

Note the situations of the communicators symbolically reaching out and melding together into a shared area. This facilitates transfer of the message. It behooves the seller to encourage such a blending of situations by identifying and nurturing customer's and seller's mutual interests. This fosters more effective communication.

The burden is thus on the sales person to create a favorable climate for his message. But seller and buyer *both* become sender as well as receiver during the communication process. This exemplifies its two-way aspect. Only by obtaining suitable *feedback* can the sales person discover whether the customer is getting the sales message. In most selling situations, the ultimate feedback sought is a signal from the customer of a decision to buy.

Barriers to Communication

The full meaning of the selling message is seldom perfectly perceived by the buyer even though this is the outcome the sales person tries to ensure. The purpose of this chapter is to identify some of the barriers that can obstruct optimal comprehension of a sales message and to suggest some techniques for penetrating those barriers.

SITUATION BARRIERS

One barrier to good communication arises from the divergent situations of the sales person and the prospect. Situation here includes a broad spectrum of factors such as size and nature of the business, its products or services, its capabilities, financial position, credit status, objectives, needs, and problems. Such situation factors relate to both seller and buyer; they influence every sales transaction to some degree. Problems in communicating are most likely to crop up for the sales person who hasn't adequately sized up the particular prospect and selling situation he faces. Indications that communication problems exist are customer comments such as "You don't understand my business" or "I doubt whether your proposition can do anything for me" or similar expressions of uncertainty.

The following anecdote, although unrelated to selling, illustrates how divergence in situations can present a formidable obstacle to good communication.

> Tony was the company's best laborer. One day while he was digging one of the perfect ditches in which he took pride, Tony encountered a big boulder. He disposed of the boulder by digging a hole in the side of the trench, rolling the boulder into that hole, and packing earth over it carefully before continuing his task.
>
> The foreman approached Tony later and told him the boulder should have been left in the trench. The trench was going to contain a concrete foundation and he told Tony impatiently that the boulder would have saved a yard of concrete if it had been left where it was.
>
> Later, Tony was working on another ditch and came across another boulder. This time he dug past it and left it where it was. The foreman came by and gruffly told Tony to remove the boulder from the bottom of the trench. It seems this trench was going to carry a pipe and the boulder would block its path.
>
> Tony was a bit confused by now. He remarked to another laborer he was working with: "Well, it's hell if you do and it's hell if you don't!"*

In this incident, the communication failure can be ascribed to Tony's boss. He didn't take into account the vast difference between his situation and that of the hapless Tony, who was trying hard to please within his understanding of what was expected of him.

The predicament of Tony and his boss exemplifies the need of all sales people to explore each customer's situation thoughtfully before making a sales approach. Too often this is done only superficially. This accounts for the ineffectiveness of many "cold calls," during which the prospect says—or thinks —"You're wasting my time!" The sales person is wasting his own time too, by not having made some preliminary study of the prospect prior to making the sales call. Otherwise, the response might have been different; or the sales person's home-

* Reprinted by permission of author, Eaton H. Conant, Professor of Management, University of Oregon, Eugene, Oregon.

work might have eliminated that prospect in favor of others more promising.

To penetrate the situation barrier, make some evaluation of the prospective customer's stature, needs, and problems *before* making your initial contact. The extent of your investigation should be in proportion to the importance you place on the outcome. Assess the prospect's situation not only as it appears to you but as it is likely to appear to him. This step is particularly important. When you're able to "speak the customer's langauge" and give evidence that you're familiar with his problems *as he sees them*, he'll become most receptive to your sales message. It can be virtually impossible for a prospective customer to understand and accept a new idea unless the seller conveys the message in terms the buyer can readily relate to factors he finds meaningful.

Concurrently, portray your own business situation and purpose in terms the buyer can accept as being reasonable or promising. For example, you might include statements qualifying you as a supplier, such as:

Mr. Prospect, I represent the Acme Chemical Company. You know of us, I believe, as a well-established producer of a group of special reagents, some of which are commonly used in other processes similar to yours. I'm aware that you may be facing a supply problem with one of the chemicals you've been using because of looming import problems affecting one of the basic elements required to formulate it. That could throw your production into a real bind, as you know far better than I.

But in many processes, that chemical can be replaced with _____, of which we're a major supplier. It should prove equally effective for your needs; however, some changes in your process would be needed and the nature of the effluent would be altered somewhat. Wouldn't it be a good idea to run some laboratory tests to determine what your results would be with a changeover? We have production capacity that we could earmark for you, and there is no risk of any shortage. This would relieve you of concern about the supply problems you may encounter otherwise.

This sales person quickly established that he is familiar with his prospect's situation. Obviously he did some homework before making this sales call. From this beginning, good rapport should develop quickly between the two. This establishes the communication climate needed for a constructive exchange of ideas.

PERSONALITY BARRIERS

This hindrance to good sales communication results from personality differences between seller and buyer. Disparities in cultural background, social attitudes, education, business and professional rank, and other personal attributes often create communication problems. The result can be distortions in your interpretation of the buyer's point of view as surmised from the buyer's responses. In turn, the buyer may misunderstand because you are not tuned in on his wave length.

As an example, this kind of barrier can arise between a college-trained sales person and a prospective customer who works in a plant and does not speak English as well as a college graduate. Turn this 180 degrees and it can also occur between the same sales person and a corporation executive or a highly skilled professional. A sales representative may be uncomfortable with either type of prospect. Hence the representative may communicate less effectively, unless he has the right attitude and is adequately prepared.

Preparation calls for suitable study of the buyer's situation, as already discussed. But it also calls for conscious, sensitive empathy with the prospect as a person. Make a serious effort to anticipate what impact your message may have on your prospect. More important, try to communicate on a relaxed basis with each prospect *at his level* of understanding and interest. Adjust your conversation to accommodate any significant differences in personal situations. For example, adopt temporarily (and carefully – to avoid sounding phony) some of the vernacular expressions or trade language the prospective customer may be using. This helps put him at ease and helps you get the feedback you need. If the executive is crisp and businesslike, or the professional is logical and objective, respond in kind. By practicing communicative flexibility on a personal basis, you project yourself into the customer's situation and begin to speak his language—all in the interest of communicating more effectively.

SEMANTIC BARRIERS

To reemphasize, the purpose of most sales communication is to convey a selling message to a prospective customer and to motivate the customer to respond positively. The primary tool for human communication is language—*words*. Unfortunately, the same words can mean quite different things to different people. Many words also have multiple meanings, depending on how they're used. This becomes evident from a brief look at a good dictionary. Compounding all these variations are regional colloquialisms. Furthermore, the meaning of a spoken word or phrase can be altered by the inflection or emphasis used.

In short, semantic barriers reflect variations in what people *think* are the meanings of words or expressions used in a message. This is why people sometimes derive a meaning from something we say that differs widely from the meaning we intended. This kind of communication problem is particularly difficult to overcome. But just being aware of some of the potential complications can help us avoid or compensate for them.

Even commonly used words can be troublesome because of possible variations in meaning. Consider, for example, the word run and some of the many different meanings it has: to move swiftly; to attempt to gain public office; to operate a business; a run in a stocking; a run on a bank or the market; the run of a train or a ship; a run of salmon in a stream. This listing could be extended for several pages. Webster's *New International Dictionary*—unabridged—fills four columns with fine print detailing countless additional variations in meaning for this one word. Add to this the hundreds of other commonly used words that also have multiple meanings and the scope of the problem mushrooms.

In addition, many expressions are "loaded" because they tend to arouse emotional reactions related to personal convictions of the hearer. In this category are terms like "excess profits," "tax loophole," and "welfare state," to mention only a few. Obviously, when possible, such provocative words and phrases should be avoided if you're seeking agreement rather than argument.

Then there is the variation in meaning brought about simply by changing the emphasis given any word in a sentence. To demonstrate, here's a simple sentence any sales person might use: "This product is the best you can buy." Consider how the meaning is subtly altered when different words in that sentence are emphasized. Try this by saying the following sentences aloud and accenting the boldface word in each:

> **This** product is the best you can buy.
> This **product** is the best you can buy.
> This product **is** the best you can buy.
> This product is **the** best you can buy.
> This product is the **best** you can buy.
> This product is the best **you** can buy.
> This product is the best you **can** buy.
> This product is the best you can **buy**.

A listener might interpret the meaning of that sentence in many different ways depending on the stress given individual words. So it is not only *what* you say but *how* you say it that contributes to the meaning conveyed.

OVERCOMING SEMANTIC BARRIERS

Penetrating the semantic barriers to good communication is a never-ending challenge because of the infinite number of variations. Can any of us ever hope to anticipate and counteract all the countless ways of being misunderstood? Probably not. But here are two basic rules for minimizing semantic distortion of meaning:

Maintain vigilant awareness of the risks involved.
Resolve to improve your semantic skills unceasingly.

Careful choice of words and clarity of expression should be constant objectives. Language should be as simple and direct as possible, considering the selling situation and product involved. Avoid ambiguous words and complicated sentences;

they seldom contribute to understanding and may aggravate other communication barriers. If prospective customers must decode complex language to discover the real meaning of a sales message, they may subconsciously reject it for that reason alone.

Every business also tends to develop its own jargon – a kind of special language used by insiders. It's usually best to make only sparing use of such trade expressions until you've ascertained that they're understood and accepted by your customers. Your customers may be reluctant to seek explanation of unusual expressions they don't understand. And they may even be offended by language that seems to imply they're not very well informed. There is no sales advantage in using the special vocabulary of your business if it causes a breakdown in communication.

Artful use of repetition sometimes helps convey the meaning of a sales message. While the prospect is pondering an idea that's new to him, express it again – but in different words having essentially the same meaning. This reinforces the concept before you go on to others, thereby giving the hearer more time to absorb it. Insight into the prospect's situation and degree of understanding is needed. A message the prospect finds perplexing may lose him unless it's quickly restated in other words. On the other hand, it may be redundant to repeat a message when the hearer is already assimilating it easily.

We've referred several times to feedback as a communication tool. One technique for obtaining feedback is adroit questioning at critical points to measure how well your sales message is getting through. The right answers will give you assurance that the prospect is understanding your message. Be sensitive to every reaction – direct or indirect – that can reveal how effectively you are communicating. This enables you to adjust your approach or emphasis instantly to clarify and reinforce your message.

It helps to become a student of language and its use. There are many fine books and courses available on this subject. And it helps to observe the communication practices of others. You can improve your own ability by studying the strengths and weaknesses of others. Communicating clearly in simple, straightforward langauge is a skill that requires resolute practice.

THE LISTENING BARRIER

Does the idea that listening can constitute a barrier to good communication surprise you? Let's explore this concept briefly. In the linear model of the communication process, sender and receiver reverse roles repeatedly; otherwise no idea exchange takes place. As a receiver, each is intermittently a listener when the message is vocal. But let's examine particularly the role of the sender, since our special interest is your role as the seller.

For a sales person, being a good listener is important in a number of critical ways. How else can you obtain the feedback you need? How else can you learn of your customer's problems and needs as a basis for suggesting solutions? How else can you cope with your customer's complaints unless you first hear them out thoroughly? The trouble is that most of us are not really very good listeners unless we work at it consciously. Too often listening is viewed only as the interlude during which we busily think about what *we* are going to say *next*. Occasionally, we even callously interrupt the other person, oblivious to what he is saying, so that we can resume talking!

For sales people, this kind of nonlistening is anathema and should be studiously avoided. They need to become skilled at listening, intently and courteously, to everything their customers have to say. It is by careful listening that they corral their cues for sales strategy and tactics. They can acquire such tips only while giving full attention to their customer's comments. For well-prepared sales people, propitious responses will flash into their minds as needed; they don't have to think them out while they should be listening. The listening side of the equation is essential to the balance and effectiveness of communication.

THE DEAF EAR BARRIER

This is a variety of listening barrier exhibited by some customers. A message sometimes fails to get through simply because it contains an idea that's contrary to what the hearer already knows or believes. His mind is set; his habitual attitudes and past experience condition him to reject anything that runs counter to his ingrained patterns of thought or reaction. Many people tend naturally to resist change; they cling to creeds or conduct that they find comfortable. This characterizes the customer who tries to dismiss you with comments like "I'm satisfied with my present supplier" or "The product I'm using now just can't be beat." This customer may be deluding himself, but he must be dealt with as you find him.

Penetration of this customer's attitude calls for friendly persistence and only gentle pressure. His resistance needs to be disarmed — idea by idea. Perhaps he first needs to be startled in some way into awareness that he may be missing out on something good. Then he'll begin to listen and to think. This is a situation in which repetition can help by presenting the same concept from different vantage points on successive opportunities. Patience is the password.

THE MASQUERADE BARRIER

This refers to an elusive but nonetheless very real characteristic of human nature; people don't always say what they think or what they mean. For obvious or obscure reasons we sometimes camouflage our true opinions or attitudes in what we say or do. We play a mummer's game — perhaps to avoid hurting someone's feelings, perhaps to conform with organizational or social pressures, perhaps only to gain time for mulling something over.

Whatever the reasons for this benign form of deception, it is a human trait that crops up frequently in selling. Your customer may prefer another product; he may want to favor another sales person; he may have an undisclosed dislike for your company; or he may simply be annoyed with you for some reason. But this is not what he says, and this leaves you nonplussed because you sense that you're not getting the whole story.

This kind of barrier is hard to detect and often even harder to penetrate. Questions that probe gently usually will eventually uncover the real reasons so you can move to neutralize them. Discreet investigation through other sources may prove helpful. Patient effort should eventually induce such a customer to level with you so that the two of you can come to a rational understanding.

WRITING: BARRIER AS WELL AS OPPORTUNITY

We've focused so far on penetrating barriers to good oral communication because most sales contacts are made in person or by telephone. Face-to-face communication is much preferred in most selling situations. Ideas as well as feelings can be conveyed much more effectively in spoken sales messages. An oral message can also be reinforced simultaneously with supporting visual or auditory media. And instant feedback can be obtained by observing the buyer's reaction firsthand; this adds shades and depth of meaning to what the buyer says.

Sales people usually favor personal contact with their customers and prospects for these reasons. Also, sales people have a legendary aversion to paperwork. However, sales people do write to their customers — sales letters, proposals, quotations, and so on. Much of our prior discussion about causes and correction of the problems of oral communication applies equally to written messages. When a written communication must be relied upon, however, the situation of the seller and the prospect changes significantly. Writing is primarily one-way communication because there's no opportunity for getting immediate feedback with which to measure and adjust message impact. You have to say it right the first time. Accordingly, several principles of good construction of written sales messages merit special attention.

Mastering the techniques of effective writing requires much study and practice. Our purpose here is to highlight some of the basics of writing good sales-oriented communications. If your particular responsibility calls for extensive writing of sales promotional material, you'll be wise to take a course or two in writing. Or study some of the excellent books available on this fascinating subject.

In writing to a customer, all you can be sure you have going for you is what you can say on that piece of paper. When your message arrives, it competes with everything else that is vying for the customer's attention at that time. So your message must be designed to arrest his attention, capture his interest, and enable him to grasp your meaning and intent clearly and quickly. Otherwise it risks and may deserve the usual fate of much junk mail.

It is just as important to evaluate the receiver's situation, personality, and receptivity when planning a written communication as an oral one. A sales prospect's attitude toward you or your organization can range from faith and friendship to distrust and hostility. Your message should take into account your best forecast of what the receiver's viewpoint will be.

A written sales message should always be as brief as possible for accomplishing its objective. Long, rambling discourses are more apt to confuse than clarify and consequently may never even be read. Don't risk wasting your prospect's time and losing his interest by writing at length about things he already knows. Introduce in one or two sentences the situation you're writing about; state your objective; then launch right into the persuasive body of your message.

Your letter should be well organized and easy to read. It should spell out your major points one by one—leaving some white space between each point. It should be confined to one page—or two at most. If you believe more detail is absolutely necessary, attach it to the primary communication on a separate page. However, the primary communication should contain all the salient points. Each point can be more completely explained and reinforced in the attachment. This ensures that the receiver will get the main thrust of your message without becoming involved in all the supporting particulars unless he wants to. In short, you start with the summary to make sure that the most important part of your message gets the receiver's attention first.

Before beginning to write, plan what you want to accomplish. Decide first on your objective, because you want the receiver's reaction to coincide with your purpose. Then use the following process or something similar for achieving it:

1. Jot down the response you want to obtain (your objective), the key points you want to make, the facts you want to relay.

2. Think through each component of your message—how you want to say it and why it is important.
3. Draft a brief outline by making notes on each point in its order of importance relative to your objective.
4. Convert the outline into your message by using simple language and the fewest words possible.
5. Review the message carefully before sending it, to make sure it conveys your meaning clearly and invites the conclusion you seek.

Write in a direct style in language you'd use if you were speaking to the receiver in person. This means using the first and second person whenever suitable—I, you, we, us—as well as the present tense and active voice—this is; our product saves; and so on. An unaffected writing style is easier to read and understand. It is also more positive and personal. The aura of your presence emanates from such a message. Write as informally as the situation warrants. Avoid stilted language forms— it is recommended (why not "we recommend"?); at an early date (why not "soon"?); in the event that (why not "if"?). Stylized, archaic expressions like these detract from clarity and even sound a bit foolish when a letter full of them is read aloud.

Early in this chapter, we mentioned that sales communication barriers can be equated with sales opportunities. This concept merits special consideration in relation to written communications. Timely sales letters written by you, a sales representative, can broaden your coverage and enhance your effectiveness. They add a touch of professionalism. There is always a limit to the number of customers and prospects you can call on within any given time frame—a function of what you sell and the size of your territory. Good sales letters—short, personalized, and perhaps including sales literature—can help you enlarge and reinforce your coverage. This tactic becomes even more important in view of travel limitations induced by the energy shortage.

Such messages serve as personal reminders of your readiness to serve and also help bridge the time lapse between sales calls made in person. The general sales letters your employer may broadcast to customers usually fill some special need. But those you write yourself can be much more effective saleswise. You can modify the same basic letter for use with many customers; write a new one whenever you have something new to say. Try writing letters as a way of strengthening rapport with your customers as well as selling them more.

So far, the suggestions about how to formulate a good written sales communication have not offered many ideas about the kinds of things it should say in order to sell. In practice, the content and structure of a good sales letter virtually parallel a good oral sales presentation; only the situation and the medium are different. How to sell an idea and how to make a good personal sales presentation are covered in later chapters. As these techniques and skills are examined, you will see that they can be translated readily into written form.

Summary on Sales Communication

The suggestions offered here for improving communicative skills will help only if you apply them resolutely. Diligent effort is the only route to skill at penetrating the barriers to good communication and turning them into sales opportunities. This summary covers the most common problems and provides a brief review of techniques for overcoming each one.

1. A frequent barrier to sales communication is one that arises from differences in situation; the seller doesn't understand the prospect's business and problems; or fails to provide assurance of the vendor's capacity to help solve these problems.

Resolve by cultivating sensitivity to the situations of prospective customers — their circumstances, problems, needs, level of knowledge, and understanding. Indicate your awareness of situation as well as your interest and ability to help.

2. Personality differences between seller and prospect often create a communication gap.

Resolve by developing empathy for and rapport with each individual *as a person;* learn to speak each buyer's language.

3. Many words and phrases have multiple definitions and often mean different things to different people – depending on their situations, locale, the context in which the expressions are used, and the emphasis employed.

Counteract by studying word meanings and by varying language used according to the nature of the selling situations; maintain vigilant awareness of the risks of being misunderstood because of semantic differences; select words and phrases carefully; use simple language.

4. Failure to hear and understand what your prospects are trying to tell you can create a communication block.

Cultivate the habit of listening intently to everything your prospects say; you owe them this courtesy, and it is also your best means of discerning what stands between you and selling them. Listening provides the principal source of the feedback you need for measuring how your sales effort is progressing and then adjusting it as needed.

5. Prospects sometimes hear only what they want to hear; they may turn a deaf ear to new ideas that conflict with their current beliefs or past experiences.

Resolve by patient persistence and by pointing out that they may be depriving themselves of valuable opportunities.

6. People don't always say what they think or what they mean; this sometimes unconscious behavior may be used to divert the thrust of your sales effort or to avoid making a decision.

If you suspect this is happening, probe gently to discover whether your prospects are expressing their *real* reasons for parrying your sales efforts; adjust your tactics accordingly.

7. Written sales messages are most likely to communicate effectively when thoughtfully prepared to generate the response desired. Good personal sales letters can reinforce sales call effectiveness; this valuable sales tactic should be employed more often.

When writing to customers, state your purpose clearly, be brief, use simple language, and personalize your messages as much as the situation warrants. Use short letters to supplement your sales calls. Employing this added touch when timely can tip more sales in your favor.

This chapter has introduced a number of basic concepts of the communication process and related them to selling. We hope this will motivate you to make a lifelong study of effective communication techniques. Because good communication is a vital part of the selling process, it behooves all sales people to work unceasingly at improving their skills in expressing themselves clearly and in understanding their customers accurately.

Turn to Learning Exercise No. 7 in Appendix

CHAPTER 4

PERSUASION – THE CORE OF THE SELLING PROCESS

The selling process involves helping customers crystallize their awareness of specific wants or needs and persuading them to purchase products or services that can satisfy those needs. Inherent in this process is a fair exchange of values benefiting both buyer and seller. Communication of ideas is the very heart of selling – constructive ideas that entail advantages for both parties. Unless the transaction involves an exchange of mutually beneficial ideas and values, a sale is not likely to take place. Accordingly, creative ideas form the very core of selling, and persuasion is the means of conveying those ideas convincingly from seller to buyer.

Emotional as well as intellectual factors contribute to this process. A prospective customer is moved to buy not only by the merit of the seller's ideas but also by the seller's motivation as perceived by the buyer. Prospects often feel constrained to respond favorably to sales people they sense are sincerely trying to help them. This is doubtless a manifestation of the emotional impulse most of us feel to repay a kindness with a kindness. This chapter examines the part persuasion plays in bringing about the exchange of ideas and values that characterizes the selling process.

The Selling Process

Viewed in broad perspective, this process falls logically into three distinct but interdependent phases:

Preparation – getting ready to sell

Persuasion—making the sale

Postsale functions—making sure the customer remains satisfied with his purchase

Each phase makes critical contributions to the viability of the entire selling process. Neglect of any phase diminishes overall selling effectiveness and involves risk of losing sales as well as customers.

PREPARATION

The preparation phase encompasses widely diverse functions by which sales people qualify themselves and make ready to sell and serve their customers. One way they qualify themselves is by acquiring comprehensive knowledge of their products or services—particularly knowledge of product features and corresponding customer benefits. This phase also includes preparatory activities such as identifying prospects, exploring their wants and needs, formulating ideas for solving their problems, assessing their readiness to buy and ability to pay, and developing sales presentations designed to persuade them to buy.

Preparatory functions are mostly creative and future-oriented. But preparation also involves certain relatively routine chores, such as organizing and maintaining files of useful data on sales prospects and established customers, planning market coverage and sales calls, recording sales call results, maintaining supplies of sales helps, and apprising supervisors of sales plans and progress. It is not easy to carry out all these tasks effectively (the more important of them are examined in later chapters). But diligent sales preparation is a prerequisite for successfully accomplishing the highly critical second phase —inducing prospective customers to buy.

SALES PERSUASION

Friendly persuasion should be the dominant although sometimes subtle theme of every interaction between a sales person and a prospect. The setting for personal persuasion is usually a face-to-face sales call. Telephone conversations and correspondence are also employed effectively—most commonly to supplement personal contacts. Sales people are on stage during every sales interview they make. The success of their every other function contributes to or depends upon the effectiveness of the dialogues they conduct with prospective and current customers. Furthermore, the relative infrequency and brevity of personal sales presentations as measured against the full scope of sales work underscore how critical it is for sales interviews to be productive.

It is vital for sales people to strive for superior performance during every sales call—whatever its purpose. Obviously, it is crucial for them to cultivate the skills of sales persuasion. Their vocation is justified by and depends upon creating maximum opportunities for persuasive presentation of their products or services to qualified prospects and customers.

Paradoxically, this most significant phase of the selling process also tends to be most neglected in many sales training programs, which often focus primarily on product knowledge and sales procedures. Although these are also important, new sales people are frequently left to learn the skills of sales persuasion largely through on-the-job experience and their own initiative. This is frustrating for those sales people as well as for their customers. While inadequately trained sales people are struggling to master this most critical challenge of sales work, their employers' sales volume and market image are likely to suffer. Intelligent investment in helping new sales people become proficient more rapidly in the persuasive skills of selling can yield substantial returns in improved sales results—which become evident even if they are difficult to measure.

POSTSALE FUNCTIONS

Postsale activities cover a wide range of sales reinforcement, follow-up, and customer service functions, from simply reassuring customers that they have made good buying decisions to handling complex delivery or service requirements, complaints, collection problems, and countless variations of other sales-related situations. As with sales preparation, this phase involves many relatively routine duties. But the sensitivity and skill with which they are handled do much to foster customer satisfaction and good will. This enhances a sales person's reputation for dependability, which, in turn, helps land new customers as well as build repeat business from established accounts.

Making sales is what the job is all about. As this book unfolds, we'll give special attention to vital aspects of all three phases of the selling process. But first let's make a quantum jump into the very heart of phase two — how to make a good selling presentation. Why? Because making successful sales talks provides reward as well as justification for the many preparatory and follow-up chores.

Acquiring skill in persuasion is not only the most critical challenge sales people face but also the most meaningful measure of their success. The widely varying procedural aspects of sales work are best learned from company programs or from on-the-job tutelage of an able sales manager who knows the company's requirements well. But the basic concepts of preparing and making a convincing sales talk apply to whatever you sell. And proficiency in the skills of persuasion also helps integrate all other components of sales work into a cohesive, forceful function.

Selling a Problem-Solving Idea

Why does a sales person call on prospects or customers? Is not the primary purpose to sell them something that will contribute to their advantage or well-being? The thrust of every sales effort is to *persuade* the customer that the product or service being offered can solve a problem or satisfy a need. Although there are many secondary reasons for making sales calls, these all relate and contribute to the main event — *selling customers on ideas that will benefit them.* Your principal challenge as a sales person when facing prospective customers is persuading them to respond positively to the sales ideas that prompted you to call on them.

In every situation, it is really an idea that you are selling. A product or service is sold by *selling the idea* that accepting your proposal will bring your customers satisfactions that represent value to them. The question always uppermost in a customer's mind is, "What can this sales person's proposition do for me?'' That question can only be answered with ideas. In one sense, the product or service involved serves only as a vehicle for the key idea or ideas that convince customers to buy. They can be induced to buy only as a consequence of becoming persuaded that owning or using your product or service will satisfy some significant need. So it is that learning how to sell an idea equips you with a skill applicable to anything you sell.

SOME EXAMPLES OF IDEA SELLING

An insurance sales representative sells a policy by selling the *idea* of the protection it will afford the policy holder or the holder's beneficiary if the risk insured against should materialize.

A fertilizer sales representative sells fertilizer products by selling the *idea* of the increase in crop productivity their use will bring about.

A securities sales person sells stocks, bonds, or other instruments of investment by selling the *idea* of the potential they provide for income or appreciation in value.

Countless industrial products or pieces of equipment are sold by selling *ideas* about the performance or service they will provide relative to the customer's specific needs; their potential for improving the products or services that the customer manufactures and markets; the savings they will generate in the customer's processes; the contributions they will make to the company's earnings.

A real estate sales representative sells a home by selling *ideas* about how well it will serve the needs of the family and the satisfaction they will derive from living in it.

Commodities of virtually every kind are sold by selling *ideas* about their capacity for satisfying the user's requirements; their quality relative to the user's specifications; their cost relative to operating or marketing budgets; their availability relative to delivery or production schedules.

Virtually all types of business equipment or services are sold by selling *ideas* about the increases in efficiency they will bring about; contributions they can make to the ease of doing business, keeping records, or retrieving data rapidly and accurately; and the savings they can generate relative to current costs.

Note the uniform theme running through all these examples. In a broad sense, it matters little whether the product or service involved is tangible or intangible; whether it's a bulk commodity or sophisticated equipment; whether it's a specialized business service or whatever — the concept of selling by selling ideas about the benefits of the product or service that are significant to the customer applies in every case. While it is simplistic to suggest that the identity of the product is incidental, it is true that the keys to idea selling — and therefore to all selling — are:

— Your knowledge of the customer's wants and needs.
— Your knowledge of how the customer's wants and needs can be satisfied by your product or service.
— Your ability to persuade the customer that you qualify personally on the first point, and that by buying your product, he'll benefit as you claim in the second point.

These, then, are the key requirements that you must master as a sales person: your knowledge of the products you sell and of their useful applications, and your skill in persuading the customer how they can benefit him. They are simple enough in concept but sometimes infinitely complex in application.

Turn to Learning Exercise No. 8 in Appendix.

Customer Buying Motives

Let's review briefly the nature of the other half of the selling equation — the customer — before delving further into techniques for luring him into buying. It must not be overlooked that parallel with the selling process is a corresponding buying process. Selling is sometimes viewed shortsightedly as a kind of marketplace drama in which sales people play all the principal parts. On the contrary, it is the customer who always occupies center stage. Closer study of his character and role contributes much to better understanding of the interplay of ideas taking place between seller and buyer as sales action moves toward a climax.

Keep in mind that for the buyer a sale constitutes a purchase. Every sale/purchase agreement comes about as the consummation of a dialogue between seller and buyer during which the expectations *of each* are explored and brought into balance. A sale/purchase isn't likely to occur unless the participants conclude that the transaction represents a fair exchange providing a satisfactory measure of advantage or profit for each.

Every sales prospect is an individual with unique problems, needs, objectives, and personal characteristics. These must be recognized and taken into account by the seller. Every customer also has his own special motives for buying. The customer can be induced to buy more readily when the seller perceives those buying motives and accommodates them in his sales presentation. A potential customer is usually aware of his reasons for considering a purchase — but not always. Motives for buying are sometimes obscure and hard to identify — even by the customer himself. Occasionally, a skillful sales person can uncover and focus on repressed buying motives, which then become factors in the sale/purchase decision.

Buying motives vary with business and industry, the problem source of the prospect's need, and even with the prospect's personality, status, and stature. Purchases are often influenced by complex combinations of buying motives. The most prevalent reasons for buying are broadly categorized below.

BUSINESS-RELATED BUYING MOTIVES

Variations of one or more of the following motives are likely to influence the decisions of prospects who make purchases for businesses that supply products or services to others. Because of their particular problems or objectives, buyers for such concerns may feel constrained to:

Increase profits.
Reduce costs — save money.
Improve use of invested capital.
Simplify a function — conserve time or effort.
Improve operating efficiency.
Improve quality, utility, performance, convenience.
Increase safety — reduce risks.

Develop a new product or service.
Expand the business.
Counter competition.

PERSONAL BUYING MOTIVES

Whether purchasing for their own businesses, for their employers, or for themselves, prospects are also likely to be influenced by one or more personal buying motives such as those typified below. They may be neither consciously aware of these motives nor willing to acknowledge them even to themselves, but this does not diminish the impact of these motives on their decision-making processes. Thus they may be moved to buy by desire to:

Demonstrate personal leadership.
Participate in a new development.
Perform well—gain approval of superiors.
Further personal ambitions—enlarge career opportunities.
Enhance sense of personal importance or pride.
Gain or give pleasure, comfort, or satisfaction.
Avoid loss, protect position, or reap advantage.
Exercise sharp buying acumen, bargain, economize.

Neither of these lists is comprehensive. Buying motives vary infinitely with the situations and the people involved. An elusive combination of both business and personal buying motives is likely to be at work in any given buying situation. The important message this conveys is that every sales presentation should reflect the sales person's best assessment of the buying motives active in the situation at hand. Your perception of the buying motives most likely to influence a particular customer helps you to formulate the *ideas* most likely to persuade him to buy. Adjust your sales appeal according to the impact you sense your message is making on those motives.

How are buying motives identified? Careful prior study of the needs of the potential customer and of his personal characteristics is the only way. Remember that buying motives must be reckoned with; ignoring them can blunt or nullify otherwise well-conceived sales efforts.

The Selling/Buying Process

Most authorities on selling agree that the selling process consists of five sequential steps:

1. Gaining attention.
2. Arousing interest.
3. Creating conviction.
4. Developing desire.
5. Implementing action.

Some analysts of selling express the five steps differently; some subdivide them into more steps; some hold that in certain situations one step overlaps another. For the most part, however, there is acceptance that a sales/purchase transaction usually adheres rather closely to this format from inception to fruition. There is no good reason for seriously disagreeing with this basic perception of the selling process.

By logical extension of our earlier review of customer buying motives, however, it becomes apparent that those five steps of selling reflect the purchasing process almost as accurately. Potential customers faced with wants or needs and variously motivated into making purchases to resolve problem situations go through a close approximation of those same five steps in arriving at buying decisions. Consider this transposition of those steps to a sale from the viewpoint of a buyer:

1. The buyer's attention is drawn in some way to a potential solution or means of satisfying a problem or need.
2. His interest is aroused as he considers the promising possibilities of the solution.
3. He becomes progressively more convinced of the merits of the solution as he studies its advantages (unless disadvantages serious enough to terminate interest are uncovered).
4. His desire to acquire the solution mounts as he weighs the pros and cons, considers its advantages in relation to alternatives, and mulls over cost considerations.
5. He accepts the solution when, upon thorough evaluation, its positive aspects sufficiently outweigh the negative to induce him to decide to buy.

Note that this process of arriving at a decision to purchase is essentially the same whether a sales person is involved or not. The attention of potential buyers may be drawn to a product or service by an advertisement, by hearing about it from associates, or in any number of other ways. Interest may arise spontaneously if latent desires are stimulated. Buyers may become convinced of the utility and merit of the product or service through their own investigations. Desire to buy is generated as they discover it will satisfy their problems or needs. Finally, they decide to buy when they conclude that the cost is justifiable and is within their means. In this context, it is conceivable that a sales person might become involved in this purchasing process only in its final stages — arranging particulars of price and delivery.

This summary of the purchasing process does not detract from the functions of selling. Instead, it emphasizes that sales people should concentrate their efforts on guiding potential buyers through this normal decision-making process, thus *helping them decide to buy*. And since these processes are predominantly mental, we are dealing almost entirely with ideas. Thus helping a buyer reach a positive buying decision can aptly be called *idea selling*.

Origins of Idea Selling

> The use of persuasive speech is to lead to decisions. . . .
> This is so even if one is addressing a single person and urging him to do or not to do something, . . . the single person is as much your "judge" as if he were one of many; . . . any one is your judge whom you have to persuade. Nor does it matter whether we are arguing against an actual opponent or against a . . . proposition; in the latter case we still have to use speech and overthrow the opposing arguments.*

* *The Basic Works of Aristotle.* Richard McKeon, ed. New York: Random House, 1941. Original source: "Rhetoric." W. Rhys Roberts, trans. From W. D. Ross, ed., *The Oxford Translation of Aristotle*, Vol. 11. Used with permission.

Those words were written by the Greek philosopher Aristotle, who lived from 384 to 322 B.C. They are presented here to point out that much of what we accept today as valid about the principles of selling—"persuasive speech"—does not necessarily result from recent discovery. On the contrary, the basic skills of selling as we know them have evolved in large measure from principles of persuasion understood and practiced by the ancients. Skillful selling as practiced today, however, reflects the significant social changes and corresponding changes in things people value that have occurred during the intervening centuries. Nevertheless, the basic principles of persuasion remain essentially unaltered. Human nature has changed little during recorded history. Our psychological makeup seems to have been little modified by the phenomenal changes in the human condition that have taken place over the past two thousand years.

To carry this analogy further, let's consider again the five steps of the selling/buying process: (1) gaining attention, (2) arousing interest, (3) creating conviction, (4) developing desire, and (5) implementing action. Perhaps these steps have developed more recently. But reflect for a moment on these additional words from Aristotle:

> A speech has two parts. You must state your case, and you must prove it. . . . These are the essential features of a speech; and it cannot in any case have more than Introduction, Statement, Argument, and Epilogue, . . . [which latter] merely reminds us of what has been said already.

The relationship between this quotation and the five steps of selling is easily traced: (1) gaining attention corresponds with Aristotle's Introduction; (2) arousing interest in his Statement of the case; (3) creating conviction is a contemporary interpretation of his term Argument; (4) reinforcing agreement and desire is the function of the Epilogue; and (5) implementing action is analogous to the brief Conclusion Aristotle recommended for closing a speech as a means of soliciting hearers' evaluations of its merits. Thus the principles and techniques of persuasive speech developed so eloquently in Aristotle's "Rhetoric" are reflected in most contemporary treatments of the principles and techniques of selling. The concepts of idea selling presented herein are no exception.

Specifics of Idea Selling

Now let's examine more specifically just what idea selling means and how it works. Although Aristotle's concepts of persuasive speech are valid today, his language requires updating to reflect the twentieth-century concept of selling—a form of persuasion little known to the ancients. The five steps of the selling/purchasing process should be phrased more positively to reflect a function as dynamic as selling. Why not express those five steps in more active words? Consider this phrasing for the five-step selling format:

Twentieth Century	*Aristotle*
1. Stimulate your prospect's interest	Introduction
2. State your sales proposal	Statement of case
3. Convince the prospect that it will work	Argument— the specifics
4. Summarize its benefits and results	Epilogue—re-inforcement
5. Ask for decisive action	Conclusion

Look upon that initial word "stimulate" as setting the mood for your entire sales presentation. It is quite proper to arouse emotion during sales persuasion—as long as it isn't a cover for fraudulence. So generate a sense of anticipation and enthusiasm about your sales presentation; it helps induce your prospect to buy.

Let's review each of the five steps separately.

STEP 1. STIMULATE YOUR PROSPECT'S INTEREST
Purpose
    This step should embody only the essentials of an effective introduction. It should be brief and to the point. It should

justify and qualify why you are asking the prospect to listen to your proposition.

You *justify* by suggesting that your message relates to something that will benefit him. This incites initial interest by answering his unspoken question, "Why should I listen?"

You *qualify* by touching lightly on aspects of his situation that you hope to help him improve. You are most likely to command his close attention by making him aware that you're familiar with his problems, limitations, wants, or needs and are about to offer ideas for their solution. This makes him want to hear more because you're beginning to answer his mental question "What's in this for me?"

Suggestions for handling

On a first call, begin by courteously introducing yourself, your company, and the nature of your business. If you've been introduced by a mutual acquaintance, acknowledge this graciously. Convey by voice and manner a subdued air of confidence that the buyer will be pleased to hear what you've come to say.

Keep in mind that any intrusion may encounter some resistance from the buyer. Even a customer who is expecting you and already knows your purpose may respond hesitantly. This reflects natural resistance to interruption or change. Offset this by placing your prospect in a receptive frame of mind as quickly as you can after greeting him.

Customary social amenities allow for some small talk at the beginning of most sales interviews. This helps establish rapport, opens the way for exchanges on topics of mutual interest, and helps build good will—all desirable purposes. But the small-talk interlude should always be brief. React quickly to any signals that the customer feels it's time to get down to business. Then adhere as closely to your planned five-step sales presentation as two-way discussion of its key points will permit.

Following is an example of a Step 1 introduction that might be suitable for a sales representative selling a data processing system featuring a small computer. The prospect is Mr. King, president of a large, local firm that distributes plumbing supplies. Mr. King is faced with mounting inventory control problems — according to information the sales representative has gleaned from several sources. This example — combined with examples of Steps 2 through 5 — constitutes a model for the idea-selling process, a prototype for developing idea-selling presentations covering the specific products or services you sell. However, the examples employed here are too imprecise for use in an actual data processing sales situation. Their only purpose is to illustrate concepts and techniques.

As the examples unfold, you'll observe that they are entirely one-sided — smooth sales presentations uninterrupted by the prospect. Obviously, it never really happens this way. The prospect usually interrupts repeatedly and often has much to say. Typical prospect responses are omitted here in order to bring into clearer focus a pattern for putting together idea-selling presentations that have maximum persuasive impact. Ways to handle prospect interruptions will be examined later. It's always easier to get back on the track, however, with a sales presentation that has been well thought out in advance.

Example of Idea-Selling Step 1

Good morning, Mr. King. I'm Alan Jones, sales representative for Apollo Data Systems. I assure you I'll be as brief as you want me to be. I appreciate very much having this opportunity to talk with you about a matter I believe you'll find very much worth your while.

I'm here to explore with you some ideas about a data processing system that can be employed to very good advantage in inventory control — along with various other applications. The experience of others bears out that our system simplifies and multiplies the efficiency of inventory control. At the same time, it also makes possible substantial reduction of overall investment in inventory, and reduction in the unit costs of many items stocked.

I'm very grateful to Mr. Smith of Central Bank for recommending me to you. He has a great many business contacts, and it seems likely he's aware of how well our MINI computer systems are working out for others—companies in other fields that also stock thousands of items. And a highly variable turnover rate is a rather common problem for those who must maintain large inventories.

You see, I've been boning up a little on the scope and some particulars of the inventory control problems besetting your particular type of business. I'm aware that overstocking as well as unexpected shortages of key items can both prove costly. Also that manual systems of maintaining inventory data are no longer adequate in the face of today's marketing demands and competitive pressures. But our data processing system can eliminate or vastly reduce many of those problems. Let me outline its key characteristics for you.

Note that the sales person *justifies* his sales overture by what he says in paragraph 2 and *qualifies* his credentials by what he says in paragraphs 3 and 4. He makes clear that he is familiar with a prospect problem that needs correction. This becomes the basis for the sales proposal he will then unfold for solving that problem, beginning with Step 2.

Let's conclude our examination of Step 1 by reviewing what Aristotle had to say about what the Introduction to a persuasive speech ought to be.

> The Introduction is the beginning of a speech . . . paving the way, as it were, for what is to follow. . . . This, then, is the most essential function and distinctive property of the introduction, to show what the aim of the speech is. . . . The appeal to the hearer aims at securing his goodwill, or . . . gaining his serious attention to the case. . . . You may use any means you choose to make your hearer receptive; among others, giving him a good impression of your character, which always helps to secure his attention. He will be ready to attend to anything . . . that is important, surprising, or agreeable; and you should accordingly convey to him the impression that what you have to say is of this nature.

Turn to Learning Exercise No. 9 in Appendix.

STEP 2. STATE YOUR SALES PROPOSAL
Purpose

This step embodies a concise statement of the core of your sales proposal. Its purpose is to fix the prospect's attention on the *specific selling ideas* you are prepared to develop in terms of their advantages to him. Your Step 2 proposal should brief him clearly on your key idea and how it can benefit him. This constitutes the main sales theme that you'll clarify, demonstrate, and perhaps prove as your presentation unfolds. State your key selling idea in terms that show you expect it to solve the prospect's problem or need as described in your Step 1 introduction. A good proposal statement intensifies your prospect's interest; it stimulates his readiness to hear and evaluate how your idea can improve his situation.

Suggestions for handling

Your sales proposal serves as conclusion for Step 1 as well as introduction to the Step 3 particulars that follow it. Your proposal provides transition from the introduction to the body of your sales presentation. Yet it should stand out as the recognizable anchor line of your entire sales message.

In planning a sales presentation, the proposal statement is a good place to start because it states the key idea — the objective — of that particular selling effort. After formulating the main purpose of your sales call, you decide how to introduce it (Step 1) and how to support it (Step 3). Although short, the proposal should be the most precisely thought-out part of the entire presentation.

Every proposal should be customized to fit the problem or need of one particular sales prospect. The ideas presented to support the proposal can then be tailored to fit that objective as the selling dialogue unfolds. But the proposal should convey in arresting langugage what you believe you can do for *that* prospect. It becomes a point of reference for all particulars of the sales interview that follow. A proposal statement should be brief — two or three sentences at most. Otherwise, it hasn't been well formulated for its purpose. Here is an example of a Step 2 proposal statement that the sales representative for Apollo Data

Systems might use in continuing his sales presentation to the prospect with the inventory control problem.

Example of Idea-Selling Step 2

> By utilizing one of our MINI series computers in your inventory control system, you can vastly improve efficiency of your sales/service functions. You may even be able to reduce inventory investment by as much as 40 percent. And this same computer can take over a substantial part of your accounting work load— thereby generating still more cost savings that can flow through to the bottom line.

This proposal statement headlines the key ideas that sales representative Alan Jones will try to sell his prospect. The prospect's willingness to buy the MINI computer is contingent on his acceptance of those ideas. Accordingly, Alan's proposal statement sets the stage for substantiating the merit of those ideas—his next step.

Turn to Learning Exercise No. 10 in Appendix.

We're now ready to move on to our idea-selling Step 3. This corresponds with Aristotle's proof of the statement, which he called the Argument.

STEP 3. CONVINCE THE PROSPECT THAT THE PROPOSAL WILL WORK

Purpose

The Step 2 proposal outlines only key aspects of your selling idea. The purpose of Step 3 is to fill in all the supporting particulars. This constitutes the body of your selling presentation by which you convince your prospect, point by point, that your proposal will produce the advantages and benefits you claim for it.

You now explain your proposition completely. In this step, you make full use of your knowledge of the features and benefits of your product or service. But select only those features and corresponding benefits that relate to this particular prospect's need. In Step 3, you "prove" your proposal is valid by employing explanation, description, demonstration, examples, endorsements, visual aids, and other suitable means.

Suggestions for handling

During this step, your sales presentation is most likely to become a dialogue with the prospect. At the outset, he may mostly listen and mentally size up you and your proposition. Expect him now to begin asking about any aspects that specially interest him or cause concern. This suggests that you should:

— Try to anticipate all critical points and cover them in your presentation.
— Be well prepared to answer questions as they arise.

Objections to specifics of your proposal are most likely to occur during this step. Expect them and deal positively with each as it arises. Handling objections successfully is a very important phase of selling that is examined in a later chapter.

Ask prompting questions of your own and listen carefully to your prospect's answers for clues to selling points that may need strengthening. It's also a good tactic to ask your prospect whether he agrees with major features as you explain them — for example, "Do you agree that this would represent a valuable advantage to you?" Obtaining concurrence progressively with parts of your sales presentation can help lead your propsect to accept the entire proposition.

Obviously, Step 3 needs to be well planned, point by point. Consider the order in which supporting ideas should unfold, if this is critical to your presentation. By having them all clearly in mind, you'll be able to resume your sales talk smoothly after being diverted by questions or objections.

The Step 3 example below particularizes why the sales prospect of Apollo Data Systems should seriously consider purchasing that MINI series computer. The dialogue covering the questions and objections that would surely arise is omitted to avoid obscuring the idea-selling techniques involved in this part of the sales presentation.

Example of Idea-Selling Step 3

Our compact MINI computer system is uniquely qualified to maintain an accurate perpetual inventory of every item you stock. Every new sales order entered into the data system becomes a commitment against the inventory. You can establish reorder points with variable lead times for every item; the computer can then be programmed to alert you when each item should be reordered. As incoming shipments move into stock, they are logged into the data system. A printout can tell you daily where you stand on every item if you wish.

These advantages together with other refinements in inventory control will position you to reduce overall inventory and still remain better prepared to serve your customers. And a reduction in inventory frees funds for other purposes. Inventory losses and waste will be minimized as will the incidence of backorders—all adding to operating profitability.

Since you'll be feeding data on all new orders into the computer anyhow, it's only logical to consider setting up the system to also handle order and shipping control, customer billing, accounts receivable, analysis of sales volume and profit margins, as well as other related functions. The MINI computer system is ideally equipped to handle all of this and more. This can give you virtually instant control of your costs of doing business because the cumulative effect of changes in unit prices and costs can be measured for any conceivable set of conditions you can project.

From this beginning, you can gradually transfer more of your accounting and financial functions into this system as rapidly as you can adjust internally to take advantage of the many options this affords you. You will then be able to undertake refinements in business management controls that are now beyond your reach.

Although an actual sales presentation of such a computer system would require many more facts, this example illustrates the nature of this phase of idea selling. Note that the sales representative concentrates on the benefits of the MINI computer system rather than on its internal electronic wizardry.

Aristotle had much to say about this phase of persuasive speech, but it is well summarized in this brief statement:

The duty of the Arguments is to attempt demonstrative proofs . . . [which] must bear directly upon the question in dispute.

How can we disagree? To reiterate, the purpose of idea-selling Step 3 is to ensure that the prospect gains a full understanding of the sales proposal and to convince him of its merits in relation to his particular problem or need.

Turn to Learning Exercise No. 11 in Appendix.

STEP 4. SUMMARIZE THE BENEFITS AND RESULTS OF THE PROPOSAL

Purpose

An old saw about how to make a good speech goes like this: "First you tell them what you're going to tell them; then you tell them; then you tell them what you told them." This incorporates what we do in our Step 4; we tell the prospect what we told him.

At this point, we undertake to wrap up the entire sales presentation by summarizing the key selling idea and the major points cited to support it. Avoid introducing anything new during this step. Concentrate now on showing how the projected results improve on the prospect's problem situation as outlined in introduction Step 1. Recap the features and benefits so the prospect can grasp the entire scope and merit of your proposal. In Step 3, you took the proposal apart to help the prospect understand each point. Now you put it all back together so he can better appreciate the overall advantages offered. This step provides a reassuring answer to his mental question, "What's in this for me?"

Suggestions for handling

Orient this phase of your presentation strongly toward *results*. Provide assurance that they will be achieved if your prospect accepts your sales proposal. Cite examples of good results obtained by others in similar situations. Employ testimonials; relate supporting facts and figures. Summarize what the prospect can expect to happen if he buys, and reassure him that all will work out satisfactorily.

If you're selling against competition, this is the time to point out any differences that you are sure are in your favor; maximize them without attacking your competitor. Emphasize the personal sales services you will provide as well as any special advantage of doing business with your company. Since price will have become a factor by this point, provide a credible comparison of the benefit values he'll receive relative to the costs. An example of this step follows in the words of the sales representative trying to sell the computer system.

Example of Idea-Selling Step 4

By installing our MINI computer, you will first of all solve your inventory control problems. A related result will be the opportunity to substantially reduce your total investment in inventory. This translates into a lower cost of doing business. And so do the reduced inventory losses this system makes possible. All this will contribute to increased operating profits.

In addition, by gradually transferring many of your order handling, customer billing, accounting, and financial control functions to the MINI computer, you can further increase your operating efficiencies. This should also result in still lower costs. And perhaps most important you'll greatly augment your management controls over your business. This may open up new opportunities for better overall business planning.

I'll be involved personally with installation of the MINI system in an overview control capacity. This will help ensure that it is set up to handle all the functional requirements we agree it should undertake. During this period, I'll be available at all times for any questions that arise. And it goes without saying that the whole installation will be backed fully by Apollo Data Systems. I gather you already have a recommendation from Mr. Smith of Central Bank. If you'd like, I can put you in touch with executives of several other companies who are using this system very successfully for similar applications.

Our sales presentation Step 4 corresponds closely in purpose and structure with the pattern outlined by Aristotle for the Epilogue of a persuasive speech. He had this to say about it:

The Epilogue has four parts. You must (1) make the audience well-disposed towards yourself and ill-disposed towards your opponent, (2) magnify or minimize the leading facts, (3) excite the required state of emotion in your hearers, and (4) refresh their memories.

That's about what we're trying to accomplish at this state as we prepare to close for the order — the primary purpose of climactic Step 5 of idea selling.

Turn to Learning Exercise No. 12 in Appendix.

STEP 5. ASK FOR DECISIVE ACTION
Purpose

There is good reason for calling this step "Ask for decisive action" instead of "Ask for the order." Getting a sales order on the spot is not always the immediate purpose of a sales presentation. Sometimes the sales order — or contract — can be landed only after several intermediate sales interviews, each building toward the climax. But when the sole purpose of the presentation is to close a sale, the meaning of Step 5 is indeed to ask for the order.

Every sales presentation must have an objective. If it is not to land a sales order, it may be to persuade the prospect to take the next step toward a major buying decision. Accordingly, the purpose of Step 5 is to obtain the prospect's agreement with whatever sales-related action you're seeking at that time.

Ideally, a point is reached during every presentation when all selling ideas have been expressed and all objections or questions have been satisfied. At that point, the prospect's decision often turns quite simply on his being asked for it. Step 5 is intended to evoke some kind of positive decision by the prospect. Yet sales people sometimes find it difficult to ask for action even when this is obviously the next logical move.

Reluctance to ask for decisive action often implies a vague hope that the prospect will volunteer a "yes" without the sales person's having to risk being rebuffed. In reality, the prospect ordinarily expects to be asked for his decision. Experienced buyers say they sometimes hold back, waiting for "the question," even though they're ready to place an order. They feel it's the sales person's responsibility to ask for it. By hesitating, the seller risks losing an order that may quite literally be his for the asking.

Asking for action is the natural close for a soundly made sales presentation. It often occurs almost as an anticlimax because both buyer and seller have gradually perceived during the sales dialogue that acceptance of the proposal is the likely outcome.

A sales person should start constructing his close for the order at the very beginning of his presentation. He can do this by sounding out his prospect periodically for agreement with key selling ideas as they unfold. These queries are sometimes called trial closes. When the idea-selling process has proceeded successfully, there remains at its close only one final question. And a positive response can be expected because of all those encouraging prior clues.

Suggestions for handling

Even though it's incumbent on the sales person to ask for action, it helps to do so in a way that makes it easier for the prospect to say yes. Try giving the prospect a little nudge if he's dallying in last-minute indecision. A number of closing techniques are effective in tilting the prospect toward positive action. Three of the most commonly used techniques – assuming acceptance, offering a choice, and asking for the order or a commitment – are discussed briefly below. Following each discussion is an example of how sales representative Alan Jones might use the technique in getting his prospect to agree to the next step in sales negotiations for the MINI computer system. Because of their scope, those negotiations might continue through several stages prior to the final decision.

1. *Assuming acceptance.* In using this technique, you reflect complete confidence that your prospect intends to accept your proposal. You ask a leading question that implies agreement. A positive response constitutes tacit acceptance of your proposition and initiates the desired action.

Example of Idea-Selling Step 5 — Closing by Assuming Acceptance

It seems evident that you're very impressed with the results you could expect from a MINI computer installation. Suppose we set up a meeting with your general manager, Mr. Prince, to begin planning the functions you'd like this system to perform at the outset. With that data in hand, we can make a specific proposal to you including costs and other particulars. If Mr. Prince is free right now, would you like to call him in so we can discuss this next step?

By agreeing with this next step, the prospect in effect indicates approval of the entire proposal. He's taking decisive action that is a move toward ultimate acceptance. But it may be easier for him to say, "Yes, let's talk with Mr. Prince" than for him to say, "Yes, I accept your proposal," especially since he's heard little thus far about cost or other particulars. This technique works just as well in less complex situations where an order on the spot is the objective. For example:

You mentioned this photo printer would come in handy for that job you have to get out late next week. I know we have several in stock; suppose I phone in right now and see if we can deliver one to you by Monday?

Your reactions suggest you'd like very much to be the owner of this particular model. And by ordering it today, you can still get in on the special price. Why don't I write up the order right now so we can clinch the deal?

In these instances, the actions instituted by the sales person — unless expressly stopped by the prospect — result in consummation of the sale.

2. *Offering a choice.* Although simple in concept, this technique requires skillful handling. It involves offering the prospect an either/or choice between two actions neither of which explicitly asks him to accept the proposal. But choosing either

of the alternatives offered is tantamount to acceptance. That's because either choice initiates the action the sales person seeks.

Example of Idea-Selling Step 5—Closing by Offering a Choice

> From your responses, I sense that you're quite interested in all the advantages a MINI computer installation would create for you. But we'll have to do a little preliminary planning with your people on the specific functions you'll want the system to perform. With that information, we can then make you a specific proposal including costs and other particulars. Should we plan to include only the inventory control functions or would you like us to go further and cover some of the order control and accounting functions as well?

Agreeing with either suggestion amounts to accepting the basic proposal because it gets things started. But it's easier to express a choice between the two alternatives offered than to signify outright acceptance of the proposal at this preliminary stage. Simpler variations of this technique of closing by offering a choice can be applied where the situation is less complex. For example:

> Would you prefer the hand-operated or the automatic model for the application you have in mind?

> Would you like to pay for this on an annual basis, or does the quarterly payment plan fit your situation better?

> Which finish would you prefer, the natural wood with the satin gloss or the high gloss, lacquered finish?

The prospect's selective response to each of these choices virtually commits him to buying.

3. *Asking for the order or a commitment.* Sometimes the situation isn't appropriate for using subtleties in closing. Or perhaps oblique closing techniques have been tried and the prospect still holds back. When this happens, it's necessary to ask the order question in more direct terms. Since the purpose

of the presentation is to gain some kind of decision, it's far better to risk a no than to leave the matter up in the air by not asking. The question can still be phrased so as to avoid seeming to be blunt. Although such an impasse would be unlikely in the MINI computer selling situation, it might be handled in the following manner if it did arise.

Example of Idea-Selling Step 5 — Closing by asking for the Order or a Commitment

You've shown a great deal of interest in the potential of our MINI computer system for solving many of your inventory and accounting problems. You've also indicated an urgent need to do something about those problems. Suppose we set up a series of meetings between some of our specialists and the department heads you choose in order to begin working out some particulars. Then we can follow up with a more precise proposal. Either Wednesday or Thursday of next week would be fine for us for the first meeting; which of those days would you prefer?

Although this tactic includes characteristics of both techniques previously examined, it is much more direct. It should produce some definite response. In less complex selling situations, approaches similar to the following may work.

Should we go ahead with a first shipment of enough material for a trial so you can check out how it works in your process?

Would you like us to ship one gross to start with for testing customer response?

Would you like to give me a deposit now as a binder so we can start on your order?

I believe we've covered every question either of us can think of and every answer has been favorable. I'm ready to write up your order; how should your billing name and address read to be correct?

The prospect can scarcely escape making some kind of definite answer to questions like these. And his response is most likely to be positive when the sales presentation has been well prepared and well expressed.

Summary of Idea-Selling Step 5

The foregoing closing techniques, and the countless variations possible, should make it easier for you to ask for action more confidently and make it more comfortable for the prospect to say yes. People are often skittish about making decisions even though they realize they should do so. We sometimes look for an excuse to "think it over." This is another facet of human nature to be reckoned with in selling. The professional sales person learns to ask for action so adeptly on concluding a masterful sales presentation that acceptance of his proposal is the natural outcome expected and is welcomed by both buyer and seller.

Aristotle recommended a very direct close for a persuasive talk, such as: I have finished; you now have all the facts and I ask for your decision. We are much indebted to Aristotle for his legacy about the principles of persuasion.

Turn to Learning Exercise No. 13 in Appendix.

Summary on the Persuasive Selling Process

1. *Write out basic sales presentations.* There is only one way to master the skills of persuasive selling; that is to practice them persistently. Practice applies to becoming proficient in selling techniques as surely as it does to acquiring skill in sports.

Professionalism in sales persuasion begins with the thoughtful working out of basic sales presentations covering the principal products or services you sell—using the five-step idea-selling format as a guide. This should be done in writing, because for most of us this is the only way we can logically think through the ideas we want to convey, consider the results we want to emphasize, and determine the best timing and all the other factors that make up a good sales talk. Writing out our ideas also enables us to visualize them mentally. This helps fix them in mind for better recall when needed. Very few sales people can make polished sales presentations — the kind that sell — without this kind of careful preparation.

After developing a set of basic sales presentations, retain them in a three-ring binder or other suitable holder for ready reference. Review them occasionally to keep your persuasive skills in good form. And update them as you accumulate new selling ideas or obtain additional data on the performance of a product or service.

2. *Canned sales talks.* Some employers provide their sales people with prepared material to use for sales talks. This ensures that sales points considered most important by the employer are not overlooked. It also contributes to some uniformity in sales presentations by all sales people involved, if this is desirable. Reciting such material slavishly results in stereotyped sales talks, however, especially when sales people parrot expressions that are unnatural to them. The best approach is for them to rework employer-prepared sales talk material into their own language.

3. *Rehearse sales presentations.* Finally, rehearse your sales presentations aloud so you can sense how you sound to others. Do this before a live audience if possible — your spouse or a friend, anyone willing to provide feedback on how you're coming across. If you lack an audience, try rehearsing with a tape recorder; the playback will sound different from what you expected. Better still, if you can rehearse before a closed-circuit videotape camera, do so. You may be amazed — even shocked — when you see as well as hear yourself as others do. This experience can do more than any other to reveal, and induce you to correct, mannerisms or peculiarities of speech that may detract from your selling effectiveness.

Creating and rehearsing basic sales presentations presumes that you possess thorough knowledge of the features and benefits of whatever you sell. That combination of knowledge and skill provides you with flexibility for mastering every sales situation that can occur—each situation is unique in some respect. The self-confidence this generates permeates your sales presentations. In-depth preparation enables you to adjust a sales presentation on the spot to meet variations in prospect problems or needs as they arise. You are then well on your way to becoming a truly professional sales person.*

Turn to Learning Exercise No. 14 in Appendix.

---

* It may be constructive to point out that the five-step idea-selling process is an effective format for other persuasive purposes. It is useful for organizing an oral or written proposal covering a new product, service, or plan. If you speak occasionally before a trade association or community group, the five-step idea-selling pattern is also excellent for preparing and delivering an orderly, interesting, and persuasive talk.

COPING WITH CUSTOMER RESISTANCE, OBJECTIONS, AND COMPLAINTS

CHAPTER 5

So far we've presented selling as a process likely to culminate in a sale whenever the benefits of product or service are communicated persuasively enough. And perhaps we've implied thereby that the prospect is always likely to accede to a good sales talk. This arbitrary hypothesis is convenient for examining the subtleties of sales persuasion from the seller's vantage point. But in the real world of selling, the unpredictable reactions of customers are forever complicating things. So if we've seemed to suggest that mastering the skills of persuasion assures success for every well-prepared sales effort, we hasten to point out that this isn't necessarily the outcome. On the contrary, sales people must be constantly prepared to make quick adjustments in sales tactics to cope successfully with subtle sales resistance and with an infinite variety of objections raised by prospective customers.

As already emphasized, it takes two to consummate a sale—a skillful seller and a willing buyer. Each has his own individual objectives, wants, needs, preferences, prejudices, stature, personal characteristics, communicative ability, and a host of other attributes. Selling involves recognizing and reconciling the many differences that can arise, and arriving at a balance between the values sought by buyer and seller for the benefit of both.

The burden of creating this balance rests with the sales person. It is scarcely likely that agreement can be brought about without some differences arising between the two. How to recognize and deal constructively with these hindrances is what this chapter is about.

A reality of selling is that prospective customers seldom accept without question a sales person's representations about his product or service no matter how skillfully they are stated. Characteristically, prospects raise objections and ask questions; they also equivocate, evade, stall, and sometimes even seem to ignore or belittle the sales person. Sometimes they also complain bitterly about some aspect of a completed sales transaction that displeases them, whether the injury is real or fancied. In other words, customers react about like people are prone to do in all other kinds of human relationships; they reflect the full spectrum of human virtues and fallibilities.

All this can be quite disconcerting and discouraging to a sales person not prepared to expect and accept such occurrences as inherent in the selling process. New sales people, especially, need to discipline themselves to deal with such frustrations in a positive way. It is important for them to learn early that these are normal features of the give-and-take that is characteristic of the selling process. So this constitutes still another challenge for which they need to develop matching skills. They must recognize that the abrasiveness that sometimes occurs in sales negotiations seldom reflects personal animosity. Adroit, diplomatic mollification of the customer is called for, nevertheless. And they must learn to discern in the obstacles that arise the tips they can often reveal about strategy or tactics that may help close the sale. It is by dint of this preparation and practice that sales people achieve command of the selling situations and rise above being buffeted by them.

It is not easy to acquire sure-footed skill in this phase of selling, which involves being constantly ready to counter resistance with little prior indication of the form it may take. But being aware of the kinds of obstacles that arise and some techniques others employ to cope with them can render sales resistance less debilitating.

Sales resistance. This encompasses both the overt and covert evasive tactics prospects may use — intentionally or unconsciously — to avoid or deflect your initial sales overtures. Falling within this category are all the negative things prospects may say or do *before* your selling effort ever really begins — primarily to avoid being disturbed or diverted from whatever is more engrossing to them at the moment. They may resist even though they vitally need the product or service about to be offered, albeit a need that sometimes goes unrecognized until a sales person points it out.

This type of "don't bother me" resistance should be regarded as a natural human reaction to any interference with whatever is comfortable or habitual. It occurs in many forms and requires skillful penetration in order to obtain even passive reception for a sales overture. Many authorities on selling call this "arousing interest" or "gaining attention." We'll examine several varieties of this genus of sales resistance and the reasons they sprout; we'll also provide suggestions for wilting them so that fruitful selling ideas can take root.

Sales objections. These also belong to genus sales resistance, but they are a more specific and virulent variety. They also require more vigorous countermeasures to keep them from smothering a budding sale. A sales objection usually arises *during* a sales presentation; otherwise it closely resembles any other type of sales resistance. Many objections are entirely appropriate; prospects properly raise them to voice exception to or ask questions about aspects of product or service that don't appear to fill their needs. But other objections camouflage the prospect's *real* reason for resisting the sale. These are usually the most difficult to recognize, interpret, and neutralize constructively.

A valuable characteristic of many objections, however, is that they tend to reveal what concerns or interests the prospect most about the product being considered. Being alert to clues enables you to zero in more closely on your potential customer's wants and needs. Such objections are blessings in disguise rather than hindrances. Often they can be skillfully converted into convincing sales points. Many sales people—the best prepared and most proficient—say they welcome objections because they guide the way toward landing an order.

A sale isn't likely to result unless all objections raised are dealt with constructively. This is another compelling reason for preparing yourself thoroughly on the features and benefits of whatever you sell, including prices, policies, and all other critical factors. Objections can be taken as an encouraging sign that the prospect is interested. Otherwise, why would he bother to question the merits of the sales proposal? Objections take many forms and can occur at any time during a sales effort. We'll examine the most prevalent types and suggest ways for turning them to advantage.

Sales complaints. These are objections that occur *after* the sale has been made—often after the product has been delivered or the service rendered. Something has gone wrong. Delivery requirements haven't been adhered to, or the product has proven faulty, or the service has not been satisfactory, or results did not meet expectations, or. . . . Unhappily, such occurrences seem to be inevitable. The best companies experience them even after taking every conceivable precaution to ensure customer satisfaction.

Related to complaints are the customer claims that often accompany them, demands for reimbursement, or offsetting deductions arbitrarily taken from remittances due. Settling such claims satisfactorily becomes even stickier if they are not entirely justified, such as when the customer himself is partly at fault for whatever went wrong.

There is seldom any one best way to handle a complaint or claim. Settling either problem satisfactorily and salvaging the customer's good will as well often require the wisdom and patience of Solomon. We'll discuss some do's and don'ts distilled from the experiences of many sales people.

Coping with Sales Resistance

Attempts to create neat lists of categories of sales resistance and corresponding remedies are usually unproductive. People's reactions to selling ideas are much too complex to permit useful cataloging of "proven methods for countering sales resistance." Even psychologists often can't agree on the reasons for what people say and do.

A more practical approach is to formulate guidelines for recognizing the most common manifestations of sales resistance. This can help you learn how to neutralize the resistance by using your own techniques. The sales resistance tactics reviewed below can arise during *any* phase of a selling effort.

But they are most typical of the reluctance likely to appear during exploratory calls or while trying to arrange an initial interview. At this stage, preliminary prospecting and qualifying steps not requiring direct customer contact have probably been completed. You're reasonably sure you have a good prospect and you're beginning your sales approach.

INERTIA AND INDIFFERENCE

Inertia and indifference are perhaps the most pervasive forms of sales resistance. Their close cousins are complacency, habit, procrastination, satisfaction with the status quo, a sense of obligation to other suppliers, reluctance to encourage a new involvement, and related negative reactions. To a sensitive sales person, any of these can represent a brushoff. It is human nature to resist change—often to fear it—even when it's apparent that some kind of change is needed.

Presence of such resistance factors can be surmised from prospect responses that include expressions such as:

"We're satisfied with our present supplier (or service or product)."

"I'll think it over. Just send me some literature."

"I'm too busy today. Call me again sometime later."

"I don't know you or your company."

"I doubt if you could help me."

"Just leave your card. I'll get in touch with you if anything comes up."

No doubt you've heard many variations of responses similar to those. Sometimes they are valid, but what they usually are shouting silently but clearly is:

> You must shake me hard and quickly with a promising new idea or I'll revert to the self-satisfied situation you're now disturbing and I'll soon forget all about you!

This is your cue to do just that—shake your prospect with an idea that will awaken in him an urgent desire to hear more from you. This must be a brief, undisguised, confidently expressed appeal to his self-interest—usually centered on something that will earn or save him money or otherwise improve his situation. The more positive and dramatic you can make it, the better. It helps immensely if you can reveal that you already possess some pertinent knowledge of his situation and needs. This bespeaks your personal interest in him, which in turn kindles his interest in you. Your appeal can take the form of a direct statement including shaker phrases such as:

> I'm prepared to offer you . . . that will save you . . . which will enlarge . . . increase . . . expand . . . improve your results . . . your position . . . or satisfaction . . . or prestige . . . or stature . . . or attractiveness. . . .

Sometimes your quick appeal can be even more effective if stated as a question that includes phrases such as:

> Wouldn't you like to learn about a new . . . that will save you . . . improve your profits . . . expand your output . . . increase your efficiency . . . provide more safety . . . broaden your coverage . . . enhance your stature . . . increase your self-esteem?

Your prospect can scarcely say no to a question like that. Your immediate objective is simply to plant a promising idea with enough enthusiasm to convince him that he might be passing up something valuable if he doesn't learn more about it. This can set the stage for a later interview at a mutually convenient time; or it may lead into a sales presentation then and there if the time is opportune and you are prepared to follow through. Adequate preparation on your part should be threefold.

1. Learn enough *in advance* about the prospect, his situation, and his needs to qualify you to discuss them with him, as well as to qualify him as a potential customer.

2. Have ready several key "shaker upper" appeals for penetrating inertia or indifference whenever you encounter it. These shakers should be condensed but exciting adaptations of the selling idea that comprises the central theme of your sales presentation for that product or service.

3. Have a well-prepared five-point idea-selling presentation that you are ready to launch whenever you've created a receptive opening for it.

It's usually a good idea to memorize a set of suitable shaker-uppers so they'll be at the tip of your tongue for instant use. Your sales presentation should be thoroughly developed and well rehearsed, but seldom memorized. This gives you more flexibility for meeting objections easily and naturally as they arise. Such preparation and action are the surest way to penetrate inertia and indifference—the forms of resistance usually most baffling to most sales people. An apt postscript might be that many people automatically resist initial sales overtures largely because of unfortunate past experiences. They have become conditioned to a need for resisting the pressure tactics of unqualified sales people who obviously haven't bothered to become familiar with the needs and interests of prospective customers.

AVOID REINFORCING SALES RESISTANCE

Some sales people unwittingly reinforce sales resistance by reflecting attitudes that raise the prospect's guard. They try to overcome resistance by applying more pressure. They feel they must prevail as a matter of honor. So they sell still harder in the hope of gaining some degree of acceptance. This only generates more resistance. A standoff results from which no one benefits. This syndrome doubtless stems from the discredited but residual concept that selling constitutes an adversary relationship between buyer and seller in which one must win by outwitting the other. A sales person's combative instincts should be exercised in outmaneuvering a competitor—never in overpowering a prospective customer.

Easy does it is the password for neutralizing sales resistance. Nothing can be gained by continuing to press an unyielding prospect. Far better to simply introduce the key selling idea in promising, enthusiastic terms and then retire graciously for another try later. If the prospect has a valid need for your product or service and your selling idea is sound, it will be working for you in the meantime. You're likely to find him much more receptive the next time you call. He'll remember you as a friendly, helpful person rather than as an antagonist.

Keep in mind that sales resistance is sometimes a temporary reflex; it may result from preoccupation with a situation entirely unrelated to your sales effort. Give the prospect the benefit of the doubt and try again later.

FRIENDSHIP AND TRUST

Abraham Lincoln is credited with having said that if you want to win a man to your cause, you must first convince him you are his friend. Lincoln would have made a great sales trainer; one would be hard pressed to give better advice than that to a new sales person. It's not only easier to sell a prospect with whom you've established a friendly relationship; it also makes selling a lot more fun.

How do you do it? Simply start out by being friendly with a new prospect, and he's likely to reciprocate. People are usually friendly to friendly people. By demonstrating genuinely friendly behavior, you virtually impel the other person to respond likewise. Otherwise, the prospect soon develops an uneasy discomfort that he can dispel only by being nice to you, too.

A show of friendliness that is superficial can wear thin very quickly, however. It must be accompanied by evidence of genuine liking for your prospect. The best evidence is doing or offering to do things that help him. This is nothing more or less than applying the Golden Rule, "Do unto others as you would have them do unto you"—and it works. It's a great neutralizer for sales resistance.

If you should drift into an at-odds situation with a prospect, readjust your own attitudes and reactions into a positive, friendly stance and watch your prospect change with you. It's an almost automatic reflex. This again reflects the facet of human nature that impels most people to appear likable to others who appear to like them.

A friendly demeanor works magic not only for quickly establishing rapport with new prospects but also for retaining established customers. We all prefer doing business with our friends. When a long, pleasant relationship can be maintained with a customer, it's far more difficult for a competitor to break in. And if one does try to do so, your customer will usually let you know soon enough for you to respond. It's axiomatic, however, that a business friendship must be accompanied by continued good quality and service in whatever you sell. It's fatal to assume that friendship will offset for very long any short-comings in the benefits of doing business with you.

WHO YOU ARE AND WHAT YOU WANT

To round out this review of antidotes for sales resistance, let's examine one more cause and remedy. This is the impression sales people make when introducing themselves — particularly to new prospects. First impressions are important; they have a lingering influence on a prospect's reaction to a sales representative and his proposals.

Besides being friendly, it is essential to develop a courteous, positive manner of presenting yourself that leaves no doubt about who you are or your purpose. A hesitant, uncertain approach can generate resistance beginning with the opening salutation. Any prospect worth trying to sell is usually a busy person; his time is valuable; he may encounter many sales people daily — all competing for his attention and acceptance. You must stand out favorably among them, gain recognition for yourself and your product, make a good impression he'll remember, preview what you propose to do for him, and do all of that quickly — unless you find yourself in the happy circumstances of being invited to elaborate on your proposition.

So announce in your opening statements who you are, whom you represent, what you came to talk about and why. Pause for small talk only as long as the prospect appears to welcome it. Then state your shaker-upper confidently and expectantly. Beyond that point, close attention to your prospect's verbal responses and visible reactions will guide you on how much of your sales story it's wise to unfold on a first call. It's a mistake to push further and faster than your prospect appears ready to accept; trying to do so will only generate resistance. But if you have captured his interest, you may be able to complete your entire sales presentation on the spot and obtain an order. This is great for those who are expected to make a sale in one or two calls.

A McGraw-Hill Publications Co. advertisement that appeared several years ago portrayed very graphically what a sales person's introduction needs to accomplish. The ad pictured a buyer facing a young sales person and saying:

> I don't know who you are.
> I don't know your company.
> I don't know your company's product.
> I don't know what your company stands for.
> I don't know your company's customers.
> I don't know your company's record.
> I don't know your company's reputation.
> Now — what was it you wanted to sell me?*

This quotation sums up quite well the challenge every sales person faces in overcoming the natural sales resistance of a new prospect.

Turn to Learning Exercise No. 15 in Appendix.

Coping with Objections

The kinds of sales resistance we've reviewed so far often bear no relation either to whether your prospect has any need for your wares or to the likelihood of his buying them. Now we'll consider various ways of coping with objections raised to particular aspects of your sales presentation. The situation is altered somewhat now, because your prospect has presumably become a willing listener. This subtly changes the nature of his sales resistance from passive and ill defined to active and specific. He now begins to evaluate what you tell him in terms of his wants or needs, the price and value of your product, his ability to buy or pay, other options for using his available funds, optimal timing for buying, and whether he even wants to hear any more of your sales story as he begins to perceive the thrust of its message more clearly.

Your prospect may express his reservations quite openly, or he may signal vaguely that he's keeping some of them to him-

---

* Reprinted by permission of McGraw-Hill Publications Company.

self. In either case your challenge as a sales person is to identify and satisfy each of his doubts; otherwise he's not likely to make a buying commitment. This human need for satisfaction surfaces in any situation involving choice and decision. Satisfying prospect objections, whether or not they are voiced, constitutes a critical juncture in the selling process.

OBJECTIONS DEFINED

Most objections are rational, inquisitive, evaluative responses of a prospect to a sales presentation. Most objections are not contentious rejections of a sales person's sales story. But some sales people irrationally fear all objections because they assume erroneously that most are raised primarily to block or undermine a sales effort.

In its most forthright form, an objection is simply a question or criticism by means of which the prospect seeks clarification of some aspect or fact about product, service, performance, cost, or whatever, that he doesn't quite understand or agree with. At the other end of the scale, an objection can be an obscure negative comment that camouflages—unconsciously or purposely—the real reason the prospect hesitates to commit himself.

Somewhat similarly, a prospect may say bluntly, "Not interested," although something in his manner suggests it might be good strategy to pursue the matter further, but with more ideas and not right now. Objections can be highly complex in manifestation and meaning.

Objections can be likened to pawns in a game of chess. They're advanced by the prospect in part to test the sales person's skill or product knowledge. Objections should never be anticipated with foreboding or guarded against as threatening moves to checkmate. Objections open up the action much as do moves of pawns in a chess game. Each should be calmly noted, considered respectfully, and countered skillfully. Each creates opportunity. An objection can provide clues to what the prospect has in mind if he is playing a subtle game with you—or with himself.

All objections constitute expressions of doubt regarding the seller's proposal—doubts that must be removed to help the prospect reach a decision to buy. Most doubts fall into two broad categories:

— Those that are *genuine* expressions of concern or requests for more information.
— Those that can be described as *insincere* because they mask the prospect's true attitude.

GENUINE OBJECTIONS

Genuine objections are generally the more common form. Most genuine objections can be ascribed to three principal motivations:

1. Uncertainties that reflect the prospect's personality and habitual reactions;
2. Uncertainties relating to the prospect's situation that prompts his possible interest in buying;
3. Uncertainties that relate to adequacy of the seller's product or service for the prospect's need.

Each of these sources of objections comprises a countless variety of relatively identifiable doubts. They can occur singly and in complex combinations. Genuine objections can be viewed as being positive, in the sense that they reflect the prospect's tentative interest in buying if his doubts can be dissolved. By raising objections, he is, in effect, asking the sales person to help him reach a favorable decision.

INSINCERE OBJECTIONS

Insincere objections result, for the most part, from two kinds of motivation. The first is a pervasive desire to avoid involvement in the selling interaction; a vague escape wish. This is characterized by a wide variety of typically transparent excuses many of which can be tactfully penetrated. Such evasive reactions are most likely to occur during the initial sales approach; they have already been reviewed in the section "Coping with Sales Resistance."

The second kind of motivation is an intentional or unconscious effort by the prospect to conceal the real reason he doesn't want the sales interview to make progress. This is characterized by doubts or delaying tactics masquerading behind every manner of oblique verbal expression or subterfuge. Sometimes the stated objection masks a bias toward buying if only certain obstacles could be removed without too much pain. This helps explain the masquerade. The prospect may even be interested, but he tries to protect the sales person, someone else, or even himself from the discomfort or damage that might occur if he admitted candidly why he can't be brought to buy.

Insincere objections must be viewed as inherently negative but should not be considered irreversible. Concealed objections, however, do present a challenge to the sales person's skill at identifying the true reasons for a prospect's resistance. Once they're known, the seller proceeds to reverse those reasons by using tactics similar to those for dealing with genuine objections.

The breakdown and analysis of the two kinds of objections on the following two pages may help clarify the motivations for objections and the relationships between them.

SEEK OUT THE REAL REASONS
BEHIND INSINCERE OBJECTIONS

How much insincerity you encounter among sales prospects depends in part on what you sell and to whom. Those selling to business and industry face comparatively little insincerity among professional buyers or others whose function requires being alert to all opportunities. Such people are apt to be direct and positive in their questions and objections; they don't like to waste time playing games. Nevertheless, they may be obscure at times in negotiations relating to price, competitive situations, and the like.

Sales people dealing with nonprofessional buyers or with the general public are more likely to encounter insincere or uncertain responses. People who buy only occasionally tend to be more reserved with sales people—perhaps out of concern about being deceived or persuaded unwillingly. They're aware that the sales person possesses special skills; being unskilled at buying, they feel impelled to hold the sales person off while they mull over what to them are weighty decisions. One way of

Motivations for Genuine Objections

Potentially positive, these motivations reflect interest in buying if doubts can be removed.

Primary motivation	Factors creating doubt or delay
1 Uncertainties generated by personal factors, such as:	Prospect's personality and habits Procrastination Indecision Doubts about own competence Personality clash with salesperson Reaction to seller's product Reaction to seller's company Reservations about proposal Reluctance due to past experience Problems with similar products Friendship with competitors Doubts about authority to buy Other factors
2 Uncertainties relating to prospects buying situation, such as:	Doubts about need for product or service Prior commitment to competitor Interest in competitive products Limitations: space, time, etc. Business conditions – sales volume Timing: availability vs. need Maintenance requirements Service requirements Profitability – margins Availability of funds or credit Other factors

3
Uncertainties about product or service being offered, such as:
	Faulty understanding of utility of
	  product or service
	Doubts about benefits claimed
	Doubts about seller's dependability
	Questions about suitability of
	  product or service relative to:
	　Quality　　　Durability
	　Performance　Safety
	　Complexity　Availability
	　Productivity.　Profitability
	　Dependability　Cost/value
	　Service　　　Other

Motivations for Insincere Objections

Predominantly negative, these motivations must be analyzed and overcome or neutralized to convert into interest in buying.

Primary motivation

Factors creating doubt or delay

1
Simple evasion marked by excuses concealing personal factors, such as:

Inertia or indifference
Satisfaction with status quo
Reluctance to consider change
Procrastination
Indecision
Desire to avoid responsibility
Desire to avoid being disturbed
Desire to avoid involvment
Inclination to belittle or
  frustrate sales person
Other negative factors

2
Camouflage for a *real* objection, which includes such factors as:

Lack of confidence in sales
  person
Lack of confidence in supplier
Delaying tactics in order to:
    Obtain other proposals
    Compare with other proposals
    Check with superiors
Desire to avoid disclosing:
    Lack of buying authority
    Need for approval by others
    Lack of funds for buying
    Inability to finance
    Commitment to competitor
    Consideration of competitive
      proposal
    Reluctance to buy for fear
      of making a mistake
Desire to avoid obligating self
Desire to favor a friend
Desire to induce sales person to
  sell harder
Desire to aggrandize self
Other concealed factors

gaining time for this is for them to mask their real feelings behind insincere excuses or objections.

So it is that many new sales people have some difficulty in becoming accustomed to insincere objections and learning how to uncover their real meaning. Just being aware that such tactics reflect a natural human reaction helps one cope with them. Patience is often the key; a cautious buyer can't be pressured. Trial and error remains the best teacher in this skill area. Here are several useful methods for identifying the real objection when it is being obscured by an insincere camouflage.

• Observe the prospect's reaction to your sales story. If he seems to lose interest after you've made several sales points that are usually effective, go over them again briefly and ask if he has any questions. This may induce him to indicate why he has been unresponsive and give you a clue for proceeding.

• Observe the prospect's reaction when you respond to an objection he has raised. If he appears unconcerned and unimpressed, chances are the objection was an insincere cover for his real reason for resisting. Try asking questions like: Does that answer your question? Is there any other problem? What is your real reason . . . ? Continued tactful questioning is usually your best tool—often your only recourse. Sooner or later the prospect is likely to begin: "Well, I'll tell you . . ." and then reveal what the problem really is.

• Guessing at the real objection and phrasing it as a question sometimes helps identify it. For example, after asking, "Could it be you feel our price is out of line?" you can follow up with more value points justifying the price. This may help uncover whether price or financing is the real point of resistance.

• Restate a suspect objection with a twist in meaning that provides opportunity for relating more selling points—preferably points bearing on a likely real objection. This will sometimes bring it out into the open.

• Questioning too persistently can be self-defeating. If it's an important prospect whom you can see again readily, it may be better to try uncovering the real objection more casually over a longer period of time.

Whatever they are, the real objections must be identified before they can be resolved. If the prospect's excuses are still impenetrable after reasonable effort, you may be wasting your time. This is all part of that sales game of chess being played out between prospect and sales person.

BE PREPARED TO MEET AND HANDLE OBJECTIONS

We've pointed out that most genuine objections double as requests for more information about your product or service, its performance, results to be expected, quality and service considerations, availability and delivery concerns, price and terms of sale, or other particulars. Insincere objections reflect prospect uncertainty that needs to be penetrated to isolate the real reasons for resistance so that you can deal with them objectively.

The right-hand columns in the two motivation charts contain checklists of a broad variety of underlying reasons that can form the basis for objections. The better prepared you are to provide the prospect with information relating to those reasons for objecting, the less likely you are to stumble over objections.

GENERAL GUIDELINES FOR HANDLING OBJECTIONS

Certain largely common-sense guidelines should be followed when responding to any objection, whatever its motivation. When an objection is primarily a request for more information, often all that is needed to dissolve the prospect's doubts is to supply that information clearly and factually. There are also a number of effective techniques for countering objections that require altering the prospect's point of view in order to win him over to your proposal. First we'll review some general guidelines for coping with any kind of objection. Then we'll examine several of those special techniques.

Listen attentively. This simple admonition should be evident, but it bears emphasizing nonetheless. When a prospect raises an objection, he wants to be heard and usually expects a constructive reply. Only by listening carefully can you make sure you understand the objection clearly enough to respond effectively. Yet some sales people jump to conclusions after hearing only part of what the prospect is trying to say. Then they reply prematurely — sometimes even interrupting the prospect to do so. Such a reflex response is often self-defeating and is discourteous as well. Lightning-like judgments in answering objections are often faulty, and they usually reflect poor strategy.

By listening attentively, you not only learn what is really on your prospect's mind, you also beam him a message that says: "Your opinions are important to me and I respect them. They deserve thoughtful consideration." When the prospect finishes voicing his objection, pause a little before replying. This provides you more time for framing the most appropriate response, and reassures your prospect that you are considering what he has said. He is therefore more likely to give your reply careful consideration in return.

Question your prospect respectfully. Tactful questioning about the doubt your prospect has expressed goes hand in hand with attentive listening. This helps clarify the prospect's objection, reinforces your stance of taking it seriously, gives you more time to consider it fairly and often increases the likelihood of gaining his agreement. Encourage him to talk by asking questions such as: Can you explain your reasons for that opinion a little more fully? or What performance would you expect of a product adequate for your need? Questions beginning with "Why" are also very useful in dealing with objections. In answering them, your prospect may find himself satisfying his own objection; he may also discover it isn't quite as critical as he thought, or he may decide that the issue really isn't worth pressing.

A prospect sometimes objects in order to clarify his own thinking. He also may simply want to reaffirm that the pending decision is his to make — not the seller's to impose. By asking questions, the sales person invites the prospect's participation. This tends to reinforce the prospect's positive feelings about both the seller and his proposition. It is a gross error for a sales person to feel he must always dominate the talking in order to make a sale. Tactful questions can sometimes help a prospect talk himself into buying.

Paraphrase objections. A more subtle variation of asking questions of the prospect is to restate his objection in paraphrased form, often closing with a question. This technique can accomplish several things:

1. It demonstrates that you haven't folded — that you intend to answer the objection but are first making sure you understand it correctly.
2. It reinforces the prospect's self-regard by showing that you take his objection seriously and appreciate his point of view. This alone often scales down the seriousness with which the prospect views the objection and may induce him to soften his stance.
3. It gives you a little more time to decide on the best response.
4. It gives you an opportunity to transform the prospect's objection into a more readily handled request for information.

For example, suppose your prospect says:

> What you say is all very interesting, but there's a lot at stake here in considering any change in the process we're now using. A small saving is hardly worth jeopardizing the highly dependable results we've been getting for a long time.

You might rephrase this as:

> I recognize that that is a very critical point with you, as it should be. As I see it, you're questioning whether there are enough advantages to justify using my product — perhaps after making a trial run first to check out its dependability. Is that about right?

That isn't precisely what he said, and it also introduces the idea of a trial. But it's not very likely that he'll disagree seriously with your restatement. This reopens opportunity for you to spell out still more reasons why your product should fill his need and at a savings as well. Also, you can now pursue the idea of making a trial run to verify your claims for the product.

Observe your prospect's reactions and control your own re-

actions. The oft-heard truism that actions speak louder than words is a factor in selling, particularly when dealing with objections. It is especially important to avoid displaying any resistance or hostility when an objection is raised; doing so will only reinforce the objection. On the other hand, a show of mild surprise or perplexity on your part can sometimes help by suggesting to the prospect that his doubts are probably unfounded, which you then clarify in words.

A positive, enthusiastic tone of voice and an assured manner are always a constructive stance for a sales person. Use expressive gestures — in moderation. Also smile — often. There are few better ways of disarming a prospect's objection than showing by a smile that it doesn't disturb you. Treat him as the personal friend you want him to become. And by all means, avoid being drawn into an argument. Even the most vigorously stated objection tends to lose some of its force when it's not resisted in kind.

This means of communicating ideas and insights works for both seller and buyer. Observe carefully your prospect's demeanor, tone of voice, points made and degree of emphasis, the expression in his eyes, and so on. All of these can provide clues to the full meaning of what he says. Today, the term body language is applied to this form of communication, which has long been employed effectively in selling.

SPECIAL TECHNIQUES FOR HANDLING OBJECTIONS

No single technique for handling objections is best for every situation. Experienced sales people usually employ a combination of approaches — selecting and adjusting tactics to meet each objection as it is raised. Such versatility calls for familiarity with a variety of techniques and skill in using them, which comes only from experience.

Several rhetorical tactics for countering objections and converting them from liabilities into assets and opportunities are much relied upon. They are techniques that have been used with good results for generations by those skilled in persuading others to alter their points of view. The origins of these techniques reach far back into the history of the arts of communication, as do the origins of idea selling. These techniques can be applied effectively in selling, so we'll examine them from that vantage point.

Agree and counter with new ideas. Perhaps the best-known and most-used technique is one often referred to as the "Yes . . . but" approach, even though those two words do not describe its use or impact very aptly. This technique comprises a flanking maneuver for deflecting the objection without affronting the prospect. It is a tactic that enables you to resume your sales story by recounting additional sales points not previously brought out. Yet you use the objection itself as the basis for doing so.

This two-step counteraction presumes that there are some aspects of the prospect's objection about which you can express limited agreement or approval. So you (1) concede that his objection may well be valid—even laudable within limited circumstances. Then you (2) proceed to use that as a reason for relating additional features and benefits of your proposal calculated to refute or outweigh any disadvantages he has cited.

For example, an account executive selling advertising for a radio station has just been confronted with this objection:

> I've always relied on newspaper advertising and that seems to work pretty well in my business. My competitors all use newspaper ads, too; so I think I'll just stick with that.

The sales person might counter with:

> (1) I can understand your reluctance to change from a medium that's been serving you well so far. Newspaper ads can be very effective—up to a point. And with your competitors using newspaper ads too, I can see it might not be wise to drop that form of promotion entirely.
> (2) However, are you aware that listener surveys show we now have a radio audience of _____ in your market area? That compares very favorably with newspaper circulation. Also, many people don't take time to read newspapers very carefully—especially the ads. They're busy and tend to rely on the radio for news—often because they can listen while they work or do other things. So they'll hear your ads even though they might never

read them. Besides, a spoken message can be much more persuasive than one that's printed. By adding radio advertising, you'll get much wider coverage of the busy people who are very likely your best potential customers.

Responding to an objection this way accomplishes several things. First, by agreeing with the prospect, you avoid engaging in a direct refutation. No one likes to be told he's wrong. By agreeing, you also show respect for the prospect's point of view; this tends to induce him to consider more favorably what you still have to say. By suggesting that your agreement is limited, you invite his curiosity about the circumstances in which he might not be right. That becomes your springboard for relating more of your selling points. These can now concentrate on the advantages you claim for radio advertising over the newspaper—the obstacle to selling him that his objection revealed. (No doubt, an equally good case can be made for newspaper advertising over radio in a suitable set of circumstances.)

Note that neither "yes" nor "but" was used in that response. It's usually better to be subtle in leading the prospect around to listening to more of your sales story. Suppose the sales person replies:

Yes, I see why you favor using newspaper ads, but radio commercials can be much more effective with some people. Let me give you some reasons . . .

Although the basic message is about the same, it could sound more like a confrontation to the prospect. Also, it does not provide for as smooth a transition to more sales persuasion. This technique can be quite effective but it must be used thoughtfully and deftly—always with a view toward fostering the prospect's continued interest and good will.

Agree and convert into a reason for buying. There are many variations of the "Yes . . . but" technique. One that can be quite effective in some situations is turning the objection itself into a reason for buying. Suppose you are a life insurance sales representative trying to sell a substantial policy to the head of a small business. He's middle-aged and has children in college but has been in business for himself only a few years. He listens attentively to your presentation but finally says in a decisive manner:

> I'm interested, but I simply can't consider taking on any more expense right now. Business has been lousy and my short-term bank obligations are up sharply. When things get better . . . maybe sometime next year . . . I'll keep your card and call you when I'm ready.

That seems like pretty logical reasoning. But here's a response that just might result in a sale:

> I can sure agree that things have been pretty tight. It's affecting us all. And you're very prudent to be watching costs so carefully during times like these. In that connection, though, have you considered that as a very good reason for taking out this policy now — without delay? Suppose the unexpected should happen. With the level of your business down and debts up, could your family manage to carry on and stay solvent? Would your children be able to continue their educations? I suggest that as a prudent manager you may not want to risk being without this insurance protection because you need it even more when business volume is down as it is now.

In this case, the sales person agrees with the validity of the objection but converts it into an even more valid reason for buying. This technique can be used only when the situation and dialogue create a suitable opening. Using it involves some risks; it may be resented as a pressure tactic or as implying that the prospect lacks astuteness in not seeing the reverse logic of his own reasoning. So be alert to the pitfalls as well as the advantages. This twist technique can be quite effective if used only when the opportunity is right.

Answer, add benefits, ask for a commitment. This variation of the usual two-step "Yes . . . but" technique adds a third step by asking for a positive commitment from the prospect after an objection has been answered. The first two steps are handled much as already described; the third step asks the prospect to agree that the features and benefits just related do indeed fill his need satisfactorily.

Suppose you're selling a building contractor on a new construction system. You have just answered an objection by agreeing with those aspects that have merit but — guided by his objection — you have also explained additional benefits of the system. You then follow up by asking for a commitment.

> Now, doesn't all that add up to some notable advantages to you — faster installation and a smoother finish without increasing costs? And wouldn't that be likely to show up as more profit on the bottom line — considering the large volume of work you do?

Your prospect will find it hard to answer anything but yes if you've substantiated some important benefits. And each time you get him to agree with some part of your proposition, you move him closer to a sale. Most people need to digest new ideas in small bites anyhow; this one-commitment-at-a-time approach helps them do that.

This is sometimes called the A-B-C technique — A for answer or agree, B for benefits, and C for commitment. It can be used just as well for answering a simple question as for handling an objection. It can be used anytime during a presentation but is particularly effective when you've covered most of your sales points and are nearing the point of asking for the order. Each commitment you obtain contributes to the final one — the prospect's agreement to buy. An opportune time to ask for the order is after obtaining positive commitments from a prospect regarding objections you've just dealt with satisfactorily. It is at this time that he is likely to be most favorably prepared for closing the sale.

Acknowledge and counterbalance detractive features. This variation of the "Yes . . . but" technique applies to occasions when the prospect identifies an actual disadvantage of your product or service as related to his need or to a competitive offering. If the objection cited is valid, the best tactic is to acknowledge it gracefully — but counterbalance immediately by singling out and emphasizing other features and benefits that will more than offset the deficiency.

Seldom is any product equal in every respect to all competing products; each usually has unique utilities and advantages. And naturally, these are the benefits on which to focus a buyer's attention. A sales person serves neither his own nor his prospect's best interests by adopting an overly defensive stance about minor product shortcomings — as long as the product can in fact fill the prospect's principal needs. It is far better to divert attention to those superior points on which the final buying decision is likely to turn. However, if the objection does disclose a bona fide reason why your product cannot serve the prospect adequately, withdraw that sales effort at once. He'll respect your honest objectivity and be more favorably disposed toward whatever else you may sell that he can use.

Postpone responding to an objection. Ordinarily, it is best to handle an objection or question as soon as it is raised. This avoids any appearance of evasion. Also, disposing of objections satisfactorily as they are brought up helps build the prospect's confidence in the sales person as well as in his product.

Sometimes, however, an objection is raised at an inopportune time. For example, it may be important for the sales presentation to be made with continuity and little interruption, so that the prospect can gain a better understanding of the utilities and benefits involved. Or perhaps the objection raised is normally covered in a later part of the presentation anyhow, so that handling it immediately would be premature. Occasionally, the objection may be so irrelevant that taking it up right then would seriously divert the sales effort. Probably most disastrous is having a price question or objection raised before the sales person has had an opportunity to tell his value story adequately.

Under such circumstances, it is appropriate to ask the prospect to hold his objection or question in abeyance for a few moments. Commend him for raising such a good point and assure him that you will handle it later. You might say:

> I'm glad you brought that up, Mr. Prospect, because it's an important point that I'll be covering in just a minute or two. But

first, if you will, I'd like to complete explaining a couple of things that have a bearing on your point, too, as you'll soon see.

When used smoothly, this technique enables you to continue your sales story to its natural climax. And by tactfully asking your prospect's permission to delay answering, you indicate respect for him. But make very sure that you do handle his objection. If you cover it normally in your presentation, ask him later:

Did I answer you satisfactorily on that very appropriate point you raised?

If it isn't covered in your presentation, bring it up yourself later for handling. If it is irrelevant, this will be apparent to both of you by then, which your prospect is likely to acknowledge.

Postponement of objections is satisfactory only if it doesn't resemble evasion. Constant alertness to the prospect's demeanor is necessary so that if a negative reaction is observed it can be offset by taking up the objection immediately.

Make a direct denial of an objection. This is so seldom the right or only way to handle an objection that it should be studiously avoided except in a few exceptional situations. By its very nature, a denial is bound to be irritating. People don't welcome contradiction even when they are wrong. And it's hardly a productive way to make sales or build customer good will.

Even so, there are occasions when a sales representative has little choice but to refute a prospect's statement or objection. For example, a buyer may say:

No doubt this paint won't stand scrubbing without fading or washing off.

The buyer is really asking for information, but he is also baiting the sales person a little in doing so. The seller can only reject the implication and try to make a selling point at the same time. The seller might respond:

It certainly will stand up, sir. This is a tough, nonfading paint that will take repeated washing—even with a detergent-type soap. It's guaranteed to be colorfast under those conditions.

Or the prospect's question or objection may imply something that's completely untrue about the seller's company, products, or policies. Again, the sales person may have no alternative to making a denial, such as:

Mr. Prospect, you have apparently been misinformed; we have always maintained a strict policy of selling only through distributors. And we sell all products in our line on a like basis with regard to prices, applicable discounts, and terms of sales. No exceptions are made, and it's proved to be a very good policy for our distributors as well as for us.

If direct denial of an objection can't be avoided, use it with extreme caution. Nothing can be gained by responding in anger —even if the prospect is hostile. If you must refute the prospect, do so with a smile even if it hurts. It could be that belligerence is part of the nature of that prospect, in which case self-control and an attempt to be friendly in dealing with him may win his grudging respect—perhaps even an order.

ANTICIPATING OBJECTIONS

Finally, the best method for handling objections is to anticipate and prepare for them. This involves treating them in either or both of two ways that require much the same kind of preparation. The first tactic is to forestall as many potential objections as possible; the second is to be ready to answer them confidently when they do arise.

Forestall objections. The best practice is to try to forestall objections by anticipating and building answers for them into the sales presentation. Essentially, this calls for telling such a complete sales story that all conceivable objections are disposed of before they can be raised. Even though this outcome can seldom be achieved, it is nonetheless a worthy objective.

All sales people soon learn from experience what factors relating to sale and use of their products or services are most likely to raise questions. It is far better to explain any potential obstacles to a sale in terms of benefits to the buyers before they have an opportunity to bring them up as objections. This tactic vastly strengthens the presentation; it also helps keep prospects from taking negative positions they may then feel compelled to defend. Even highly professional sales people cannot realistically hope to prevent all objections. But it should be possible to forestall those that can be most troublesome. The objections that still arise are then much less likely to thwart a sale.

Prepare for objections. Wise sales people prepare for objections in order to forestall as many as they can as well as be ready to answer those that are raised. Attempts at handling them off the cuff can be awkward and unconvincing. Good preparation involves listing systematically the questions and objections most likely to arise and working out persuasive, factual answers for each. By thinking through credible, logical answers before you need them — and even rehearsing them — you will be able to handle them much more easily. This will also reinforce your self-confidence, which in turn will augment your persuasive skill. Moreover, by being so well prepared, you can create a presentation so complete that incidence of objections is much reduced.

How can you do this? Start by jotting down all the questions or objections you might raise if you were a prospect being offered the product or service in a like situation. Then seek any needed information that you don't already have from those in your organization who can supply it, and work out convincing answers. Some companies provide checklists of objections and suggested responses as a part of sales training. If yours does so —fine; use them. But do study each objection and recommended answer until you understand it well enough to explain it clearly to others. Also, improve upon it if you can. As an alternative, start developing your own list of objections and answers. Add to your repertoire as you encounter new objections and develop responses that work for you.

One excellent way to maintain this information is in a card file — one objection and answer per card. Update the file as you become able to refine the answers through gaining more information and experience. This helps fix those ideas well in mind for instant use and provides a ready reference before making

Figure 5. Objection/answer reference form.

Product or Service _____	Objection No. _____
Application _____	

Objection or Question	Appropriate Response

sales calls on important new prospects. The objection/answer cards can take the form shown in Figure 5.

The record of objections and answers can take whatever form you find most convenient. Some may prefer a loose-leaf notebook format with all the more critical questions and objections logged on one or two sheets. Some may prefer to substitute "Customer type" for "Application" in the example in Figure 5. The nature of objections usually varies somewhat with the use or user.

COPING WITH PRICE OBJECTIONS

Objections relating to price are often the toughest kind to handle — even for an experienced sales person. When the prospect says, "Your price is too high," or "I can buy it cheaper," what do you say to save the day? Surmounting a price objection successfully can be the ultimate test of selling skill because when price is at issue, the sales order is usually hanging in the balance.

Virtually every technique discussed in this chapter can be applied appropriately in countering objections centered on price. Something more is called for, however — notably, a sensitivity to the relationships between product price and value combined with an ability to explain them convincingly to a prospect who is considering several competitive proposals. Since handling a price objection is so closely involved with all other aspects of selling competitively, this topic is covered in Chapter 7, "Coping with Competition."

Turn to Learning Exercise No. 16 in Appendix.

Coping with Complaints and Claims

Resolving customer complaints and the monetary claims they often generate is one phase of selling that most sales people would much rather avoid but usually cannot. Almost invariably, the sales representative is caught in the middle of a complaint situation even though he may have no personal responsibility for whatever has gone wrong. Nevertheless, he feels the full brunt of the conflict; he faces the ire of his customer as well as the pressure of his employer to get the matter settled as quickly, amicably, and economically as possible. Often, the sales representative is the only one who can represent supplier as well as customer fairly in working out a suitable settlement. The sales representative with a responsible attitude toward his work always strives for a prompt, equitable conclusion of every complaint or claim.

Fortunately, complaint handling can also have a positive and rewarding aspect. Settling complaints quickly, fairly, and considerately provides opportunity for strengthening a good sales relationship between customer and supplier. The sales person can demonstrate the validity of his prior claims — that he represents a responsible, service-oriented company. Such a constructive approach usually reinforces rapport with the customer. Conversely, an ineptly or tardily handled complaint can destroy customer confidence and good will built up through years of sales calls, advertising programs, and superior products or services. A highly valued customer can thereby be lost, perhaps irretrievably — an expensive way, indeed, to settle a complaint.

CAUSES OF COMPLAINTS

Complaints or disagreements with customers arise from such a variety of mishaps that it is pointless to try to catalog them individually. They vary widely with the nature of the product or service and the particulars of sale, distribution, and use. Most complaints, however, are likely to fall into one or more of these categories:

— Wrong product or service was supplied.
— Shipment or delivery was delayed, misdirected, or shorted.
— Quality of merchandise or supplier service hasn't measured up to customer expectations.
— Customer has unilaterally rejected or returned merchandise.
— Differences have occurred between amount customer was charged and what he expected to pay.
— Other misunderstandings have developed regarding price, sales, or credit policies, terms of payment, or related business practices.
— Disputable deductions have been taken by customer in remitting payment of an invoice.

Most complaints result from minor misunderstandings that can be rectified without substantial harm to either buyer or seller. The matter is cleared up satisfactorily and soon forgotten. In a well-run business, complaints deriving from fault of supplier or sales person are relatively uncommon. If such complaints do occur frequently and follow a pattern, it is likely that the supplier has internal problems requiring correction. An alert, concerned sales person can contribute much to bringing about the improvements needed through fair, factual reporting and handling of complaints.

Complaints do not always result from error by the supplier or sales person, however. Occasionally, certain customers become chronic repeaters with complaints that objective investigation cannot ascribe to deficiency of product or of supplier service. The complaints of such "problem customers" become suspect and must be handled with extreme care — particularly if the business of these customers is important to you and your company. At some point, it may become a matter of business judgment whether troublesome, costly complaints incurred repeatedly from the same few customers warrant trying to retain their business.

The question of liability always lurks in the background in these situations. It can be dangerous to imply that a customer is dishonest; he may be convinced that his complaint is justified even if the evidence appears insufficient to you and your company. A sales person needs good managerial and legal guidance when dealing with this kind of problem.

TECHNIQUES FOR HANDLING COMPLAINTS AND CLAIMS

Many of the same sensitivities and skills that prove effective in surmounting sales objections are useful in disposing of complaints satisfactorily. However, some of the proven approaches to constructive handling of complaints may run counter to the instinctive reactions of many people. This is a good reason for reviewing these techniques.

Act promptly on every complaint. Initiating corrective action quickly is of top importance in handling any complaint. As when a fire breaks out, any delay in bringing it under control only gives it time to get worse. So acknowledge every complaint directly to key customer personnel as soon as you learn of it. In this day of instant communication, this usually means a phone call. During this initial conversation, you may accomplish little more than learning the general nature of the complaint and reassuring your customer somewhat. It's unlikely that the problem can be corrected and settled in a single phone call. (If it can be done, that's great!) But it does enable you to assure your customer that his complaint is receiving attention and to outline for him how you propose to resolve it. At this point, what your customer wants most is *attention.* Giving it to him promptly and courteously is a long stride toward a mutually satisfactory resolution of the problem.

Let your customer unburden himself. Occurrence of a complaint often creates an emotionally charged atmosphere. The customer tacitly accepted your representations of potential benefits, advantages, service, and satisfaction when he gave you the order. He placed his trust in you and your company, but now something has gone wrong; he feels deceived, exploited, cheated. And he feels a strong urge to vent his fury on someone. You provide a logical target. Expect him to voice his anger, and let him do so — without interruption or rebuttal even if he's unreasonable and excessive. Encourage him to talk by saying something like:

> I'd appreciate it if you'd tell me exactly what has happened; I want to make sure I understand all the particulars fully. I'm very sorry you've had all this trouble, but I'm also quite sure we'll get it all worked out satisfactorily.

Then *listen* — attentively, sympathetically, and with no suggestion of antagonism. Obviously, you'll learn some of the circumstances, but more important you'll be helping to set the stage for rational examination of the problem later when a more reasonable atmosphere inevitably returns. Then begin working toward a solution by first reviewing those aspects of the situation that are still favorable or on which you can both agree.

Start a complaint investigation at once. When a customer reports that your product, service, or handling of a sale has somehow created a problem for him, it's up to you to learn all the pertinent facts in order to clear up the difficulty. This usually requires that you make a personal investigation. Often, it also calls for review of the circumstances by others in your company. Whatever the need, act on it at once. Your customer will want to know all the details — and so will your employer, as a basis for correcting the problem and preventing a recurrence. No equitable adjustment is possible until all the facts have been determined and accurately reported.

Every complaint investigation imposes special requirements upon you for tact and diplomacy. As a sales representative, you bear a responsibility to your company as well as to your customer. Considering the unhappy circumstances, the customer may well be biased in his own favor. So take care that this doesn't influence you unduly. Avoid making premature commitments. But reassure the customer that his problem will be resolved fairly.

It's always best to make a personal, on-the-spot investigation in the presence of your customer. This often elicits more pertinent information than could be gleaned in any other way. Ask him to show and explain what went wrong. If there are contributing factors unrelated to product quality or performance, these are likely to appear during a joint review of the problem.

Sales people are usually indoctrinated to look for signs of customer misapplication, damage during shipment, or other causes extraneous to product or service. While this is most certainly your duty, keep an open mind. Your customer's complaint may be entirely justified. Your even-handedness in working out a solution will then do much to strengthen his confidence in you and in your company. But should you find the fault is indeed the customer's, you'll need all the tact you can muster to gain his willing acceptance of the explanation. No one likes to be told he's wrong — especially about an issue he created. And although it might be far easier just to accept blame and settle in the customer's favor, this will not prevent a recurrence. Some companies provide for policy settlements in situations like this, but they also try to make very sure the same complaint will not occur again with the same customer.

Work out a solution and act on it. Once all critical facts have been gathered and causes of the problem established, work out an equitable solution and make sure it is acted on promptly. Let your customer know what will be done and when. If your company is to blame, strive to ensure that corrective action is taken at once. This helps make amends and also helps restore the customer's trust and high regard for you and your company. Avoid any appearance of stalling. Excessive delay of a justified adjustment tends to magnify rather than rectify the damage done by a complaint. This further angers the customer and may even lose him completely in spite of the settlement finally made.

If the causes of the complaint turn out to be extraneous to your product or service — perhaps even due to customer error — you still have a responsibility to help correct them. If the problem results from product misuse, you have an educational job to do to prevent a recurrence. And if blame is traced to faulty products or services provided by others, help make sure that these causes are eliminated too. This is all part of the kind of customer service that characterizes a professional sales person.

COMPLAINTS AND CLAIMS – CONCLUSION

No sales person ever relishes handling complaints or settling claims. But when they do arise, the best approach is always to get them over with quickly. This is the most promising way to salvage something from a situation that can become even worse if neglected.

The positive side of every complaint is the opportunity it affords for reselling your product, your company, and yourself. Although the circumstances are unfortunate, they do provide occasion to prove the validity of what you've been contending since your first call on the customer – that yours is a responsible firm and that you are personally concerned with the customer's satisfaction and success. Again and again, top sales people report that they have been able to reinforce good sales relationships with important customers through expeditious and satisfactory resolution of serious complaints. There is much merit in striving to give real meaning to the motto, "The customer is always right."

The following is a checklist for good complaint handling.

1. Always acknowledge a complaint promptly.
2. Listen attentively to your customer and avoid antagonizing him further.
3. Reassure your customer that his complaint will be resolved promptly.
4. Investigate the complaint fully and promptly.
5. Establish complaint causes promptly.
6. Expedite solutions and inform customer promptly of what will be done.
7. Carry out corrective action promptly.
8. Make any monetary adjustment due promptly.
9. If customer or others contributed to the problem, explain fully, tactfully, and promptly.
10. Make the most of every opportunity to resell the customer on your company and yourself – *promptly!*

Turn to Learning Exercise No. 17 in Appendix.

---

6 REINFORCING THE APPEAL OF SALES PRESENTATIONS

We have explored various skills of employing language persuasively for communicating sales messages to prospective customers. Language — especially the spoken word — is unquestionably the selling tool most used by most sales people. It is our primary means for communicating ideas. But to generate maximum sales appeal, language is best employed in conjunction with other supportive modes of communication. Often words alone, though eloquently expressed, won't suffice.

We humans possess five senses with which to absorb and measure the meaning of matters that concern or interest us. Vocal messages can be very motivating. But their impact is usually enhanced remarkably when augmented by appeals to senses other than hearing — that is, touch, smell, taste, and especially sight. Scientific research has demonstrated that we are far more receptive to — and remember longest — knowledge received through the sense of sight. We also tend to consider what we see to be more reliable than what we hear. This is exemplified in two age-old maxims: "One picture is worth more than ten thousand words," and "Seeing is believing." We grasp and accept most readily communications that allow us to visualize as well as hear key aspects of the message. Some authorities hold that at least three-fourths of the impressions and knowledge we *retain* reach us through the sense of sight.

When the message activates other senses as well — such as touch, smell, and taste — the potential impact is increased even more. One familiar example is the appeal the typical bakery shop has for most of us. The tantalizing aromas wafting out the door tend to lead us inside as though we were drawn by a magnet—just to see what they have. There we are tempted even more by viewing the artfully created pastries on display. When small samples are also freely provided for tasting, our sales resistance is virtually demolished; yet not a single sales word has been spoken. By the time a sales clerk cheerfully asks, "Would you like some of those delicious danish pastries?" our pleasurable anticipation has been so aroused that even the often formidable price objection no longer exerts restraint. And so we're likely to find ourselves buying without any verbal selling effort ever having taken place.

The message in this for all sales people must be apparent: always find a way to enlist one or more of the senses other than hearing as a means of reinforcing the appeal of every vocal sales presentation. There are countless opportunities for doing this appropriately—from displaying a sample or a piece of sales literature to conducting an elaborate product demonstration. And every sales presentation becomes more vividly arresting when sharpened by showmanship. Suggesting some readily available techniques for accomplishing these extra appeals is the purpose of this chapter.

Display and Explain

Let's first review some simple methods that require a minimum of planning and skill. All techniques for enhancing the sensory appeal of a sales presentation are fundamentally an adult version of "Show and Tell"—a communicative tool many of us learned in grammar school. We learned early that it's much easier to hold others in rapt attention by telling about something that we can show at the same time. The listeners' interest and understanding are thereby reinforced by an object they can see and perhaps also feel and examine, as well as hear about—or even experience in combinations of those sensations. We also learned that it is easier for us to talk before others when we have something in hand to talk about. And all of these very basic principles of communication are just as applicable in selling.

So during any sales talk, it behooves all sales people to have something to use for "show and tell," or "display and explain," as we'll call it here. At a minimum, this arouses your sales prospect's curiosity; he wonders whether what you've brought with you will really relate to his particular concerns, and he expects you to show him. This tactic helps hold his attention far better than words alone can do. It establishes a unifying frame of reference for your sales talk. It helps reassure your prospect that your call has a meaningful purpose. It makes him less likely to woolgather during your sales talk and less anxious to resume whatever activity you interrupted. It can even help ease any awkwardness that might arise by giving you both something on which to focus besides each other.

The sales person who makes a call empty-handed discounts the outcome even before he begins his sales story. And eloquent though he may be, he also relies, unwisely, on his verbal persuasive skills alone. His reluctance to use even simple props may signify great personal confidence — or perhaps just laziness. But it isn't very likely to indicate that he possesses exceptional selling skills.

Visual Props for Sales Talks

PRODUCT SAMPLES

The props most commonly available to virtually all sales people are product samples. Most marketers provide samples in some form — from simple but attractive segments or swatches of the product to elaborate displays contained in costly sample cases. Sometimes miniatures are provided, or even fascinating working models that can be highly effective for demonstration.

Whatever the product or service, inventive people can always devise some kind of representative visual aid on which to focus attention during a sales talk. If need be, you can sometimes prepare your own visual aids. Often this can be more effective anyhow because of the personal ingenuity and showmanship exhibited that set you out favorably among competitors.

Even a sales person handling bulk commodities can put together — or have constructed — small, attractive carrying cases for samples of his wares that display their special qualities or grades. This provides a useful focus for interest and discussion even when not vital for supporting the primary purpose of a sales interview.

The sales person handling intangibles or services can likewise procure or create props serving much the same purpose as samples. An insurance sales representative can carry copies of typical policies, tabulated data, charts, and other items attractively prepared for ready examination by, and explanation to, his prospects. The person selling services can carry artfully assembled portfolios of photographs, sketches, and other unique representations of the functions he sells.

The possibilities for devising effective props for selling are as diverse as the imagination is fertile. Whatever the product or service, all sales people should equip themselves to *display as well as explain*. Naturally, a multisensory sales presentation is most effective for early calls on new prospects or customers. But the principles involved apply to repeat calls as well. When it becomes redundant to display samples on every return call, other visuals can be used to incite renewed interest and help hold the customer firm against competitive enticement.

VISUAL SALES AIDS

A wide variety of visual sales aids can be very effective when used selectively for emphasis and to focus interest. They can be employed in conjunction with product samples or to support a demonstration. They can also be used instead of either samples or demonstrations where these are precluded by the selling situation or by the nature of the product or service. A broad selection of visuals can also be used as features for return calls on established accounts. Such display items contribute importantly to maintaining or strengthening customers' commitments to product and supplier.

This list covers most types of visual sales aids commonly used:

Advertisements	Easel pads	Portfolios
Audiotapes	Exhibits	Posters
Calculations	Graphs	Sales literature
Catalogs	Guarantees	Sketches
Chalkboards	Manuals	Sound-slide films

Charts	Models	Testimonials
Diagrams	Movies	Test reports
Drawings	Photos	Videotapes

Among the types of sales aid identified above, several can be very elaborate and expensive. A few are audiovisual, and some can be designed to appeal to other senses as well. Such sophisticated sales help equipment is usually provided only by those larger marketing concerns that are satisfied that the substantial investment involved is warranted by the sales results expected. The more elaborate exhibits and audiovisual aids are generally employed primarily for sales promotion to large groups such as those attending trade shows or conventions. For those marketing unique, expensive lines of products or services, the use of costly, complex selling aids is often justified — even essential. Ample prior rehearsal is always necessary to ensure facile handling of such equipment.

But certain other types of visual sales aids need not be either elaborate or expensive. Several kinds of visuals can even be prepared by the sales person himself if necessary — or with a minimum of professional help. Such relatively simple sales aids often prove surprisingly effective, in part because they reflect the kind of personalized sales effort most appreciated by most customers. The recommendations that follow cover several categories of visual sales aids that most sales people can use readily to good advantage.

Advertisements. Tear sheets or reprints of magazine ads make excellent resource material for use on sales calls. If the customer is a reseller, the ad reaffirms the media sales support being provided by the supplier. An ad often contains illustrations that are convenient for pointing out product characteristics. Copy content of an ad frequently provides a useful visual checklist for giving a sales talk that explains more completely the points being featured.

Calculations. Arithmetic supporting the savings or advantages offered by a product can be very convincing. The figures should be computed previously and organized neatly by the sales person for review during the sales interview. Such calculations provide a compelling focus for prospect attention; they also provide evidence of the sales person's desire to serve. If some revision of the math proves to be needed, sales person and prospect can work it out together; this involves the prospect in the sales interaction—another plus.

Diagrams, drawings, and sketches. As with calculations, these sales helps can often be customized for superior effectiveness. Even simple sketches prepared in advance to show how the product or service will function are likely to rivet prospect attention on the key aspects of the sales proposition. And they also impress him with the sales person's sincere desire to help.

Charts and graphs. These visuals provide another means for clarifying how the product or service can fill the prospect's needs. Complex facts and figures may remain obscure when recounted in words alone but can be crystallized into vivid meaning with well-designed charts and graphs. Marketing concerns often provide charts presenting typical data in support of product merits. But it's even better to custom prepare charts or graphs that relate product advantages and applications to the prospect's specific needs.

Photos, posters, and portfolios. Such items are excellent for display whenever it's difficult to show the product in use or to portray the results of a service. A well-organized series of good photos enables a sales person to lead prospect attention from one feature-benefits combination to another in optimal order; the photos also double as prompters as the sales person makes his presentation. The term portfolio can mean many things; one example is a collection of photos, drawings, and data specially assembled to support a particular sales presentation. It is sometimes left with the prospective customer for study when negotiations are continuing. And it provides an excellent visual display on which to base a sales-oriented talk.

Test reports and testimonials. In some fields it is established practice for competing products to be tested by independent testing laboratories to ascertain whether they meet or exceed certain minimum standards. One familiar example is Underwriters Laboratories whose "UL" insignia of approval appears on many home appliances and other products. Copies of published reports covering such tests make excellent sales helps— particularly when the product exceeds minimum standards.

Some manufacturers also test their own products and provide reports covering the results; these are also useful as sales aids. Somewhat related are testimonials — usually in letter form — obtained from satisfied customers who have given you or your company permission to show copies to prospective users as an endorsement of your product or service.

Easel pads and chalkboards. Props of this type enable one to make points visually as well as verbally during a sales presentation. As each point is cited verbally, it can be spelled out for the prospect to see as well as hear — for emphasis as well as for reference. Diagrams or sketches can be worked out on the spot to delineate applications and benefits of product or process. Color can also be employed. Such techniques help clarify critical points as well as sustain attention. And these tools also provide many opportunities for subtle touches of showmanship. As might be expected, these techniques are particularly productive for making sales presentations to groups. But small, portable chart pads can be used similarly to provide visual support while explaining a product application to only one person.

Sales literature and catalogs. This is a chronically neglected group of ready tools for dramatizing sales talks — the sales folders, brochures, catalogs, and other sales promotion materials commonly available to most sales people. Too often these valuable items are simply left with the prospect at the close of an interview, with little special comment. Some sales people even habitually overlook bringing literature with them on sales calls; then they lamely offer to send it by mail or to drop it off later.

Most sales literature has been carefully developed for maximum appeal to prospective buyers and users. It portrays in words and pictures the principal selling messages considered important by the marketer. It follows that sales people should preplan to feature selected items of sales literature to best advantage during sales calls. Sales folders provide convenient visual sales support. These pieces can help guide sales people through complex sales presentations as well as provide focal points of interest; they can help them illustrate and explain products; and they provide a sustained selling impact for them long after the interview is over. But sales literature needs to be well merchandised with a bit of showmanship in order to maximize its potential. Consider these guidelines:

- Display only fresh, clean literature during a sales call; dusty, dog-eared pieces discredit the sales person and detract from his product and company as well. Carry sales literature cased so it will remain clean and can be located quickly.
- Select a specific piece of literature for use during a call and prepare to use it well. Review the salient points it covers and note which apply particularly to this prospect's needs.
- Underline key statements for accenting during your sales talk; then leave that marked piece with the prospect as a reminder of the points you've made.
- Use the literature as a sales talk checklist — explaining the key features and benefits in your own words and emphasizing how each relates to that prospect's situation.
- Point out key statements and illustrations in the literature, but try to retain possession of it during the interview if possible. Relinquishing it too soon risks prospect preoccupation with it so that he may miss other important features and benefits as you stress them.
- Invite the prospect's agreement with major selling points before you go on to others; this helps lead to a successful close.
- Always enlarge on the benefits. Good sales literature usually presents product features quite well but may translate them into benefits only in broad terms. Particularize the benefits to apply to your prospect's special needs.
- Adapt these guidelines appropriately when presenting a sales promotional package for use by a prospective reseller who in turn will market your product to his customers.

By making creative use of product samples and visual sales aids — often in combination — sales people find they are usually able to handle the display-and-explain phases of most sales presentations quite satisfactorily. This helps to reduce the time required to close individual sales, thus optimizing overall use of the total selling time available.

Turn to Learning Exercise No. 18 in Appendix.

Demonstrations

For many products and services, demonstrations are the most convincing means of showing prospective customers the performance and results they can realistically expect. This is often what it takes to achieve the degree of conviction that will induce prospects to buy. Giving demonstrations is part of the normal, expected routine of selling for some product lines. For a product that will contribute to a sophisticated industrial process, a demonstration is likely to be staged as the decisive climax of an extended selling effort. Such a demonstration typically follows much prior discussion and evaluation of the seller's proposed solution to a customer problem. Sometimes trial use of the product in an actual production run is involved. Most demonstrations are less complex, however; they are employed selectively in those critical selling situations for which less thorough display-and-explain tactics aren't sufficiently persuasive. This need frequently arises in situations where it is important to clearly demonstrate superior product performance relative to that of a competitive product.

Opportunity to make a demonstration should be sought out and welcomed whenever this is obviously the action needed for closing an important sale. But selling wisely also dictates that a demonstration should be opted for only when it becomes evident that less comprehensive tactics won't suffice. Truly meaningful demonstrations usually require much valuable time to prepare and conduct them well; balanced against this is the sales person's need to allocate his available time judiciously to attain optimal overall sales results.

Some demonstrations are relatively easy to conduct — perhaps requiring only product samples and simple equipment. Other demonstrations involve a comprehensive trial of product or service under actual conditions of use. Whatever the circumstances justifying a demonstration, its central purpose is always to *prove* conclusively to the satisfaction of the prospect that the product *will perform as represented.* Following are some advantages of demonstrations and recommendations for planning, preparing, carrying out, and capitalizing on them in order to bring about the sales results sought.

ADVANTAGES OF DEMONSTRATIONS

Below are capsulized some characteristics of good demonstrations that appeal to sales people as well as to buyers. Accordingly, these ideas should be considered when deciding whether to make a demonstration and when planning how to carry a demonstration out most effectively.

- Demonstrations absorb the prospect's attention; help generate a desire to own and use the product.
- Demonstrations afford opportunity for appealing to several senses; provide three-dimensional realism; create more vivid impressions; motivate buying decisions more forcefully.
- Product performance and benefit potentials become manifest more quickly and cogently by demonstration than by explanation alone.
- When the prospect is shown how the product or service functions, elusive concepts can be more readily understood.
- Demonstrations occasionally make it possible to show procedures or results when verbal explanations might be resented.
- Prospect buying resistance is most effectively neutralized by what is seen and experienced.
- Objections and interruptions are minimized during demonstrations; sales person appears to be operating, displaying, and explaining rather than selling.
- Prospect can sometimes participate in a demonstration, thereby helping him sell himself.
- Demonstrations amplify a sales person's persuasive ability; also visibly augment the enthusiasm and confidence he displays about his product; this all reinforces his proficiency at getting orders.

PREPARATION FOR DEMONSTRATIONS

Planning a demonstration is just as important as planning a verbal presentation. The five-step idea-selling concept that we discussed earlier should be paralleled as nearly as possible when planning a demonstration and the discourse describing it. The verbal and the visual presentation can then proceed together — the one supporting the other. In other words, plan your demonstration so you can state *what* you're going to show, tell *why*, display and explain *how it works*, and, finally, reaffirm what you have shown by emphasizing the *results and benefits* exhibited.

Let your first planning step be that of deciding what to demonstrate and what to omit. This relates to practical considerations of what can be shown within the time available. Determine what other limitations may prevail and plan to observe or overcome them. A demonstration should be selective — concentrating on those features and benefits of prime concern to the prospect involved. A good approach is to prepare a standard demonstration encompassing all important features in optimum sequence. Then you can tailor this to fit the needs and circumstances of each selling situation that entails a demonstration.

Preparation *must* include careful prior examination of whatever will be exhibited or operated to make very sure it is in good order. Nothing is more certain to scuttle a promising sale, as well as destroy the aplomb of the sales person, than failure of the product to appear or perform as anticipated. It follows that this phase of preparation must include enough practice with the procedures involved so that they can be performed smoothly with no fumbling and no mistakes. The skill of the demonstrator vastly reinforces the results he obtains.

In planning the sales talk to accompany a demonstration, always prepare the prospect for what will take place. His anticipation of the expected outcome is much enhanced when he has been briefed on what will happen, when, and why. Such prior indoctrination is especially necessary when noise or other distractions render explanation during the demonstration difficult or even impossible. Telling the prospect what to expect and then proceeding to show him sets the stage for emphasizing the results and moving confidently to the close.

CONDUCTING DEMONSTRATIONS

Many of the more critical admonitions for carrying out a demonstration well are implicit in the recommendations already provided for its preparation. Perhaps several more merit spot emphasis, however.

- Stage the demonstration under the most favorable circumstances possible — lighting, ability to hear, temperature, personal comfort of the prospect, and so on; try to forestall distractions.
- Always synchronize what you are saying with what is happening; point out critical action to make sure it isn't missed.
- Explain what is taking place and why; never depend on the prospect to interpret properly — he may misunderstand completely. Besides, your words reinforce what the prospect sees.
- Make all points clearly — one at a time — and recheck to make sure each is clearly understood. Clarity is aided by brevity, so long as nothing important is omitted.
- Maintain good control of a demonstration throughout; don't digress from planned purpose and course; tactfully but firmly dissuade the prospect from dwelling on peripheral matters; and stay within the time allotted to you.
- Dramatize what you are displaying or what is happening; employ showmanship.

Attention to all pertinent details while conducting a demonstration is certain to magnify its impact. And remember — if it's worth doing, it's worth doing well.

REAPING THE REWARD

When a demonstration has been successfully carried out and the prospect has obviously been favorably impressed, that's your cue to ride the momentum to the natural climax — closing for the order. Yet many otherwise competent sales people tend to fumble at this point. When the peak opportunity does arrive for reaping a reward, it sometimes catches them by surprise. While working so hard to prepare and carry off the demonstration well, they overlook the need to also prepare themselves for capitalizing on a propitious outcome. The familiar old adage "Strike while the iron is hot" very likely evolved from a millennium of similar situations.

On concluding a demonstration, a sales person should move promptly to a summary of all salient features exhibited and the special advantages and benefits they represent for that prospect. During this review, ask selective questions designed to make sure all pertinent aspects have been clarified. At this point, the time is right and the prospect is as receptive as he'll ever be; so *ask him expectantly for the order.* If he should still hesitate, then quietly but quickly reinforce those benefits that you're aware by now are most meaningful to him — and ask for the order again. Chances are excellent that you'll leave with the order in your pocket as well as with the great satisfaction of knowing you've established a pleased new customer. And with good service and follow-up, you can both look forward to a mutually rewarding relationship.

Showmanship

Showmanship. A selling skill? Doesn't that word mean the kind of pizzazz that characterizes much nightclub, television, and circus entertainment? Yet the need for showmanship in sales presentations and demonstrations is referred to several times in this chapter. So let's explore briefly just what showmanship in selling means — and what it *does not* mean.

One dictionary says that showmanship is "skill in presenting anything in an entertaining and dramatic manner." Dramatic is defined as "striking in appearance or forcefully effective." And sales presentations and demonstrations should most certainly be interesting, visually striking, and forcefully effective. But few sales people view themselves as possessing any noteworthy flair for the dramatic. Don't despair; that need not be a handicap.

Showmanship in selling is *anything extra* that sales people say or do that adds sparkle to a selling effort, that makes a sales story more impressive, that results in a presentation being better remembered, that lifts it out of the drab and above most sales calls in terms of stimulating sales appeal. Astute, creative sales people consider how to incorporate a bit of showmanship into every sales call. Their call plans cover not only what they will explain but *how* they will say it; not only what they will display but *how* they will show it. They are well aware that adding a subtle aura of drama enhances the impact of every selling message.

Everyone is attracted to a show. We've all observed how a crowd gathers around a pitchman or pitchwoman making a colorful, verbal-visual demonstration of the many marvelous things their wares can do. Most observers pause to watch simply because they become fascinated by the demonstrator's dexterity and smooth line of patter. Such showmanship draws attention like a magnet; it also induces some to buy who only stopped to watch out of curiosity.

Earlier, we cited the appeal a bakery shop has for most of us. A subtle form of showmanship is involved in setting those tempting tidbits out for tasting. And even more showmanship is at work if it turns out that those irresistible aromas are being propelled outside by a fan over the door. No deception or misrepresentation is involved in such subtle appeals. They are simply methods of sharpening sensory impressions and crystallizing a prospect's awareness of latent wants and needs. Buying decisions remain entirely voluntary, based on each customer's evaluation of the merits of the merchandise as balanced with his desire to possess it. But showmanship *is* a factor in arousing that desire, in bringing about the recognition of wants and needs, and in creating the conviction that moves a wavering prospect to buy.

Showmanship in selling begins with an attitude and flowers through imagination. It consists of seeking out simple but arresting ways to attract close attention, arouse curiosity, enlarge receptivity, create a sense of suspense, reinforce proof of performance, and appeal to a prospect's emotion as well as his reason while he weighs his need for a product or service. In short, the sole purpose of showmanship is to enhance the effectiveness of any sales presentation or demonstration. Appropriate techniques for doing this are as diverse as the wares offered for sale and the ingenuity of the people selling them.

SHOWMANSHIP APPLIED

The most characteristic form of showmanship in selling is the very process of making a demonstration. This may consist simply of suitably displaying product samples. At the other end of the scale is the elaborate, sometimes spectacularly staged demonstration of a product or service in actual use. Most applications of showmanship fall somewhere in between. Many involve only the adroit use of visual aids and sales literature in support of an oral sales presentation. Whatever its expression, showmanship always involves special effort to focus prospect interest on the product or service more vividly.

Showmanship is reflected in the studied care and respect with which a skillful sales person handles, displays, or operates a product. Another component of showmanship is simply the enthusiasm evident in a capable sales person's tone of voice. These manifestations of personal style, which are relatively easy to cultivate, can be quite influential. For perspective, consider your own reaction to a sales clerk's casual, indifferent, or even abusive handling of merchandise you are considering for purchase. It dampens your interest, doesn't it? Especially your interest in buying from that particular sales person.

Showmanship can consist of using simple visuals to highlight critical points in a demonstration as they occur. For example, if the demonstration is too noisy for talking, try using a felt board on which to affix small placards bearing symbols or words accenting features and benefits as they take place. This thoughtful touch helps hold attention and create expectancy.

Almost any use of visual aids — including use of sales literature — constitutes an element of showmanship. The critical consideration lies in the skill with which the visuals are employed. Manipulate them with as much poise and as little self-consciousness as possible. This takes practice. Uncomplicated extra touches render visuals still more arresting. To cite some examples: Using black lettering on charts for listing customer problems, then using red for spelling out product features that can solve these problems, and using blue for the corresponding customer benefits. Or other uses of color such as for marking important features in literature given to a prospect — or mailed to him. Or optimal use of timing when displaying visuals — showing each when most opportune and dramatic rather than haphazardly. This tactic can also be used to create suspense and thereby hold attention. The possible variations are countless.

Your best source of suitable ideas for showmanship is your own imagination as applied to knowledge of your products and a keen awareness of your prospect's princpal interests. The ensuing half-dozen commonplace examples are provided only to trigger your own more imaginative ideas appropriate to your particular selling situations:

- Applying the flame of a blowtorch to an incombustible product to dramatize this critical feature.
- Striking an unbreakable product a blow with a hammer to demonstrate this feature convincingly.
- Immersing a product in water to dramatize its moisture-proof properties. (Remember the startling introduction of ball point pens by showing their ability to write under water?)
- Dramatizing the thermal insulating properties of a product by using it to shield something frozen from a heat source that would otherwise quickly melt it.
- Forcing a nail through an inflated, puncture-proof tire or inner tube to show that no air escapes through the hole.
- Using a dollar bill in any number of imaginative, startling ways — ways for example, to underscore the need for insurance or the merit of an investment.

PRECAUTIONS RELATING TO SHOWMANSHIP

The tactics employed in showmanship should always be tailored to fit the personality and dexterity of the individual sales person. Attempting techniques for which the demonstrator lacks any natural aptitude only invites disappointment or even disaster. Some experimenting is in order until each

Figure 6. Planner for sales presentations and demonstrations.

Selling situation	Sales prospect:		
	Key decision maker:		
	Others involved:		
	Date:	Time:	Place:
	Product/service:		Quantity:
	Prospect's problems and limitations:		
	Objective of this sales effort:		
	Other relevant factors:		

Preparation required	Props needed: (incl. samples)	
	Visuals needed: (incl. sales lit.)	
	Showmanship needs: (props and effects)	
	Facility needs: (space, lights, power, equipment)	
	Prospect preparation: Will he participate? What results should he expect?	
	Sales person or team assignments:	

Presentation plan	Notes for sales presentation
	Key selling ideas: (also specify demonstration and visual support)
	1.
	2.
	3.
	4.
	5.

Continue presentation plan on reverse side, if necessary.

practitioner discovers and settles on the types of showmanship he can carry off with aplomb and enjoy doing as well.

And by all means avoid exhibitions of pseudo-showmanship that denigrate professionalism in selling. This rules out show-off-manship, which is never a substitute for genuine show-manship. Flamboyant attire, manners, or stunts that center attention on the performer rather than on the performance of the product or service are not in keeping with the creative selling principles and techniques advocated in this book. Showman-ship in selling should always be tasteful and in keeping with its purpose of helping prospects identify and satisfy wants and needs that serve their own best interests.

In concluding this chapter, we offer a form to guide you when planning sales presentations and demonstrations (see Figure 6). Adapt this form, if you wish, to reflect more closely the nature of your particular business. It can help you make sure that you are adequately prepared for every sales call. This applies particularly to calls in which it is desirable to employ some variation of display-and-explain tactics to enhance the likelihood of making a sale.

Turn to Learning Exercise No. 19 in Appendix.

CHAPTER 7

COPING WITH
COMPETITION

Competition. Very likely no other word in the lexicon of selling evokes more diversity of meaning and emotion among sales people. To some, competition looms as an annoying frustration — an unwelcome interference without which selling would be a breeze. To a diminishing few, any competitive activity constitutes a threat to be thwarted by any tactic — fair or foul. Today, however, most sales people recognize and accept competition as a constructive challenge inherently beneficial both to consumers and to suppliers. On sober reflection, it is apparent that most of the problems characteristic of sales work are generated by the interaction of competitive forces — problems related to competing successfully, profitably, ethically, and legally while furthering the best interests of buyer as well as seller.

Attitudes toward competition vary widely among sales people — as among all people — depending on the heritage of ideas and experiences that have contributed to their ethical and economic beliefs. And personal moral values influence competitive selling practices. The competitive stance of every business enterprise reflects a composite of the standards of the people working for it — particularly its managers. This applies to companies and individuals who buy as well as to those who sell.

Obviously, not all people subscribe to quite the same standards of what is right and what is wrong in business practices — just as moral norms vary within all other spheres of social interaction. In this country, however, the trends of ethical business conduct move steadily in the direction of serving the greater good of society as well as of individuals. Witness the increasingly prevalent concept that business enterprises should subscribe to constructive social purposes as well as to profit and productivity goals. Reputable business organizations and their sales people function at a higher ethical level than is generally realized. The strident publicity given to occasional notable exceptions unjustly clouds the image of the vast majority who are steadfastly committed to exemplary business behavior.

At intervals during this continuing evolutionary process, the business practices of some have come to be viewed as intolerably abusive of the rights of others. Under public pressure, these episodes have resulted in legislation creating certain major acts governing business conduct. Other regulations having few ethical implications have also been legislated largely to provide equitable rules facilitating the flow of commerce. Whatever their relative significance, all laws impinging on competitive selling practices should be scrupulously observed.

One pervasive theme in all this, however, is that there are relatively few absolutes governing competitive selling — other than the legal restraints cited. And even these restraints are subject to recurring reinterpretation because of periodic testing in the courts. This reflects the constant shifting in economic and political forces as much as it does readjustment within the moral dimensions of business practice. But competitive selling often creates subtle and not so subtle ethical stresses, particularly when the personal standards of the people involved differ. Resolving such situations satisfactorily sometimes poses some perplexing problems. But when in doubt, the Golden Rule still serves as an excellent guide in selling as in other vocations.

Comprehensive study of the origins and current state of the ethical/legal climate surrounding sales work can be quite enlightening. But that is beyond the scope of this book. The purpose of this chapter is to provide some basic guidelines for competitive selling, and to urge you to study this subject more extensively in accordance with your own particular needs.

Competition: Genesis of the Selling Function

Coping with competition calls for a balanced perspective of the true nature of this free enterprise phenomenon. Competition constitutes the definitive force fueling the American economy. And competition is sustained by freedom of choice, which is a trademark of our democratic society. We are free to choose among the countless goods and services offered us by competitors seeking consumer favor and thus their own fortunes.

Profits are one reward earned by those who compete successfully. Profits provide recompense for those who invest in business. But profits also comprise one source of the capital needed to create more goods filling new consumer needs – thus contributing to economic growth. Constant, vigorous interaction among competitive forces tends to hold profits to reasonable levels and to develop lean, service-oriented enterprises among those able to stay the course.

Competition also creates the need for selling as the sensitive, highly personalized means of helping consumers make well-informed choices among the many options offered for satisfying their wants. In response to competitive stimuli, salesmanship has evolved into the sequence of skills we've been studying. A monopolistic enterprise has little need to sell its wares. But it takes a significant measure of skill to outsell a comparable competitive product in a free market.

Disciplined by the increasingly high standards for quality and performance that prevail today, few products ever attain clear superiority in *all* respects. Competition thus motivates suppliers to upgrade and innovate constantly in order to retain customer favor. This in turn keeps sales people in trim for their competitive roles of garnering equitable and compensatory shares of the markets for their products and services – an altogether stimulating challenge that is never easily met.

Strategy and Tactics of Competitive Selling

The artful strategist conducts every sales interview as though he has no competition. He studiously avoids even suggesting that any competition exists. Yet his sales presentations embody tactical selling points shrewdly planned to neutralize or surpass every sales advantage his competitors might be expected to claim. We stressed earlier that as a sales person, you should become familiar with the characteristics of all competing products. You can utilize this knowledge subtly in out-selling your competitors, but never employ it overtly as a means of discrediting them.

SELL YOUR ADVANTAGES – NOT COMPETITORS' DISADVANTAGES

It is wise to avoid becoming involved in discussing competition with a sales prospect. Concentrate instead on emphasizing all particulars in which you're convinced your product excels. Your responsibility is to sell your goods or services on their own merits. Allowing yourself to be drawn into a discussion of a competitor or his wares only dilutes your sales effort. Sales interviews are brief at best; use the time for talking about the virtues of your products – not the faults of competitors. Your prospect will make his own comparisons with competitors' offerings. The best way to bring about a favorable outcome is to present thoroughly every advantage of your product that represents value to him. Strive to establish your product and your salesmanship as standards competitors are hard pressed to match.

Never speak disparagingly about competition. Your most effective strategic stance is to reflect an attitude of reserved respect for your competition. If a prospect persists in wanting to discuss a competitive product, acknowedge respectfully that of course it has some merit or it wouldn't be marketable. But immediately resume explaining the superiority of your product relative to the features in question; or emphasize other favorable features that outweigh any disadvantages he may see in your product. Avoid speaking disparagingly about a competitive product. Doing so involves risks you need not invite. For example:

— The prospect knows that you're probably not an expert on competitive products; detractive statements can be erroneous and may get you into trouble.
— Any discrediting comments you make about competitive products are likely to be discounted as being biased even though they may be valid.

- Knocking a competitor lowers you in the prospect's esteem; his sense of fair play is insulted because you are attacking someone who isn't on hand to rebut your charges.
- The prospect may be a personal friend of a competitive sales person or of others in the competitor concern and so may be offended by your unfavorable comments.
- If the prospect happens to be using the competitive product, he may resent your detractive comments as impugning his judgment for having chosen it.

Magnify all favorable differences. A positive approach involves searching out all meaningful differences between your wares and competition that you can exploit to advantage. In addition to differences in product or performance, look for other disparities such as in sales policies, availability, delivery schedules, technical service, warranties, advertising, marketing support, and other customer services. Variations in these areas may amount to advantages on which you can capitalize. Sellers of goods customarily classed as commodities can make particularly good use of such differences. Often these items are so nearly uniform that buying decisions turn on questions other than product characteristics.

Explore your competitors' performance. It helps to become familiar with the selling strategies and tactics of competing companies for clues on how to counteract them successfully. Find out about the performance of competitive products and services, discreetly and ethically, as well as the degree of customer acceptance they enjoy. There are many sources for this information—friendly customers, service or maintenance people, trade show attendees, and trade journal articles, for example.

It also helps to learn something about the sales people with whom you compete regularly—especially about their personalities and selling habits. Such insights can guide you in formulating your own countervailing tactics. But it is risky to establish close personal friendships with competitive sales people. Unfortunately, such friendly relationships can become the sources of ethical conflicts. And they can sometimes lead to compromising situations—such as giving the appearance of en-

gaging in collusive practices even though this is not the case.
So it's wise to keep any such acquaintanceships at arm's length.

CULTIVATE GOODWILL

The competitive selling strategy that is perhaps most powerful is also the most pleasant to employ. This is cultivation of
goodwill among all customers and prospects. All of us prefer
doing business with friends if we have a choice. Other things
being equal — or nearly so — the sales person who is well liked
has a distinct advantage in landing the order. And good will
can be generated in many relatively simple ways. Some examples:

— Voluntarily performing small services and favors, personal
  as well as business-related.
— Accumulating and suggesting unique ideas that customers
  or prospects can use to advantage.
— Asking for advice occasionally; it's a compliment.
— Keeping all customer confidences faithfully.
— Being courteous, such as:
  showing respect for customers and their time;
  demonstrating interest in customers' families
  and other nonbusiness interests;
  being prompt in keeping all appointments and promises.
— Just being a genuinely friendly person.

Earning and reinforcing goodwill requires time and patience;
but it pays off big in helping you to gain and retain customers in
the face of aggressive competition.

Coping with Price Competition

The skill with which sales people handle questions about price
is another critical determinant of their ability to cope with competition. At some point in every sales transaction, price becomes the dominant consideration — that is, the amount of
money the buyer is willing to exchange for a purchase and the
terms he finds agreeable for the transaction. Discussion of price
should always be deferred as long as possible during the creative phases of selling. But when a buyer reaches the point of

making a final decision, price becomes — for a time — the paramount concern. Quoting the price constructively marks a very sensitive step in consummating a sale. Several discriminative aspects of competing on price are reviewed briefly below.

PRICE VERSUS VALUE

It is very important to understand that *price* is essentially a monetary measure of the relative *value* of a product or service — and that value varies in relation to the specific wants or needs of any given customer. And it is value that a customer really buys. Thus the price of a product should be considered only in relation to factors such as *quality, utility, and service,* which are the true measures of its value. It follows that comparing prices of similar competing products is largely meaningless unless those prices are considered in terms of relative values to a customer. The price of one product may be lower than the price of another; yet it may be more costly in terms of real value. It is vital to gain a clear perspective of these relationships in order to convey them persuasively to your customers whenever necessary.

Value is also relative in terms of the needs and resources of any given customer. For example, one item of industrial equipment may be distinctly superior to another in quality and durability. Yet it may not be suitable for a prospective customer because the intended application doesn't require that degree of quality or service. Furthermore, it may involve a greater investment than the prospect can justify for that purpose, or perhaps it is simply more than he can afford.

Competitive buying decisions are usually based on value and need — seldom on price alone. A customer buys only when he concludes that a specific purchase is the best value available for his needs and that its value is well worth its price tag. Some companies, when functioning as customers, refine this concept into an elaborate purchasing process called value analysis. In this decision-making procedure, competing products being considered for purchase are subjected to meticulous comparative analysis, performed by the buyer, to determine which is best in terms of purpose, quality, performance, and ultimate overall cost. Obviously, sales people selling such value-conscious customers must be thoroughly prepared to present the features and benefits of their products to maximum advantage, and make sure that none are overlooked.

YOUR PRICE IS TOO HIGH!

To many sales people, the price objection is the most chilling customer confrontation they ever have to face. How does one overcome or circumvent it? Ideas already offered can contribute much to neutralizing price resistance. But here are several more tactics to consider.

Prevent price objections. Your best strategy is to prevent price objections as much as possible by shrewdly anticipating them. Predetermine your prospect's needs accurately and match them well with your product or service. Then concentrate on selling thoroughly all features that fit the prospect's needs *before you even mention price.* Add advantage to advantage, point by point; build up values that qualify your price as reasonable when you do disclose it. The price always seems high to a prospect who has not yet been sold adequately on value.

When a prospect asks about price prematurely, try to defer answering with a tack like this:

> I'm about to tell you about the price, but first I'd like to explain several more things that will give you a better perspective on costs. You'll find this an excellent value.

If you reveal the price too soon, your prospect may be unable to think of anything else and will miss the impact of your key selling points.

Don't flinch. Some buyers habitually object to the price because they've discovered such pressure may produce a price concession. Face the issue calmly. Summarize again those features and benefits that make up value. Reaffirm quietly that your price is not negotiable. Price objections are not always sincere; they often dissolve in the face of tactful, reasoned rebuttal.

Review the facts. If the buyer claims to have been offered a lower price from a competitor, check out the specifics involved. Are you and the competitor quoting on the *same* requirements? Perhaps you offer more advantages, higher quality, better utility, performance, or service. If so, reemphasize these factors. Is the competitive price based on corresponding discounts, taxes, delivery provisions or terms? Is the competitor's price a recent, firm quotation? And don't overlook possible disparities in contingent costs to the customer — such as maintenance and operating costs of competing products.

If every tactic proves ineffectual and you become convinced the prospect actually does have a better price for equal or greater value, try to obtain suitable substantiation from the prospect. Your company is likely to require some tangible evidence with which to justify meeting the lower price — if it elects to do so.

A Brief Anatomy of Pricing

Technical knowledge about pricing doesn't qualify a person to sell, but incompetence in computing and quoting prices can cancel out otherwise masterful selling skills. Handling pricing particulars well is a very sensitive phase of selling. Customers rightfully expect sales people to know the prices of their products well enough to quote them quickly and accurately. They should not need to recheck every price with the sales office before quoting it. And sales people should always try to express prices in a context that reinforces value. They must also be aware that certain aspects of pricing have legal ramifications; errors in quoting — even though accidental — can involve a sales person and his company in a lot of problems. Some reasons for this are touched on later in this chapter under "Some Legal Aspects of Selling."

So it's highly important to become thoroughly familiar with the particulars of pricing your products correctly for every class of customer you sell. Acquire sufficient understanding of your company's pricing philosophy and policies so you can believe in them and feel comfortable about them. The self-assurance thus generated enables you to handle price questions constructively. Sales prospects quickly sense a defensive attitude and begin to wonder, "Why is he so hesitant about the price? Maybe his proposition is not as good as it sounds. Is his price perhaps too high?"

TYPES OF PRICES

Computing prices can be amazingly complex even when competition is not directly involved. Prices are quoted in a great many ways, reflecting wide differences in distribution patterns within various industries. Competitive forces influence evolution of pricing methods as companies strive to compete equitably, legally, and profitably even though some are better situated than others relative to markets and sources of supply. Most pricing accommodates variations in quantity of sale, allowable discounts, shipping costs, and applicable taxes. The location at which ownership passes legally from seller to buyer is sometimes also a pricing factor; among other things, this can affect placement of responsibility for any damage occurring during shipment. Many complications can be involved, some of which have legal implications.

Although pricing details also concern customers, their interest transcends the particulars of price structure. Mainly they want to know "What is my total cost?" for a purchase delivered or installed ready for use. Total cost is a critical consideration in every competitive selling situation. When sales prospects are comparing prices, try to make sure they compare ready-for-use costs on the same basis — with all applicable charges included. If they should omit some items in totaling up gross costs — taxes, for example — one quoted price may appear to be significantly, though deceptively, lower than another. Substantial variations in costs to customers for installing, operating, or other contingencies may also be critical factors when they're choosing the best buy.

It is impractical to go deeply into the intricacies of pricing here. We can only touch on several of the more widely used pricing methods for illustration. Particulars vary so widely between industries and companies that it is incumbent on each sales person to master the pricing procedures used in his own business. Our purpose here is to focus on some of the reasons why pricing competence is an essential component of competitive selling.

List price — a maximum published price usually subject to various discounts when computing a customer's actual cost. Published list prices often remain unchanged over long periods; price modification is effected through changes in discounts from the list price allowed to various classes of customers according to their function. Discount levels are adjusted in response to changes in competitive marketing conditions. Printed discount sheets are ordinarily provided the marketer's sales people for their own confidential use. List prices seldom include shipping costs.

Net price — represents the customer's price after any allowable discounts or other deductions have been subtracted from a list price but before addition of transportation costs, taxes, etc.

F.O.B. price — translates as "free on board" price. This pricing method has countless variations. For example, a price quoted "F.O.B. truck — shipping point" usually means it includes loading the goods on a truck at the seller's shipping point from which transportation charges to destination are paid by the buyer. Title to the goods is also deemed to pass to the buyer when merchandise has been loaded and turned over to the carrier for shipment.

But if the price is quoted "F.O.B. car — destination," it usually means the price includes loading into a railroad car at the seller's plant and transportation charges to destination. In this instance the seller also remains responsible for any loss or damage to the goods during transit.

Another variation can be stated "F.O.B. car — shipping point, freight allowed." This ordinarily indicates that the price includes payment of transportation charges by the seller, but the seller is relieved of responsibility for any damage to the goods after loading into the railroad car.

Many more examples of F.O.B. pricing could be cited — each having a distinct meaning depending on the precise wording used. Somewhat related are F.A.S. prices — meaning "free along side" — used in pricing sales for overseas shipment. The technical and legal ramifications of all such forms of pricing can become very involved and warrant careful study by all sales people who must quote them.

Zone price — a delivered price that applies uniformly for all sales within a geographical area or zone. Shipping costs included comprise an average of charges applicable to all likely destinations within the zone. A major market — such as the continental United States — may be divided into a number of zones. This is a very practical method of pricing when transportation charges are not a dominant factor in total delivered costs and sales volume is substantial. Functional discounts and other variations may apply as with list pricing.

"Guaranteed price" — an expression used when buyers are given some degree of protection against price changes — up or down — for a limited time when competitive market prices are fluctuating considerably. The effect is to protect customers against potential loss resulting from such fluctuations. Price guarantees obviously have many legal implications; they should be used only with great care.

PROFICIENCY IN PRICING

The foregoing sketches only a few of the many types of pricing that are in use, and particulars vary widely. Thorough training and diligent study are the only routes to competence in pricing matters. Most companies try to ensure that their sales people are well trained in pricing procedures and in recognizing the legalities involved. Comprehensive price bulletins are customarily provided that explain sales policies, prices and their application, and all restrictions involved. Guidance is provided for handling the pricing problems most likely to be encountered.

Drill yourself on pricing your goods or services and on all necessary precautions until you feel confident that you understand them well. And seek out qualified people to explain any factors that aren't clear to you. No other aspect of selling demands clearer understanding or greater skill than the computing and quoting of prices.

Turn to Learning Exercise No. 20 in Appendix.

Some Legal Aspects of Selling

It is impossible to provide more than token coverage of this complex subject in a few pages. Nevertheless it is important to point out that the very nature of selling constrains sales people to become more than casually familiar with the legal environment within which they work. Obviously, no sales person can be expected to become knowledgeable about all aspects of the many laws covering business functions. Yet ignorance is no excuse for flouting the law. Some prudent middle course is in order. At minimum, all sales people should become cognizant of the kinds of selling situations that can have legal ramifications. They should also be aware of the risks these situations portend. They can then observe due caution in all sales negotiations that might involve legal complications. And when in doubt, they should always seek competent advice.

Many of the legal statutes regulating business have evolved from rules of commerce developed over centuries of trade. They have been modified and updated periodically to keep pace with modern-day problems. Other major legislation of more recent origin has been enacted primarily to control and sustain competition on a basis deemed ethical and fair to all who are affected. Some of the more critical legal aspects of selling are identified here for your guidance.

THE SALES PERSON AS AN AGENT

Whether sales people are payroll employees or quasi-independent manufacturer's representatives, they function as agents for the company whose goods or services they sell. What they say or do can obligate the firm they represent. They also bear personal obligations to that firm, which in turn has obligations to them as its designated agents. The deeds of sales people in behalf of a company can be legally binding on that company. And they are obliged to carry out their selling functions in the best interests of the company they represent.

Thus the relationship involves many mutual obligations having ethical as well as legal implications. Obviously, it is important to understand the nature of those mutual accountabilities. Yet they are often covered only sketchily in the indoctrination given new sales people. Nonetheless, they exist and are embodied in various legal statutes, often collectively referred to as "the law of agency." It can be very constructive to explore these obligations with your employer to ensure good mutual understanding of their scope and intent.

UNIFORM COMMERCIAL CODE

In their role as agents, sales people constantly make offers to sell that, when duly accepted, can become binding contracts. Thus they need practical, perceptive knowledge of the legalities pertaining to terms and conditions of sales contracts and related aspects of commercial transactions. And they must be aware that in many situations offers to sell that are accepted orally can constitute valid contracts. Sales are often consummated much too rapidly to await the formalities of written quotations and acceptances.

Most of the specific rights and obligations of those involved in the sale or purchase of goods and services fall under legal jurisdiction of the states in which the transactions take place. State laws controlling commercial transactions were once widely divergent, having evolved out of common law and local custom relating to other kinds of contractual matters. As companies expanded and began to do business in many states, these variations created much confusion.

In response to the need for standardization, a Uniform Commercial Code was promulgated during the dozen years or so following 1951, and has since been adopted and placed in force in virtually every state. Broadly stated, the purposes of the code are:

1. To simplify and clarify the laws relating to commercial transactions,
2. To facilitate the general conduct of business,
3. To unify the applicable laws among the jurisdictions involved.

The code covers such matters as

Offers to sell	Transfer of title
Acceptances	Bills of lading
Sales contracts	Delivery of goods
Bulk sales	Rejection of goods
Cancellations	Breach of contract
Terms and conditions of sale	Damages
	Remedies
Price terms	Payments
Warranties	Collections
Title to goods	Lien rights

It includes countless variations of these and other topics too numerous to list here. The code is very comprehensive.

The need for such laws governing commercial transactions arises in part because, by long custom, business people often enter into sales or purchase agreements very informally — orally in person or by telephone, or by exchanging letters or other brief documents. Lacking the time to work out comprehensive documents for every transaction, each party relies on the other to abide by the accepted practices of doing business in the industry involved, which usually works out satisfactorily. But when something goes wrong, they are likely to resort to the law to resolve their problems equitably.

At the other extreme, large companies often use printed sales order forms and related documents that embody complex provisions designed to safeguard their rights as sellers. By signing the order, the buyer signifies that he accepts the offer to sell — including the seller's terms and conditions. However, large buyers often counter by using equally complex printed purchase order forms as a means of safeguarding their rights. Not surprisingly, the purchaser's terms and conditions are likely to vary with those of the seller. Resolution of the differences is normally worked out to the satisfaction of both parties, but sometimes disagreement ultimately leads to recourse to the pertinent laws involved.

It is evident that you need to acquire good understanding of the fine print on your employer's sales order forms, because the restrictions within which you are expected to sell are usually spelled out there. You should also acquire a practical familiarity with the Uniform Commericial Code and become conversant with any of its provisions that regularly impinge on sale of your products or services. But keep in mind that the code, as enacted, varies somewhat between states as a result of amendments. Your best source for this knowledge is qualified persons in your company, who can give you thorough explanation. The reading references at the end of this chapter will also be informative.

MISREPRESENTATION

A risk to be carefully avoided in competitive selling is claiming more for a product or service than the facts can justify. Abuses of this type can run afoul of various legal statutes against fraud — especially if it can be shown that the misrepresentation or exaggeration was a deliberate effort to influence a sale. A difference is ordinarily recognized between the well-meaning exuberance of a sales person extolling the advantages of his product and outright attempts to mislead or to withhold pertinent information.

Most buyers are presumed to be wise enough to use good judgment when evaluating the relative merits of enthusiastic sales presentations. And buyers can always exercise free choice in deciding whether or not to buy. But they also have access to legal redress against deceptive sales practices. Unfortunately, misguided or unscrupulous buyers occasionally attempt to claim misrepresentation where none has occurred; this sometimes makes this aspect of sales work a delicate one to handle. The best insurance against such problems is:

— Comprehensive, accurate knowledge of the features, benefits, and performance characteristics of the product or service being sold, and
— Resolute resistance of any temptation to claim more than the facts can support in order to land an order.

INFLUENCE OF THE ANTITRUST LAWS ON SELLING

As already suggested, the thrust of most legislation within the broad classification of "antitrust" is to prevent monopoly and preserve competition as well as to establish rules for doing business that will help accomplish these goals fairly and equitably. The principal impact of these laws is on the conduct of business enterprises at management or policy-making levels. However, their pervasive influences reaches into some phases of field sales activity.

It is not possible for us to examine all the facets of antitrust legislation that have some bearing on the duties and responsibilities of sales people. We can only identify some of the guidelines a sales person should observe jointly with his employer to comply fully with the law — an objective of every reputable concern.

Here is a list of the principal federal legislation involved. The letters in parentheses provide a key to the laws referred to in the listing of the rules below.

Sherman Antitrust Act	1890	(S)
Federal Trade Commission Act	1914	(FTC)
Clayton Act	1914	(C)
Robinson-Patman Act	1936	(RP)
(Amendment to Clayton Act)		
Wheeler-Lea Act	1938	(WL)
(Amendment to FTC Act)		
McGuire Fair Trade Act	1952	(M)
(Amendment to FTC Act)		

These federal acts regulate *interstate* commerce only. But the 50 states individually regulate *intrastate* commerce — in some instances extending provisions of federal law to business conducted entirely within a state. Most states have also enacted various laws that are often collectively referred to as the "Unfair Trade Practices Acts."

Following are brief, paraphrased statements of some of the more critical rules established by the federal laws identified above that impinge on sales functions:

- Attempts to restrain trade in interstate commerce are forbidden. (S)
- Attempts to monopolize business in interstate commerce are forbidden. (S)

— Use of unfair methods of competition in interstate commerce is forbidden. (FTC)

— Price discrimination between different purchasers of commodities that tends to lessen competition or to create a monopoly is illegal. (C)

Exceptions:

1. When a lower competitive price is encountered, it can be met, provided this action is taken in good faith.

2. Sellers can select their own customers in bona fide transactions as long as no restraint of trade is involved.

— Tie-in sales are forbidden. (Example: making the sale of one item contingent on the sale of other items needed in connection with its use.) (C)

— Refusing to sell a customer one item in a line unless he agrees to purchase all items in that line is forbidden. (C)

— Establishing exclusive dealerships is forbidden. (C)

— All quantity discounts offered must be supportable by lower distribution costs resulting from such larger sales of goods. (RP)

— Private-label goods cannot be sold at substantially lower prices than comparable goods sold by the same supplier to competing buyers. (RP)

— Promotional allowances and/or promotional services offered to large buyers must be offered proportionately to all competing buyers. (RP)

— Unfair or deceptive practices in interstate commerce are prohibited. (This relates particularly to false or misleading advertising practices applying to consumer goods.) (WL)

The McGuire Act qualified the legality of a number of so-called Fair Trade Acts enacted by various states over a period of years to prevent price cutting on nationally branded merchandise. Somewhat similarly, many of the state Unfair Trade Practices Acts prohibit selling unbranded goods below cost as loss leaders or for similar competitive purposes. The status of the various fair trade laws is currently clouded due to continued court testing and should be delved into carefully by those whose sales activities may be affected in any way by such pricing provisions.

CONSUMER PROTECTION LAWS

The legislation reviewed above is directed primarily at preserving competition in business. In addition, various federal laws have been enacted to protect the consumer. One of the most far-reaching of these is the Pure Food and Drug Act of 1906. Other acts in this category apply to other kinds of products and commodities that enjoy wide consumer markets. The principal thrust of these laws is to establish quality standards and to prevent inaccurate or deceptive labeling or pricing practices. There are also the "Truth in Lending" laws that require full disclosure of interest rates charged for consumer loans or for credit sales. The primary purpose of the consumer protection laws is to regulate supplier practices and establish uniform disclosure requirements. Inasmuch as sales people function as suppliers' agents, they need to be well informed about the provisions of these laws that apply to products or services they sell.

RESPECT THE LEGAL RULES OF SELLING

A balanced perspective on your sales job should reflect the attitude that all laws affecting selling have been enacted to *help* you, your customers, and the company you represent. The law should be viewed as a favorable factor in selling — not as an obstacle. Your efforts should always be directed toward complying with the law — never toward circumventing it. The circumvention route involves taking needless personal risk — perhaps even inviting disaster. If you find that you're expected to disregard known legal prohibitions affecting sales practices, perhaps you should reconsider whether you have chosen the right employment situation.

This cursory review of the legal aspects of selling should be viewed *only as a guide* to subjects you may need to learn more about. Most larger companies provide comprehensive indoctrination in this important area. If your employer does not offer an adequate program — perhaps because of limited size or resources — or if you are a self-employed sales person, you owe it to yourself to explore and absorb enough about legislation affecting your work to feel comfortably well informed. Several helpful books are listed at the end of this chapter and many more are available. Check with your local library.

Dealing with the Unethical Buyer

As pointed out earlier, all people do not conform to the same standards of ethical conduct. This includes customers and prospects as well as sellers. And one cannot very well choose customers according to whether their business ethics measure up to a prescribed set of standards. Instead, sales people learn to deal with customers as they find them—observing special safeguards when selling any they suspect may be inclined to discount ethical norms and legal restrictions.

Conceivably, you might someday face an oblique suggestion from a prospect that you participate with him in some kind of selling illegality. What should you do? You cannot agree to break the law; yet you can scarcely handle the situation by simply fleeing in alarm. After all, you may be misinterpreting the prospect's implication. And the business involved may be very desirable—provided no compromising conditions are attached.

Suppose the prospect seems to be suggesting that as a prerequisite for landing the order, you must provide some kind of rebate—either to his company or to him personally. Here are suggestions for responding, from which you might improvise a conversational reply:

> Mr. Prospect—we're just getting acquainted and I may be misinterpreting your meaning entirely. If so—just set me straight and we'll move on to other aspects of your requirements. But you seem to be saying that some rebate arrangement could assure my getting the order. In any case, perhaps I should explain our policies on such matters. Reaching a good mutual understanding now will contribute much to a sound relationship later on.

> If you're asking me to lower the price through some type of special discount to you or your company, I can only reply that my company would never go along with that—for reasons I'll

explain. And I can't personally afford to offer any monetary inducement to get the order — nor would I participate in such an arrangement.

My company's prices on this product are uniform to all customers whose function in business is the same as yours; variations in shipping charges account for the only material differences in delivered costs. This pricing pattern adheres to Robinson-Patman Act requirements for companies engaged in interstate commerce — as both our companies are. Giving you an unjustified price advantage through a rebate could land us both in jail and I know neither of us wants that! Am I right?

Perhaps what you really mean is that you've been quoted a lower price by a competitor. If so, that's an entirely different matter. If you're willing to provide me with tangible verification of the lower price and terms, when it was quoted, and other particulars, my company may be willing to meet it. But we can't undercut it; sorry — but that's the law. Have I explained the situation satisfactorily? I hope so, because I'd like to be able to work with you.

You'll find there are a great many advantages in doing business with us — the stature of our company, quality of our product, dependable service. . . .

Such a tack effectively rebuffs an invitation for hanky-panky, but it also gives the buyer an out — an opportunity to save face if he chooses to do so. It's unlikely you'll ever face a sales situation for which these somewhat stylized responses would be precisely suitable. But they do exemplify the kind of low-key reply that may set matters straight if a prospect should make an unethical request as a condition for placing an order.

This concludes our examination of some of the many aspects of sales competition and various strategies and tactics for coping with them. Clearly, competition provides the challenges that characterize selling as an exciting career demanding superior wit and wisdom from every successful practitioner.

Turn to Learning Exercise No. 21 in Appendix.

Recommended Supplemental Reading

In the following books you will find amplification of some of the topics covered in this chapter. Check the tables of contents or indexes for pertinent sections.

Corley, R. N., and Black, R. L. *The Legal Environment of Business* (4th ed.). New York: McGraw-Hill, 1977.

Grief, E. C. *Personal Salesmanship*. Reston, Va.: Reston Publishing, 1974.

Marsh, U. G. *Salesmanship: Modern Principles and Practices.* Englewood Cliffs, N. J.: Prentice-Hall, 1972.

Pederson, C. A., and Wright, M. D. *Selling Principles and Methods* (6th ed.). Homewood, Ill.: Richard D. Irwin, 1976.

Raphael, J. S. *The Uniform Commercial Code Simplified.* New York: Ronald Press, 1967.

CHAPTER 8

PROBLEM SOLVING AS A SELLING SKILL

We have stressed repeatedly that problem solving is a critical component of the selling process. A premise can even be justified that solving problems is the primary function of all sales people. Successful selling can be said to depend upon skill in:

1. Searching out and identifying customer problems that can be solved by the seller's product or service.
2. Creating solutions for those customer problems through use of the seller's product or service.
3. Persuading customers to accept those solutions, symbolically, by purchasing the seller's product or service.
4. Maintaining customers' continued satisfaction with the problem solutions they have purchased.

Those four skills embody most of the challenges faced by sales people. To meet those challenges, they engage in strategic sales planning, prospecting for customers, various preliminary selling tactics, making sales presentations, closing for orders, following through on sales made, and providing customer service. They also perform countless secondary chores that contribute to translating those key phases of selling into results benefiting both buyer and seller. But every step in the selling process involves making decisions through some variant of problem solving.

Enterprising sales people face a never-ending series of challenges: determining *what* their markets are, *how* to identify them, *which* prospects represent good sales potential, *why* they are promising, *where* to find them, *how* to sell them, *when* to approach them; *what to do* next month, next week, tomorrow, today, or even during the next hour. Within the realities of any given selling situation, each of these questions can constitute a sales problem. And not least of all sales people's problems is how to find enough time for everything that needs to be done.

This chapter explores some of the reasons for saluting the sales person as a problem solver. It also provides guidelines for a reasoned approach to solving sales problems. Emphasized throughout is the concept that problem solving comprises a principal tool for identifying and capitalizing on sales opportunities. Learning to use such a potent selling tool skillfully merits conscientious study and practice.

The Sales Person as a Manager

Selling is the very antithesis of every well-structured vocation in which the work pattern is readily apparent or predictable. In most marketing organizations, sales managers provide broad guidance through communication of overall objectives, marketing plans, sales policies, sales volume expectations, product pricing, and administrative procedures. They may even help sell and maintain good relations with major customers. But planning and carrying out the day-to-day sales activities that produce the results sought from a particular territory are responsibilities of the sales representative assigned to cover it. No one will do this work for him. In a very real sense, he is the manager of his own business — something of an entrepreneur, as discussed earlier. And like every manager, he becomes deeply involved in problem solving as the primary means of accomplishing his objectives.

Problem solving and the closely related processes of decision making, planning, implementing action, and measuring results are generally regarded as management functions. They are examined here as selling skills, because practicing them intelligently is a vital aspect of effective selling. Yet many sales people seem unaware of any need to cultivate these capabilities. Many who possess other talents qualifying them highly for sales work nevertheless fall short in performance. This often reflects deficiency in the disciplined thinking and planning needed to harness their many other abilities more productively.

Unfortunately, some sales people are only vaguely aware that the problems constantly besetting them can be dealt with rationally — not just intuitively. Skill in solving sales problems by orderly reasoning is one prerequisite for fruitful selling. Perceptive sales people conceive solutions for customers' problems. Those solutions then become sources for the key selling ideas around which convincing sales presentations are created. So let's explore the skills of problem solving and their application. They can contribute importantly to improved sales results as well as to better sales territory management.

The Nature of Sales Problems

Most problems faced by sales people fall into two broad categories: (1) functional problems related to planning and carrying out their multiple role so as to produce optimal sales results, and (2) customers' problems — sources of all the sales they make.

These two groups of problems are very much interrelated. The first group includes the problems of determining market potentials, planning how to capitalize on them, and administering the various sales work chores of one's territory. These functions lay the groundwork for solving customers' problems, which comprise the second group and provide all sales opportunities. Skillful sales people become adept at solving both kinds of problems in good balance.

Internal problems. Functional problems, those in the first group, comprise phases of sales work that are largely internal. For the most part, they relate to situations and functions over which sales people can exercise considerable control. For example, functional problems pertain to how they organize and carry out their day-to-day activities, how they allocate and use their time, and how perceptively they analyze and act on the potential of their markets.

External problems. Customers' problems, those in the second group, are primarily external, in the sense that they are *not* within sales people's control except as they can turn them to their advantage through the knowledge and skills they employ. For example, these problems relate to economic and industry trends, to business conditions within the markets being sold and to the prosperity, problems, and needs of individual customers and prospects. Also looming large among sales people's external problems are the activities of their competitors and the degree of market acceptance enjoyed by them.

Observe that virtually all types of sales problems are highly nonspecific — especially those classed as external. It is hard to define them precisely or to say of them "these are the facts" or "this will work" and be entirely sure you are right. Yet these are the very kinds of uncertainties that create the climate in which all sales work is conducted. This relative obscurity of sales problems often leads to a presumption that they are not susceptible to solution by logical reasoning processes such as are applied in scientific pursuits, and that sales intuition is the only available guide.

The perception that comes with experience is indeed valuable to the truly professional sales person who couples it with thoughtful problem analysis. For new sales people especially, however, it is very important to employ logical reasoning in the solution of problems precisely because they do involve so many uncertainties. This helps enterprising sales people accumulate the successful experience that is the real origin of the sales person's legendary "nose for business." Lazy sales people who avoid the mental work of studying their problems objectively in favor of selling strictly on hunches seldom acquire outstanding, enduring skills. They are more likely to join the thousands of mediocre, moderately productive sales people that employers are constantly striving to train and motivate — or wondering whether to replace.

Problem Solving Starts with Sales Objectives

Now let's back up a little to point out that every sales problem constitutes an obstacle to carrying out some sales objective. The goal may be making a specific sale, landing a new customer, introducing a new product, improving territory management, and so on. The list could be added to endlessly. But note that each includable item is synonymous to some degree with sales opportunity.

A sales problem thus comes into being whenever a sales objective is established. And it is very important to determine clearly just what that objective is. Unless an objective or goal is distinctly defined and understood at the outset, how can one know for sure when it has been accomplished? Furthermore, how can one determine what problems need to be solved, plans made, and actions taken for reaching any sales goal until the objectives and their derivative problems have been identified?

Objectives are often said to comprise the starting points for all productive business activity. The concept of management by objectives has become so widely accepted that it is employed to some extent by most sales organizations. Most sales people are now assigned objectives, or asked to develop their own — usually subject to approval. In practice, however, many modes of selling by objectives do not adequately take into account three critical requirements:

1. Every sales objective should be defined so clearly that its intent, scope, and limitations can be fully understood.
2. Every sales objective should be agreed upon by both the sales person and his supervisor as being appropriate and attainable.
3. An orderly reasoning process should be employed for delineating and solving problems found to stand in the way of accomplishing sales objectives.

It is vital to realize that sales problem solving begins and unfolds with the formulation of sales objectives. Sales problems and the objectives that create them are prime, interdependent factors in the selling process.

Sales problems are often multifaceted. In tackling the sales problems obstructing achievement of a major sales objective, you're likely to need to establish one or more *contributory* objectives. You may find it advantageous to subdivide the primary objective into several more easily managed parts — some to be tackled first and others later as you develop and pursue a sales strategy. The scope of the problems uncovered on analyzing a sales situation may dictate that you can't handle all the problems at once. Instead, you may need to set up a hierarchy of contributory objectives and then strive to accomplish those objectives in stages to reach your ultimate goal. Those contributory objectives provide the basis for formulating sales strategy and tactics. In one sense, then, the first step in problem solving is to divide in order to conquer.

ORIGINS OF PROBLEM-SOLVING PROCESSES

The mental processes involved in problem solving have been the subject of countless studies and are well presented in many excellent books and courses. The historical beginnings of a reasoned approach to problem solving can be found within many ancient chronicals of man's first insights into his own thinking processes. Certainly one of the most penetrating sources of the early twentieth century is John Dewey's "Analysis of Reflective Thinking."* More recently, various authorities on business management have promulgated many worthy models for analytical decision making.

There seems to be general agreement that about half a dozen stages of thinking are definable in sizing up a problem situation, devising a promising solution, taking action on it, and evaluating the results. The steps may be followed in logical sequence; or one's mind may skip about from one step to another as the implications of each are pondered. In any case, most of the steps are likely to be touched upon – some repeatedly – in reaching a considered decision. Figure 7 offers seven steps leading to identification and solution of problems standing in the way of accomplishing a sales objective or goal. The need for a *primary* sales objective or goal is prominently set out as the starting point because the existence of that objective initiates and justifies the entire problem-solving process.

Primary objectives are usually assigned to a sales person; if not, he should set them for himself. He is likely to receive or need a number of them. They may remain relatively unchanged over a long period of time, like the beacons toward which ships steer their courses. Or they may be changed or modified with some frequency – as when changes in sales situations or strat-

---

* John Dewey, *How We Think* (First Gateway Edition). Chicago: Henry Regnery, 1971.

Figure 7. Sales problem-solving process.

Primary sales objective or goal: _____

Step 1. Appraise sales situation to define the problems it involves.

Step 2. Develop contributory sales objectives.

Step 3. Create alternative courses of action for attaining each contributory sales objective.

Step 4. Evaluate relative merits and probable results of all alternatives; choose the most promising course of action for achieving each objective.

Step 5. Plan how to implement actions decided upon for reaching each objective selected.

Step 6. Carry out sales plan(s).

Step 7. Evaluate sales results in terms of the primary sales objective.

Repeat this process, if necessary, starting with Step 1.

---

egies require adjustment of tactics. But they must always be clearly defined. Otherwise, sales problem solving and the selling process lose meaning and direction.

After Step 7 of the sales problem-solving process outlined in Figure 7 has been completed, the process should be repeated, if necessary. Problem solving is *never complete* in an absolute sense. It is a continuous process because even the best solutions are always subject to refinement. Sales results considered satisfactory when attained yesterday — whether from a market or from one customer — are judged inadequate and in need of improvement tomorrow. Sales situations are never static; sales prospects and potentials are forever changing. Hence most sales objectives need constant review and readjustment — especially the ones you establish for yourself. Thus sales problem solving continues unceasingly as it adapts to or takes advantage of constantly changing conditions. The degree of reevaluation deemed necessary may vary widely, but the mental steps involved remain essentially unchanged.

Developing Sales Objectives

The *primary* sales objectives or goals we're considering here are broad in scope as these examples indicate:

- Increase sales of (product or service) by 25 percent in your territory by (date).
- Establish ABC Company as a distributor of (product or service) within the Central City market by (date).
- By (date), obtain at least 25 percent of the business of XYZ Company for (product or service) now supplied by a competitor.
- Introduce (new product or service) in the Central City market area by establishing customers purchasing (dollar volume) by (date).
- Realign pattern of sales coverage in order to increase concentration in the rapidly expanding Central City market without jeopardizing customer establishment elsewhere in your territory.
- Explore and adopt methods for improving your ability to perceive and analyze customers' problems as an aid to selling more of (product or service).

Contributory sales objectives supporting primary objectives such as those exemplified above should be defined as precisely as necessary to provide good direction of sales effort.

Techniques for formulating well-conceived objectives merit amplification as a separate topic. Those with a special need or interest can find much helpful material published on this subject. However, our main purpose here is to point out that objectives are inextricably involved with problem solving and the selling process. Each primary objective cited above constitutes a rather specifically defined goal. But observe that undertaking its accomplishment would very likely generate a number of contingent problems to be identified and surmounted in the process. Note also that four of the objectives include a completion date, and that a date could plausibly be added to the other two. Establishing a target date is an important component of most objectives as well as of most sales plans; without time limits they can be too open-ended to serve their purposes well.

Turn to Learning Exercise No. 22 in Appendix.

Must Sales Problem Solving Be This Complex?

Let's pause to reconsider where this chapter is heading. The problem-solving concepts presented so far may seem rather complex for daily application to sales work. And the ideas offered on the pages that follow may magnify that impression. A painstaking process is outlined for sifting through the maze of conflicting facts and assumptions that often complicate a selling situation. A method is propounded for reaching decisions for sales action. You may view these techniques as too involved to be practical for busy sales people who must close orders constantly. If so, you're quite right; the procedures presented here cannot be followed meticulously in making every sale. But please read on.

Our purpose is to formulate *a pattern for thinking through any sales problem to reasoned conclusions* on the most promising courses of action for making a sale. You are guided through this process carefully, step by step, as a learning experience that embodies explanation, example, and practice. But such thoroughgoing analysis cannot and need not be applied to every routine sales problem that comes along. Usually there simply isn't time for this. However, there is always time for bringing to bear the *attitudes* implicit in a reasoned approach to problem solving.

Imaginative objectivity is needed at the outset to think through and absorb the concepts involved. We recommend that you couple this with enough systematic, persistent practice so that a workable adaptation of these mental processes gradually becomes a part of your individual selling style. In time, an inquisitive, orderly pattern for solving sales problems that is compatible with your personality will evolve as habit. This is the goal we urge you to set for yourself. Disciplined ability to discern the pivotal points of sales problems quickly will help you reach constructive conclusions surely and act on them decisively.

MAKE NOTES ON YOUR FINDINGS AND PLANS

In analyzing your sales problems, it always helps to jot down data and ideas pertaining to the various steps involved. This enables you to visualize better the relationships between disparate factors as well as to identify and separate facts from assumptions. An orderly approach contributes to reaching sound conclusions more confidently.

Also make notes on the steps of the sales plan you decide on for surmounting the problem. Your notes can be brief or extensive depending on the complexity of the problem. Writing down the particulars helps you crystallize your plan and fix it in mind. Without notes for reference on plans decided upon, actions taken, and results achieved, you can find yourself in a constant state of anxiety because you're unable to remember clearly the current status of every selling effort you have under way. There's an old saying that "the strongest memory is weaker than the palest ink."

It's good practice for new sales people to make notes on their deliberations and decisions on *all* problems; this needn't become overly time-consuming. It is especially wise to apply this technique when dealing with a major problem situation — such as how to land an important new account. This kind of care adds a powerful multiplier to the likelihood of devising and carrying out successful sales strategies. Now let's return to the sales problem solving process and examine each of its seven steps in turn.

Particulars of Problem Solving

Remember: All problem solving starts with identification of an objective or goal. Then proceed this way:

STEP 1. APPRAISE SALES SITUATION TO DEFINE PROBLEMS IT INVOLVES

In this context a situation refers to any circumstances that create a problem in handling any phase of your selling activities. This includes functional problems faced in carrying out

your assignment. It also includes the specific customer problems you hope to resolve through sale of your product or
service.

We will concentrate heavily on situation appraisal because
this is a critical phase of sales problem solving. Yet this often
receives only cursory consideration or is neglected entirely.
The tendency of too many sales people is to jump hastily to
conclusions for sales action only to discover belatedly that situation factors they should have reckoned with — but overlooked
or ignored — have cost them an order or other sales-related accomplishment.

In this mental step, all identifiable factors in the problem situation are sized up and their relative importance weighed. Separate those factors you can do something about from those you
must accept and deal with as you find them. Garner this information by remaining constantly alert to everything happening
in your territory and industry that can affect your sales opportunities. Obtain ideas pertinent to your problems from customers and other trade contacts. Glean data from trade publications
and local newspapers. Gather information from business direc-
tories or government reports. Elicit information needed by asking the sales prospect himself. Potential sources are as infinite
as you are imaginative.

Situation appraisal boils down to careful determination of
what your problem really is. Without a perceptive approach,
you risk setting out to solve the wrong problem or only part of
the right one. The legendary Charles Kettering of General
Motors fame once pointed out that it takes just as much effort to
solve a useless problem as a useful one. Most dangerous is
jumping to a conclusion about what the problem is without
thinking it through objectively. This escalates your chances of
being wrong. On careful evaluation, you may even find you
have no serious problem; somehow it tends to shrink when a
little clear thinking unclouds your point of view.

To reiterate, a sales problem can be viewed as any situation
that interferes with achieving a sales goal or objective. Two examples of typical sales problem situations are described below.

Selling a major account now supplied by a competitor
Suppose the assignment or personal objective of a sales rep-

resentative is to sell a major prospect who has long been purchasing a competitive product. The overall problem is how to go about it — especially since the prospect is apparently quite satisfied with the product he's now using. The sales person is convinced that he sells a better product offering outstanding benefits; but it is somewhat more costly. He's also aware that close personal friendships have developed between the prospect's key personnel and the competitive supplier. But that's about all he knows.

So it's a tricky situation. *What other factors* may impinge significantly on the scope of the sales person's problem? Could additional particulars provide guidance for determining a course of action that would overcome known obstacles? Until the sales person has considered all the ramifications he can reasonably uncover, he is not well prepared for deciding how to proceed in selling this large customer and thus achieve his objective.

What steps might he take to gather additional pertinent information?

Introducing a new product

Consider the situation of a sales person who has just had a promising new product added to his line. His assignment (objective) is to introduce it to most (but not all) of his present customers as well as to many new prospects he's had no reason to call on before. Some present customers have no application for the new product. His primary problem is how to accomplish this introduction rapidly in order to capitalize on the impact of new product appeal. But it is also very important not to jeopardize any established accounts through inattention in the meantime.

Obviously, his task must be well planned. He can't carry it out successfully by jumping in his car and driving off in all directions at once. *Who* are the new prospects and *where* are they located relative to present customers? *Which* new prospects offer the most potential? *Which* might be deferred in sales call priority, with the least risk? *How much* additional time will a good presentation of the new product require? With new prospects? With present customers? In *what new ways* might relationships with established accounts be well maintained while introduction of the new product proceeds? *What other factors* have a critical bearing on this problem situation and its optimal solution? The sales person won't be ready to exploit his new opportunities until he has studied all aspects of the problem and has arrived at well-considered decisions for the best course of action.

What can he do that might help him size up the situation better?

Turn to Learning Exercise No. 23 in Appendix.

In evaluating a sales situation, it is critical to ask the right questions of yourself and of others. This requires sensitivity to the variables in the situation and the relationships between them. The variables include all the *facts* you can be sure about as well as the *assumptions* you must make that you cannot be sure about. No sales person ever has all the facts. Yet decisions for sales action are often urgent. So he must base decisions on a combination of assured facts and reasonable assumptions

Figure 8. Outline for problem-solving Step 1.

Purpose: Appraise sales situation to define the problems it involves

Primary sales objective or goal: _____

_____

Factors involved in sales situation	Fact or assumption?	Subordinate problems uncovered
1. _____	_____	_____
2. _____	_____	_____
3. _____	_____	_____
4. _____	_____	_____

(continue as needed)

while distinguishing carefully between the two. Hasty conclusions based on assumptions confused with facts provide a dubious basis for creating good sales plans.

Figure 8 is a schematic outline of the thought processes involved in sizing up a problem situation. Try adapting this format to your own problem-solving needs and style.

Note that this format traces thought processes through only the *first* of the seven steps of sales problem solving presented in Figure 7. Additional outlines in similar format lead one's reasoning through the ensuing steps. In effect, this first step breaks down the overall problem situation into several more manageable problems. It identifies the factors involved and considers whether each can be tagged as true or only probable. This process crystallizes the lesser problems that, taken together, comprise the whole. Tackling each subordinate problem when timely actuates a divide and conquer strategy for mastering the overall sales problem situation.

Turn to Learning Exercise No. 24 in Appendix.

STEP 2. DEVELOP CONTRIBUTORY SALES OBJECTIVES

The right-hand column in Figure 8 identifies the various subordinate problems uncovered in appraising a sales situation. Those subordinate problems deemed sufficiently important can now be restated as "working" or contributory objectives, accomplishment of which will contribute to realizing the *primary goal* initially defined.

The potential impact of each contributory objective on winning the main event should be clearly thought out. Sales strategy and tactics are now being formulated and priorities established. The question of *why* each contributory objective is important must be faced squarely. There should be compelling reasons for carrying out each objective in order to avoid unproductive diversion of effort. For example, answering the question "why?" at this point may bring reluctant realization that your friendly contact within a prospect's organization is not the real decision maker, and that accordingly it is important to

Figure 9. Outline for problem-solving Step 2.

Purpose: Develop contributory sales objectives

Subordinate problems	Reformulate as contributory sales objectives:	Why is each important?
1._____	_____	_____
2._____		
3._____	_____	_____
4._____		
	(continue as needed)	

make sure others having authority to buy also hear your presentation. This may create still another problem to solve. Or facing up to the question why may crystallize an uneasy awareness that the product or service you are planning to offer doesn't quite satisfy the prospect's needs; thus more homework should be done before you make a specific sales proposal.

Figure 9 is an outline of thought processes in this step of the problem-solving process. Note from the figure that not every identifiable subordinate problem need be reformulated into a contributory sales objective. Thorough appraisal of a complex sales situation is likely to bring to light a profusion of subordinate problems; those that are less compelling should be set aside in favor of those that are more critical. Also, carrying out one well-formulated contributory objective may solve several subordinate problems. Examining *why* each problem uncovered needs to be solved helps eliminate those least likely to favorably influence the customer's buying decision. This reduces contributory objectives to those likely to be most helpful in accomplishing the primary goal.

Turn to Learning Exercise No. 25 in Appendix.

STEP 3. CREATE ALTERNATIVE COURSES OF ACTION FOR ATTAINING EACH CONTRIBUTORY SALES OBJECTIVE

We've seen that subordinate sales problems become opportunities when recast into positive contributory objectives. Once an objective has been identified, it is necessary to perceive and consider all viable alternatives for carrying it out. This calls for creative thinking.

It is a rather common error to overlook the fact that a choice can usually be made among several courses of action. One alternative may hold the promise of better results or involve fewer risks than another. When several choices are available, some are likely to be mutually competitive; only the best should be selected after the merits of each have been weighed. But sales people sometimes rush to act on the first solution that comes to mind without realizing a more propitious choice may be open to them. Conversely, others sometimes see so many options open that they equivocate—unable to decide and act on any. Doing nothing is always an alternative, but it's seldom the right one. The reasoning involved in this problem-solving step can be outlined as shown in Figure 10.

Consider again the sales person who has just had a promising new product added to his line. His assignment is to introduce it quickly to all potential customers in his territory. That becomes his *primary* objective. One of many problems facing him is how to maintain satisfactory, uninterrupted sales and service to his present accounts while launching the new product. Through creative rethinking, this becomes *one* of his contributory working objectives. What, then, are some alternatives for sustaining his existing customers? Here are several courses the sales person might consider:

- Personally explain the situation to each present customer during the next regular sales call whenever that happens to occur.
- Write or phone each customer to explain the situation and ask for his forbearance.
- Phone each to solicit reorders about the time they would normally fall due.

Figure 10. Outline for problem-solving Step 3.

Purpose: Create alternative courses of action for attaining each contributory sales objective

Contributory sales objectives chosen	Alternatives for attaining each	Relative merits of each alternative
1.		
2.		

(continue as needed)

— Ask each to place somewhat larger orders than usual to offset any possibility of service interruption.
— Provide each with forms and preaddressed envelopes for mailing in orders.
— Arrange to have sales and service calls continued by others in his organization during the new product campaign.
— Make no special provisions at all and hope for the best.

With a little imagination, many more options could easily be added to this list.

Among several alternatives, each usually has inherent advantages as well as disadvantages when weighed relative to all others. Evaluating all available options and choosing the best among them comprises the next problem-solving step. It is essentially an extension of the step just examined but is treated separately to help clarify the sequence in reasoning processes.

Turn to Learning Exercise No. 26 in Appendix.

STEP 4. EVALUATE RELATIVE MERITS AND PROBABLE RESULTS OF ALTERNATIVES AND CHOOSE THE MOST PROMISING

After creating several viable alternatives for achieving any sales objective, the next step is choosing the best course of action. Take into account the probable consequences of each alternative if adopted. Consequences are always future-oriented; evaluating the options involves making judicious predictions. Weigh the pros and cons of each alternative. If one particular alternative is acted upon, what is the most likely outcome? Is this course more likely than another to accomplish the result sought? Consider the relative risks as well as the prospects for success.

This is a step into the unknown for which the only available guide is careful initial appraisal of the sales situation during the first problem-solving step. A choice of sales actions must be made. But on what basis? This predicament exemplifies the need to employ objective reasoning for solving sales problems instead of relying blindly on speculative hunches. The outline in Figure 11 may clarify the purpose and application of this mental step.

This figure outlines thought processes for deciding on the best course of action for attaining *one* contributory objective selected to help reach the primary sales goal. If several contributory objectives are adopted, this process applies for each. Obviously the problem-solving process can fan out broadly when complex selling situations are involved. Well-reasoned preparation for sales action is always warranted, however, especially when major opportunities are at stake in a sensitive sales situation.

One alternative likely to occur to the sales person faced with introducing a new product is simply to explain it all to each established customer on his next regular call. But what if he's delayed because of time devoted to new prospects? Will this

Figure 11. Outline for problem-solving Step 4.

Purpose: Evaluate relative merits and probable results of all alternatives; choose the most promising course of action for achieving each objective.

Contributory objective: _____

Alternatives for reaching objective	Possible outcome of each alternative		On appraisal, the best alternative
	Favorable factors	Unfavorable factors	
1._____			
2._____			

(continue as needed)

jeopardize his standing with current accounts? Might some become irritated enough to listen with renewed interest to a competitor's coaxing? Does the sales person risk losing some existing sales accounts as an unwarranted cost for landing customers for the new product? This kind of questioning should be applied to each option. Chances are that objective evaluation of his relationships with current customers will lead to somewhat different plans for handling each of them. The sales person's approach to new prospects should also take into account realistic estimates of the relative opportunities each represents.

Having chosen the best options for sales action, we're ready for the next step — sales planning.

Turn to Learning Exercise No. 27 in Appendix.

STEP 5. PLAN HOW TO IMPLEMENT ACTIONS DECIDED UPON FOR REACHING EACH OBJECTIVE SELECTED

All prior problem-solving steps prepare for this one — planning how to carry out sales actions decided on. Sizing up the sales situation and all viable alternatives for mastering it clarifies what a good sales plan should encompass. It remains to organize components of the plan, review their adequacy, and implement them. We've pointed out that a combination of several contributory objectives and courses of action may be strategic for reaching the primary sales goal. Thus the overall sales plan opted for may include several parts — one for realizing each contributory sales objective adopted.

A workable sales plan answers these questions: *What* actions are needed? *Why* are they needed? *Who* is to carry them out? *When, where,* and *how* is each to be accomplished? A sales plan anticipates future results and establishes means for bringing them about. It can be as simple or as complex as the primary objective and selling situation prescribe. It may consist of a few notes or comprise a detailed document. It may be short- or long-range. It may cover only sales work to be done tomorrow or anticipate market results to be sought next year and spell out steps for accomplishing them.

A sales plan concludes the decision-making process on sales actions to be taken. When formulated, a sales plan signifies the climax of situation appraisal and the beginning of active selling. Accordingly, a sales plan deserves to be written out — whatever its scope. It is a commitment for action — subject to any approvals required. A sales plan also serves as a checklist for progress made toward the primary sales goal. Thus it becomes the basis for measuring results.

Figure 12 contains an outline for preparing a sales plan. Note the provision for restating the contributory objectives that have perhaps been modified during problem solving. If precise ob-

Figure 12. Outline for problem-solving Step 5.

Purpose: Preparing a sales plan

Objective(s) decided upon: _____

_____

Specific sales plan components

What actions   Why is each
are needed?   action needed?

1. _____   _____

Alternative course   2. _____   _____
of action chosen
for achieving   3. _____   _____
objective
(describe briefly)   4. _____   _____

_____   (continue as needed)

_____   Who will carry out each action?

_____   When? Where? How?

_____   1. _____ _____ _____ _____

2. _____ _____ _____ _____

3. _____ _____ _____ _____

4. _____ _____ _____ _____

(continue as needed)

jectives are missing, a sales plan can be misleading or even
meaningless. The outline diagrams thought processes for preparing a sales plan to carry out *one* objective. When several
contributory objectives are involved, planning is required for
accomplishing each, and the resulting overall sales plan becomes more complex.

Within this context, that sales person assigned to introduce
the new product will doubtless need a number of sales plans.
After appraising his overall problem situation and reaching

conclusions about the sales opportunities and risks involved, he'll need an overall plan for his entire campaign. This should set out just what he plans to do and why, whom he'll call on and when, as well as how he plans to get everything done within the time available. Then he'll need a plan for accomplishing his *specific objective* for each current customer and each new prospect. Individual call plans, though similar, should accommodate the unique opportunities afforded by each customer and prospect—as uncovered by the sales person's situation appraisal. And he'll need to plan his basic sales presentation covering features and benefits of the new product by employing the five-step idea-selling format.

Thus, having appraised the sales situation, developed objectives, created and evaluated alternative ways of achieving them, selected the most promising options, and planned how to carry them out, *the sales person is now ready to sell.*

Turn to Learning Exercise No. 28 in Appendix.

STEP 6. CARRY OUT SALES PLAN(S)

We may seem merely to be stating the obvious, but several aspects of this step warrant emphasis. So far sales problem solving might be characterized primarily as a mental exercise—more passive than active. At this point, however, *action* is unquestionably called for, lest all prior appraisal and planning come to naught. Sales people vary widely in personal ability and motivation. Some are very good at planning but slow in acting decisively to carry out their well-conceived plans. Others jump into action without considering sufficiently just what is to be accomplished and how. A middle course is needed; *both* good planning *and* positive action are essential for fruitful selling.

Decide for yourself which is greater—your need to cultivate your ability to appraise and plan or your need to develop the drive to carry out sales actions decided upon. It's a common truism that most sales people find doing more to their liking than planning. That's why we've examined problem solving so thoroughly—to emphasize that much purposeful thinking should go into deciding *what* to do and planning 'how to do it.

An eminent professor of management once expressed very well the need for good balance between planning and doing in this "Prayer for Sales People":

> O Good Lord, give me the strength to refrain from rushing into the *how* of things until I know *what* is to be done and *why*.

A well-conceived sales plan is always easier to implement and is more likely to lead to the desired results. With a good plan, a sales person can move smoothly and confidently from one step to the next; he doesn't lose momentum by having to stop to figure out what to do next.

Some sales people are dashing, charismatic characters. An interesting personality is always an asset as long as it doesn't obscure the reality that the payoff in selling results from closing orders—not from colorful conduct. This brings into focus the last of the seven steps in problem solving—measuring results.

STEP 7. EVALUATING SALES RESULTS IN TERMS OF THE PRIMARY SALES OBJECTIVE

The premise for this step is that it is impossible to anticipate with certainty precisely what course of action will succeed in solving any given sales problem and landing the order. Good sales planning helps ensure that nothing will go wrong; nevertheless, something often does.

The forces of change are always operating; market conditions and customers' needs are constantly shifting. The specifics of a sales situation may change even while superb plans for capitalizing on it are being carried out. And competitive action almost invariably adds to the uncertainties. So it is that sales results don't always measure up to expectations; objectives aren't quite achieved or may even be missed completely. This doesn't necessarily signify that the game is over. But it does signal need for readjustment of strategy and tactics. In selling, as in our other endeavors, we learn from our mistakes.

This is what takes place in the results-measuring step. Its purpose is to appraise sales achievement in terms of the *primary sales objective* as well as the sales problems actually encountered. When accomplishment falls short but the sales opportunity remains within reach, *reappraisal should lead to modified sales plans and renewed sales action.* Thus evaluation of sales results leads to innovative renewal of the selling process based on actual experience. Tentative results should be tested whenever they begin to appear; any unwanted deviation is your cue to adjust sales action for zeroing in more closely on the objective.

With the results-measuring step we have come full circle in examining the particulars of sales problem solving. We hope it is now clear why problem solving should be viewed as a repetitive, continuing process—as suggested in Figure 7, which introduced this concept.

Those practicing the techniques of problem solving by carrying out the exercises provided will find it difficult to continue beyond problem-solving Step 5 on an armchair basis. Role-playing comes up short when compared with actual practice in carrying out sales plans and measuring the results achieved in the marketplace. On-the-job experience in real selling situations with live customers and prospects is indispensable for learning and refining these phases of selling. However, after-the-fact reconstruction of an actual selling episode is an effective means of analyzing how it might be done better next time. The learning exercises provided for this chapter suggest a pattern for devising case problems drawn from authentic selling experiences that can be used as the basis for group learning seminars, if desired.

Summary on Sales Problem Solving

This chapter has outlined and examined a functional pattern for creating sales strategies and applying sales tactics designed to improve results. The principal tool involved is mental—a rational, systematic method of analyzing sales problems and synthesizing solutions for them. Sales objectives and plans thus formulated become the basis for sales actions. Results are then measured against the sales objectives as initially established. If achievement has fallen short of expectations, the process is then recycled—with modification, to benefit from the experience gained.

The seven problem-solving steps that we have examined are summarized below. Let's begin by reemphasizing that problem solving commences only after we have identified an *overall sales objective or goal*. This may be any *primary* goal that initiates the need for problem solving. It may be one of several goals assigned to a sales person, or it may be self-established. Three random examples are (1) selling an important new account, (2) opening a major new market, (3) launching a new product.

1. *Appraise sales situation to define sales problems.* In this first step, the overall situation is sized up in order to break it down into manageable sales problems, solution of which will contribute to achieving the primary goal. This entails astute examination of all that can be learned about the situation—facts as well as reasonable assumptions.

2. *Develop specific contributory sales objectives.* Each critical problem formulated in Step 1 is restructured into a specific contributory sales objective. Achieving the primary overall sales goal can be expected to culminate from attaining these contributory objectives. The question of *why* each contributory objective is important is considered exactingly to preclude all unproductive sales effort.

3. *Create alternative courses of action for attaining each contributory sales objective.* Often several potentially successful approaches can be devised to accomplish an objective. In this step, all reasonably promising alternatives for reaching each contributory sales objective are developed.

4. *Evaluate the relative merits of each alternative in terms of potential results; choose the best option available.* By weighing the advantages and risks implicit in each alternative, the most promising courses of sales action for accomplishing each objective are selected. The basis for evaluating each alternative is the relative likelihood of its contributing as desired to the sales results sought.

5. *Plan how to implement the most promising alternatives selected.* A step-by-step plan is created for those sales actions chosen for achieving each contributory objective selected for pursuit. This plan is the vehicle for converting probability into

reality. A good plan always answers the questions of what, why, who, when, where, and how for every sales action to be undertaken.

6. *Carry out sales plan.* Resolute, timely action is now required for placing the plan into operation by all appropriate means deemed most likely to bring about the results sought. Performance is now the key to results; since appraisal and planning are now complete, any unnecessary delay can prove costly.

7. *Evaluate sales results in terms of the* primary *sales objective.* In this final step, actual accomplishment is compared with the sales results anticipated as represented by the initial goal or objective. Any shortfall in achievement becomes the basis for recycling the sales problem solving process—in modified form to compensate for changes in the sales situation and inadequacies in the sales actions as carried out.

We have conducted a highly clinical examination of the process of solving sales problems in order to help you understand the concepts involved and learn to adapt them to your own selling style. Real-life market exigencies rarely afford any sales person the luxury of such laboratory-like scrutiny of sales problems and alternative ways of capitalizing on them. Time pressures seldom permit this. Nevertheless, the study and practice outlined here represent a good way to acquire or improve these skills. They comprise an approach to sales problem solving that stimulates creative thinking and encourages innovation—abilities that are indispensable for professional selling. When accepted and absorbed, the concepts embodied in this approach are certain to be reflected positively in your selling performance.

CHAPTER 9

TERRITORY MANAGEMENT AND PERSONAL DEVELOPMENT

Here are two aspects of sales work that correlate very well because they involve so many of the same attitude and skill factors — territory management and personal development. All sales people who set out to manage their work well also tacitly commit themselves to a continuing pattern of self-improvement. Progress toward either goal is contingent on simultaneous pursuit of the other. And superior performance depends on cultivation of one personality trait in particular — *self-discipline*. This attribute is doubtless more motivating than any other for those aspiring to achieve success and self-realization in selling. As we have explored the skills of selling, it should have become apparent that skill in managing the procedural chores of selling is also required. Examining some of the personal disciplines imposed by these aspects of sales work is the purpose of this final chapter.

Freedom to Succeed — Or Fail

One of the alluring features of outside sales work also constitutes a subtle risk for the credulous. This is the virtual independence with which outside sales people appear to function. Except for the directives supplied by a sales manager they seldom see, they are free to come and go much as they please. They can arise when they like, go to work when they wish, and work as much or as little as they choose. They can elect to toil long hours or goof off at will. What a utopian situation! Few other occupations provide such a wide degree of personal freedom. It is a vocation that does, indeed, afford many advantages; but it also involves many pitfalls for those ill prepared to cope with all that freedom. Because there is a catch.

Those privileges must be earned to be retained — earned by sales performance for which the ultimate measure is the quantity and quality of sales orders obtained. Landing those orders provides the chief justification for all sales jobs. Sales people soon learn that their *real boss* is that little piece of paper — the sales order — and that the requirements it makes on them are unrelenting. That glow of satisfaction generated by closing an important sale is very gratifying but transient; it fades as realization returns that the next sale is waiting to be made . . . and the next . . . and the next after that.

So outside sales people discover that their freedom is somewhat elusive and deceptive. They retain it only by acquiring skill at landing enough sales orders, at serving their customers satisfactorily, and at handling the many administrative chores that keep everything going. No one tells them precisely how to manage all this, but manage they must. This is the obligation that comes with that freedom they cherish. Those who love to sell wouldn't have it any other way. But they also know that the price of that privilege is the self-discipline they must apply in order to manage their territories and themselves well.

Territory Management

The functions comprising good territory management vary widely among industries, businesses, and even among sales representatives who work for the same company. Each situation is unique and individual sales people cope with similar situations differently. Presented here are broadly valid concepts of good territory management that sales people can relate selectively to their own needs. The *specific* tasks and routines deemed essential for handling the sales work of any given territory can be explained only by those having inside knowledge of the sales functions of that company. But many norms for effective territory management have evolved that have virtually universal application. We'll review some of them.

FUNCTIONS OF TERRITORY MANAGEMENT

Good territory management involves planning, organizing, controlling, and measuring the results of *every aspect* of sales work that contributes to generating an optimal volume of profitable sales and to serving all customers satisfactorily. Accomplishing this requires sales people to manage personal performance capably. This entails application of the skills of sales problem solving discussed in the preceding chapter.

Systematic prospecting for new customers is one relentless requirement of good territory management. Markets, economic conditions, buyer preferences, sales opportunities, and competitive activity shift continually. Attrition among customers for diverse reasons compels constant recruitment of replacements. In addition, most suppliers of goods or services are committed to growth objectives — ever larger shares of the markets available.

Astute use of time is another imperative for good territory management. The proportion of working hours devoted to actual selling must be kept high to maximize order-getting opportunities. Conversely, time used for sales supportive chores must be minimized but not to the point of neglecting these essential duties. So good use of time is of the essence in sales work. Other key functions of territory management include:

- Analyzing long-range market potentials and identifying near-term sales opportunities.
- Appraising present customer establishment to evaluate which accounts offer good growth potential and hence merit close attention, which are static but valuable, and which are declining and hence may need to be replaced.
- Sustaining satisfactory territory profit margins through constant scrutiny of the credit worthiness of customers and sales prospects — in accordance with company credit standards.
- Providing customers with adequate services such as ensuring timely shipment of orders, informing them on proper product usage, and resolving any complaints promptly.
- Fostering clear channels of communication with custom-

ers and prospects as well as with company sales management in order to carry on all sales functions smoothly and
assure good customer relations.

— Maintaining adequate reference notes on all pending sales
  opportunities as well as concise records of sales relationships with established accounts.

— Keeping company sales management accurately informed
  about market opportunities and competitive conditions
  through clear, timely reporting based on personal observation.

— Controlling costs of selling by maintaining them at reasonable levels consistent with sales opportunities.

Carrying out such an exacting set of territory management responsibilities satisfactorily — *besides selling productively* — obviously calls for a sales superman. Exemplary performance in
all these activities is rarely, if ever, attained by anyone. Nonetheless, these represent appropriate objectives for most sales people. Good balance needs to be maintained between the requirements of face-to-face selling and those of the inescapable
secondary chores of sales work. Self-discipline is the key to
improving performance in these tasks — several of which are
explored further below.

Prospecting for New Customers

Skill at identifying and qualifying sales prospects ranks second
in importance only to skill at selling them. Before sales people
can sell, they must find prospects who are willing and able to
buy. Qualifying potential customers is a critical aspect of the
prospecting function. It is unrewarding to invest time and effort
in a prospect only to discover belatedly that although interested he doesn't have the means or authority to buy.

Prospecting is a logical function of territory management.
Without effective prospecting, all other phases of territory management become meaningless as does the entire selling process.
Good prospecting entails systematic methods that are interrelated with all other aspects of territory management. What-

ever the procedures followed, they must be carried out assiduously. The circumstances that characterize this function and the time it requires vary greatly with what is being sold and other contingencies. Look to your sales supervisor for guidance on a pattern suitable for your business. As a rule of thumb, however, most sales people can expect to devote 20 percent or more of their time to prospecting in order to stay ahead of customer attrition.

PROSPECT FILE

An orderly, well-maintained file of active prospects is indispensable for effective territory management. There is no better way to keep tabs on where you stand saleswise with each of a constantly changing assortment of potential prospects. The kind of prospect file you adopt is immaterial as long as it is utilitarian and can be kept current with a minimum of time and effort. It should enable you to locate quickly and grasp at a glance all data collected relating to any active sales prospect.

Your company may supply forms as well as leads and data for a prospect file. If so, great; use this data and improve on it. If not, develop your own system streamlined to fit your personal preferences and needs. One convenient method features a portable loose-leaf or card file. It should include one durable sheet or card for each prospect. It's best to have the form preprinted with prompter headings that allow space for recording every type of information about a prospective customer that can be useful for selling him. Provide ample space for notes on those particulars that experience proves are most helpful.

Information collected about a prospect remains valuable when he becomes a customer. One good format provides for pertinent prospect data on one side of the form and for essential customer sales record notes on the other. When the prospect is sold, the form is simply transferred to a customer file and all data are retained. Two cards can be stapled together if more space becomes needed.

Select headings for the prospecting side of the form that best serve your special needs. Here are some suggestions to consider:

Prospect (name & address)	Buyer/decision maker (name & title)
Shipping Address	
Nature of business	Principal contact (name/title)
Annual volume	Other VIP contact (name/title)
Financial strength	Problem situation
Credit needs	Product(s) to be sold
Special factors	Estimated annual sales potential
Notes on sales plan and call results	Probable competitors

SOURCES OF PROSPECTING INFORMATION

How do you go about identifying prospects and accumulating data on them? The possible answers are legion. Check with your sales supervisor for specific ideas germane to your business. Following are several general recommendations.

Surprisingly, perhaps, established customers can be an excellent source of sales prospect information. Listen attentively when they talk about their markets and their competitors. Ask questions tactfully when you've become well enough acquainted with them. Contacts developed in other businesses can be helpful — especially sources in banking, real estate, insurance, and related fields. People in such concerns are usually well informed about what's going on in the business community. Chambers of commerce are a good source of prospecting ideas within the trade areas they cover. Credit service agencies are useful too, particularly when financial and credit data are needed.

Then there are many traditional published sources of sales prospect information.

Trade publications	The Yellow Pages
Trade assn. directories	Government publications
Business and industrial directories	Selected commercial lists of prospects
Newspapers	Magazines

Public libraries also contain much published reference data useful to sales people. Ask the librarian for help.

The ultimate source of prospect information is the prospect

himself. If he has survived your preliminary investigation, verify his potential as a live prospect by skillful questioning and alert observation during an exploratory sales call. Avoid making a completely cold call, however. Learn beforehand the name and title of someone on whom to make an initial call; if possible, obtain an introduction or a personal reference. Call already knowing something about his business and possible problems. It reassures your prospect to find you've taken the trouble to prepare before calling; it flatters him, as well. Have an idea ready about how you may be able to help and with what product or service. And be prepared with pertinent questions that can help you decide whether to keep him in your active prospect file.

A well-maintained file of active prospects is your launching pad for new account development. Keep your file alive by adding new prospects regularly and weeding out the most doubtful. Also, update your notes on each card constantly. It is good practice to rank all active prospects according to your evaluation of their immediacy and relative potential — A, B, C, and so on. This helps remind you to give your best prospects preferred attention. Good prospecting depends on an alert, inquiring attitude and prepares the way for informed, confident selling.

Turn to Learning Exercise No. 29 in Appendix.

Customer Credit Considerations

A sale effects an exchange between supplier and buyer. But until the goods or services are paid for, the exchange is not complete. And if they are *not* paid for, the supplier faces loss not only of the profit expected but also of his investment in the goods sold. To obviate these risks, selling inevitably calls for prudent inquiry about a buyer's ability to pay. It is incumbent on every sales person to seek out and sell only those who have adequate means to buy. The prosperity — even survival — of every business enterprise depends in part on responsible performance by its sales people in helping prevent credit losses.

Business is transacted largely on credit in our free economy. Not many substantial purchases are paid for in cash on the spot. The relative ease with which an astronomical volume of business is transacted annually in this country relies in large measure on tacit acceptance of good faith and mutual trust among all participants. It is presumed that those who buy will pay promptly when billed. Most do — usually by bank draft. But not all are equally able to pay. And some occasionally overextend their financial resources unwisely. So it is imperative that a supplier satisfy himself that each customer can pay, or decide how much risk he can prudently accept and on what credit terms if customer finances appear dubious. Responsibility for such decisions rests with the supplier's credit management people.

Most sales people become involved in customer credit processes to some extent, however. Often credit managers must depend on sales people to provide part of the information on which to base credit decisions. The sales person is frequently the only supplier representative having any personal contact with the customer. So he is commonly called on to serve as an emissary on credit matters — either seeking financial data or communicating the supplier's credit policies, or both.

THE SALES PERSON AS A CREDIT REPRESENTATIVE

Sales people sometimes plead shortsightedly that their duties should extend only to finding customers and selling them, and that others should attend to all credit and collection responsibilities. But sales and credit are largely inseparable functions. Responsible administration of credit policies is an inescapable aspect of good territory management. The specifics of the credit procedures delegated to sales people can be explained only by those in charge of credit for any given company. Situations similar to the following commonly occur, however.

Item:

You may be asked to supply your company's credit manager with information about a new customer's financial condition and credit needs as a basis for determining his credit worthiness. To obtain the data needed, you have to ask the customer some pertinent questions — perhaps even ask him to send your credit manager confidential copies of recent balance sheets and income statements. These will then be analyzed with data from other sources such as bank references or credit service agencies.

Inquiries about customer finances should always be expressed positively but tactfully and with ample assurance of complete confidentiality. Progressive business people *expect* such requests and are usually willing to discuss their financial situations freely — even with pride — when the inquiries are justified and tastefully handled. They are accustomed to seeking similar credit assurances from their own customers. Courtesy is the key.

Item:

Your credit manager may ask for your candid evaluation of the customer's business operation based on your own observations and local inquiries. He is likely to seek a profile on characteristics such as

Evidence of good business management.
Capability of managers and key employees.
Past record and present trend of the business.
Standing among other businesses.
Reputation for personal integrity of the key executives.

Because you have a firsthand opportunity to size up a customer, your opinions constitute valuable input for credit evaluations. Provide them factually and fairly.

Item:

When customer credit worthiness has been established, it seldom remains unchanged indefinitely. Constant monitoring of credit risks and variations in credit needs is a function of good territory management. Customers sometimes face temporary financial problems due to unexpected business reverses; they can also experience surges in credit requirements due to sudden expansion of sales. Remain alert to such changes and enlist the cooperation of your credit manager in working out solutions before any problems become acute. This is a highly constructive use of credit as a sales tool for mutual benefit of supplier and customer.

Item:

Collection of overdue payments, together with adjustment of differences between buyer and seller on amounts owed, is sometimes delegated to sales people. And in some fields, collection by the sales person on all sales is standard operating procedure. You may not relish this responsibility, but as the sales person you are in the best position to handle collections and adjustments when required. You know the particulars and have a personal rapport with the customer. A direct, friendly approach is invariably the most effective. Sometimes you'll find the customer's claims are valid or that the circumstances call for compromise. By employing astute, tactful methods, you can retain or renew a strong customer relationship even while making a collection or resolving a difference.

Item:

Many companies provide incentive for prompt payment by offering discount terms such as "2% — 10 days, net 30 days," or variations. This permits the customer to deduct 2 percent of the net amount owed for a purchase if he remits within 10 days of billing date. Always urge customers to take advantage of whatever prompt-payment terms are available. That seemingly small discount often adds up to a substantial sum for a year's purchases. It sometimes even represents the difference between profit and loss on a year's business volume.

Countless sales people find that handling credit problems forthrightly boosts not only their sales but also the satisfaction they derive from selling.

Plan Your Work and Work Your Plan

A cliché? Almost. Sales people recieve this advice so regularly that it tends to be discounted as routine. This is unfortunate because those seven words are loaded with significance. They cut to the core of what good territory management is all about. They have become stereotyped only because their message often is not taken seriously enough.

Constant planning and resolute performance are the very essence of sales work. But the problem for many is how to get a handle on what looms as an overwhelming task. Customers, prospects, inquiries, leads, credit and service problems, complaints, traveling, sales literature and samples, objectives, records, reports, endless other demands and details — where to begin and what to do next? Some muddle along forever frustrated because they need to acquire more skill at planning their work and working their plans. Let's examine several approaches that may help.

FIRST THINGS FIRST

Resign yourself first to the premise that successful sales people never have enough time for all the tasks constantly besetting them. If you should ever find yourself caught up with your work, be wary — you may not be needed much longer. The significance is that with so many demands for your attention, selectivity is the key to survival. It becomes critical to choose the most important things to do first. This calls for *selective planning* — what to do to get results and how to do it. Become habitually busy doing the things that count *most*. Let the lesser chores and trivia wait. It may never matter if they don't all get done, but getting bogged down in tasks of little consequence can be disastrous.

SET UP A SYSTEM

Productive planning must be based on accurate, current information — data you can refer to quickly and easily. Sales people who plan poorly often profess not to have enough time for it; they're always too busy putting out fires. Usually their real problem is they've never made the effort to set up a workable system for handling their inside work — records, reports, files, literature. These chores can create chaos unless they've been organized to help — not hinder — your primary order-getting functions.

We've already reviewed the need for active prospect files. Current files covering your active customers are equally necessary. Depending on your particular situation, you may need a dual system — a simple loose-leaf notebook or card file of essential information you can carry with you, supplemented by a more complete file on each customer, which you maintain at your headquarters. But restrict *every* file or record you maintain to critical reference data you need at fingertip convenience for active selling and customer service. No need to duplicate the comprehensive customer files usually maintained at the company home office — data you can obtain by a phone call when necessary.

COMPUTERIZED SALES RECORDS AND PLANS

With the advent of computerized data processing systems, many companies now supply their sales people with periodic printouts providing most records needed covering sales made, sales cost and profit particulars, and related data — all by individual customer and by territory totals. This vastly simplifies the sales person's record-keeping chores. Home office electronic equipment and expertise now also provides some sales people with market research data highly useful for effective sales planning. And some companies are even doing a great deal of computerized market analysis and sales planning *for* their sales representatives. But it is still necessary for those fortunate sales people to plan responsibly for optimal application of all the sophisticated data provided them. Computers still cannot call on prospects, close orders, or service customers.

TYPES OF PLANS

All plans should first encompass the big picture and then focus on the specifics. Applied to territory management, this means that sales people should prepare and periodically update some kind of master plan for optimizing sales results in their markets. Such a plan starts with their personal analysis of sales opportunities based on their own market studies or on survey data provided by their home offices, and preferably on both. A territory sales plan should establish reasonable long-range goals and outline the steps deemed necessary to achieve them. It should also include an approximate timetable. The plan should incorporate well-reasoned objectives and plans for each significant customer and prospect. Some companies require their sales people to maintain such territory master plans.

But all sales people should prepare their own master plans even if the boss never sees them, because such plans multiply the likelihood of selling effectively.

Monthly or weekly working plans based on the broad objectives of the master plan are needed. Weekly plans should contain a concise outline of all specific customer and prospect calls to be made plus a few reminder notes on what is to be accomplished with each. A weekly plan may also include travel routing and stopover reservations made for overnight trips. Providing the office with a copy enables others to get in touch with you if necessary.

Finally, prepare a daily plan to organize each day's activities as efficiently as sales work ever permits. Granted that daily or weekly plans can seldom be carried out very closely. Somehow, urgent, justifiable deviations from the plan invariably become necessary. But having a carefully thought out plan makes it that much easier to get back on course.

TAKE TIME TO PLAN

The hours devoted to genuine planning usually prove to be the most productive in terms of sales results. Planning saves time — travel time, time lost waiting to see customers, and even time applied to routine chores. When newly assigned to a sales territory, it's always wise for a sales person to take a few days to study, plan, and organize sales coverage in some detail. Put together a tentative master plan. If you inherit sales records and customer files, review them carefully and update them as much as is practical. Establish an efficient territory management system if none exists. Work out basic travel plans for covering your territory effectively in terms of cost, time, energy, and results. Equip and prepare your home base with samples, literature, and customer records and files so it can serve you adequately when you start active selling. By beginning with a good strategic overall plan, you'll find it much easier to make tactical adjustments rapidly when necessary. Astute sales managers also recognize that good preparation by new sales people ensures a better start and quicker results.

A MASTER PLANNING PROCESS THAT WORKS

Here is a master planning technique that works for many. Subdivide your territory into a number of areas or markets, each of which you usually work at one time — perhaps on the same day or same trip. Prepare a *master plan sheet* for each market segment. On one side of each plan sheet, record very brief data about all current customers, their locations, purchase records, and other pertinent items, together with your sales plans for each. On the other side, record essential data on each prospect in that market and brief sales plan notes for each. Classify each customer and prospect A, B, C, and so on, according to relative sales potential. In another area of the sheet, jot down your overall sales plan for that market segment. Also summarize the sales establishment and the strength of competitors active in that market. Add any other data that augment the utility of the plan sheet for you.

When planning your work for a day or a week, refer first to the master plan sheets for the market segments you intend to cover. And take those plan sheets along with you. Should the need arise, they can make it easier to change call plans or tactics quickly with little lost effort. The master plan sheets can also help prompt you to prepare adequately for every sales call you're likely to make while working in the market area they cover. They serve as ready checklists. Update them often enough to keep them current. In addition to their value for sales planning, they can be useful for reference when preparing reports to your manager on market and competitive situations or on sales plans and progress.

Time Management

Good time management is a fundamental function of good territory management. These parallel requirements are virtually inseparable in any study of the skills of selling. The primary purpose of each is the development of ways to organize and utilize time and effort for optimal results. Learning to use time wisely and effectively is critical in every endeavor in which performance is the key to success. Time management characteristically receives special emphasis in sales work because sales people are perhaps more prodigal than others in the way they employ their time—often without even realizing it.

Let's set out some basic precepts about the nature and use of time as a framework for examining time management techniques:

- All of us have the same amount of time at our disposal; differences arise only in how we use it.
- It is literally impossible to save time; we can only improve on the way we use it.
- We waste time only when we use too much of it for activities ranked low on our personal value scales.
- Good time management consists of purposefully improving the ratio of high- to low-priority uses of time. This entails resolute reassessment of values and redirection of habits.

Most sales people concede readily that good time management begins with setting worthy goals and objectives. But many have trouble in allocating and controlling time use for best results in achieving those objectives.

THE "TOO BUSY" SYNDROME

Among sales people, the most profligate time-wasters are seldom even aware of their malady. The telltale symptom is constant busy-ness without ever accomplishing very much—especially not the most important things. Yet they insist that's because they have too much to do. Recovery begins when those so afflicted agree to keep a realistic time log for at least a week to determine precisely where and how they spend their time. A record by half-hour intervals usually suffices.

The truth must be faced squarely. The log should record time devoted to sales interviews and to necessary travel. But it should also account for time spent dawdling over coffee, in protracted happy talk, in long lunches, in unneeded travel, in excessive waiting, on personal matters, in paperwork, in procrastinating. Invariably, the self-probers are chagrined by what they discover on measuring actual time use against plans and intentions. This in itself can mark a corrective turning point, but a cure will result only from regular doses of self-discipline.

SOME READY REMEDIES FOR TIME LEAKS

Much could be written about each remedy itemized below for correcting time management problems. But sales people can usually sense which are most likely to apply to them and what they should do about them. If you're in doubt try them out anyhow.

— Make a daily list of critical calls to make and things to do; assign a priority to each; work on only one item at a time — starting with the most important.

— Start early; much paperwork or planning can be completed before 9 A.M. Also, some customers prefer receiving sales callers early.

— Evaluate critically whether each sales call or trip is really necessary. Can its purpose be accomplished as well by telephone or letter?

— Prepare fully before each call or trip. Make sure you take with you everything you'll need; use a checklist.

— Eliminate casual good will calls; visit customers only when you have something constructive to discuss.

— Make appointments in advance whenever possible. This helps ensure that your contact will be available when you arrive and reduces time lost in fruitless travel.

— Place limits on waiting time; make a new appointment for another time and leave. If it's about an urgent matter, telephone later.

— Use waiting time productively; review sales presentations; handle routine chores; plan or phone ahead.

— Control sales interview time. Some friendly conversation is always constructive, but don't waste customers' time or let them waste yours.

— Control lunch time — especially when entertaining customers. Long, congenial lunches often prove less productive than short office calls; they may even ruin the rest of the day for other sales work.

— Avoid driving between calls when in congested areas; save time by walking or by taking a taxi or bus.

— Conserve travel time; maximize sales calls per trip; preplan routing to minimize travel and backtracking.

— When traveling out of town, stay over where you'll work

the next day. You can then start the day fresh and early after reviewing sales call plans and preparation the evening before.

— Always reserve prime working hours for your most important personal selling calls.

— Reduce paperwork and reporting to a bare minimum. Handle these chores during time that is least productive for personal selling.

— Use a 31-day "tickler file" to help remember things to be done on specific future dates. But review it regularly; don't lose things in it.

THE TELEPHONE AS A SELLING TOOL

Unabated inflation in the costs of selling necessitates an unceasing search for ways to improve sales performance while holding the line on expenses. One outcome is the rapid expansion of use of the telephone in selling. A survey conducted by McGraw-Hill determined that the average cost of an industrial sales call reached a record high of $71.27 in 1975.* A telephone call costing $5 — or even $25 — is obviously much more cost effective whenever it can accomplish the same purpose. The time, money, and energy saved thereby can be applied to other sales efforts.

There are now available a number of comprehensive studies and training courses explaining how the telephone can be used with good results for selling — not only to supplement, but even to substitute for, personal sales interviews. The merits of such extensive use of the telephone for selling should be explored wherever it may offer unique advantage.

But the telephone can also contribute in many practical ways as a valuable tool for time and territory management. Consider the following items; each offers opportunity to conserve time, reduce expense, and increase selling efficiency.

— Use the telephone freely for sales and service contacts with local customers. This is its traditional and most common application.

* McGraw-Hill Research, Laboratory of Advertising Performance, LAP Report #8013.3.

— Make appointments by telephone to ensure being received by your customer when you arrive.
— Make follow-up calls by telephone to reinforce rapport with customers between calls made in person.
— Use the telephone to maintain closer sales contacts with distant customers who cannot be visited regularly.
— Follow up by telephone soon after a personal sales call. This can help reinforce a sales message or reassure a customer about a recent purchase decision.
— Use the telephone to further qualify a prospect after having accumulated positive but inconclusive preliminary information by other means.
— Use the telephone to initiate contact with an important new prospect. A long-distance phone call can sometimes arouse interest where a personal call or letter risks rebuff. A telephone call obtains a few minutes of undivided attention that could otherwise be hard to get. But *be prepared* with a message thoughtfully designed to convince the prospect that agreeing to learn more about your proposition could be to his advantage.

Whatever the purpose of a telephone call, plan for it adequately before touching the dial. Make an outline of points to be discussed and have all needed reference data arranged at your fingertips. Earn the right to intrude and be heard by having something to discuss that the hearer will want to listen to and talk about. And deliver your message clearly, concisely, and courteously. Used wisely, the telephone can be an extremely effective selling tool.

Turn to Learning Exercise No. 30 in Appendix.

Continuing Self-development

Our review of the skills of selling would be incomplete without touching on the importance of continuing personal growth in sales ability. Capable sales people sometimes become complacent after several years of successful performance. They reach a middling plateau of competence from which they seem loath to climb further. They earn a better than average living and feel reasonably secure. And many reflect a certain smugness that seems to say there's nothing more they need to learn about selling.

Perhaps some have, indeed, reached their maximum capabilities. But most possess talents they have never fully developed. Instead, they have settled into a comfortable rut, which they mistake for a smooth road. But this need not happen to you. Why not keep right on refining your skills throughout your career, not only to increase earnings potential but also to gain more satisfaction from self-realization?

You can avoid that rut by accepting the concept that *improvement of selling skills should continue throughout your career.* Much research into human behavior has demonstrated that few of us ever fully utilize our talents. There's also the human obsolescence that sets in when we don't keep up with the increasing scope of applicable knowledge and skills in our vocations. This allows others with more current information and skills to pass us by.

A three-step process for continuing self-improvement involves (1) establishing attainable personal objectives, (2) striving to reach them, then (3) resetting new goals — and repeating that pattern. Does that seem somewhat familiar? If so, it's because those three steps transpose to personal development the very same problem-solving and managment skills we've already examined as applied to sales work.

This book introduces the principal skills of selling. It also provides personal involvement exercises for broadening insight into applications for some of the sales work techniques presented. But on candid evaluation, it is apparent that many topics are covered only briefly. It is not possible to present within the covers of one book the full scope of the selling process together with the countless variations in selling techniques that can be effective. From this beginning, it remains for you to continue studying and polishing your skills of selling as a means of further enhancing your ability to serve the needs of others — your customers — and thereby achieve a measure of personal success as well.

Take careful stock periodically of the strengths and short-comings in your abilities. Jot down the pluses and minuses and study them objectively. Select one of the minuses that, if over-come, could effect a meaningful boost in your performance. Concentrate on conquering that particular shortcoming until you've transformed it into a strength. Then take stock again and select another deficiency for attention. You'll recognize in this approach an adaptation of that sales problem solving process.

There are many good books available on selling that can help you maintain a fruitful self-development program. A few are listed in the Bibliography of this book. Read those that promise to convey a message about selling that will be meaningful to you. Study diligently the sections that relate particularly to any troublesome selling problems you encounter. And heed the advice they contain that applies to your special needs. Practice the techniques recommended; you'll find some that will work well for you.

In addition, many short courses on salesmanship are offered regularly. Consider carefully their stated purposes, contents, and reputations among those who have taken them. Some can contribute significantly to furthering your competence and confidence as a sales person.

Continued self-development should also encompass broad-ening your knowledge in other fields — economics, business management, the sciences, and social affairs, to offer a few suggestions. Sales work involves intellectual exchange with people of widely diverse interests and accomplishments. Sales people can gain much satisfaction from becoming conversant in subjects having special importance to their customers, and will find that having a wide store of knowledge is often a great help in selling them.

And so we close. This book has served its purpose if it has heightened your appreciation of the tremendous contribution sales work makes to the quality of life and has helped you to become a true professional at selling. You can be proud of the career you have chosen; do it justice by steadily improving your selling skills.

Happy selling.

APPENDIX: THIRTY LEARNING EXERCISES

Presented here is a series of 30 learning exercises that can be carried out by those who choose to use this book as the basis for a sales training course — either for individuals or for groups. Working through the exercises can amplify understanding and develop ability in the phases of selling skill involved. For suggestions for applying the learning exercises, refer to the introductory section "How to Use This Book." Recall from that section that in each exercise, Part A is addressed to the individual sales person and Part B is addressed to the seminar moderator, for use in group training sessions. Additional recommendations relating to two important groups of exercises are offered below to enhance their potential effectiveness.

Continuity of thought and effort is very important in assimilating and practicing the concepts of idea selling. For this reason, we recommend that sales managers or sales trainers using this book for training seminars consider conducting Learning Exercises Nos. 8–14 consecutively at one time, rather than at intervals. This may require devoting one full day or more to study and practice of these skills of sales persuasion.

Similarly, Learning Exercises Nos. 23–28, covering the concepts of sales problem solving, will be much more effective if conducted consecutively at one time rather than at intervals. Otherwise, it becomes difficult to maintain continuity in the reasoning involved in problem solving, which is the very concept and skill these exercises are designed to demonstrate. We also suggest that seminar moderators gain familiarity with these particular exercises by devising means of working through them prior to conducting them with learner groups. Such preparation will contribute to carrying out this series of exercises effectively.

Relatively little advance preparation is necessary for moderating other group learning exercises. They can be employed selectively, separately or in consecutive combinations as desired. However, ample familiarity with purpose and subject matter always enhances impact and results of any group learning activity.

Learning Exercise No. 1   *Chapter 1*

Part A

Chapter 1 advances the proposition that all private enterprise and most private institutions serving the public must embrace three basic functions — production, sales, and finance — in order to fulfill their purposes. Consider whether each of these functions exists in your organization, even if known by other names. Jot down all intrinsic operations you can identify with each of the three basic functions. Are there any that don't relate to one of the three? Can you think of any way your enterprise could serve its purpose successfully without some kind of sales function? If so, make notes about it; this would provide a basis for interesting discussions with others in your organization, when opportune.

Also apply this analysis to customers' businesses. Does it hold true? Can you think of any type of business that this three-part functional pattern does not fit?

Part B

For a group learning seminar, assign exercises similar to Part A to each participant — as prior homework, if desired. Then conduct group discussion of participants' opinions about how, or whether, various activities in your business (or others) fit the tripartite functional pattern. Solicit participants' ideas as to whether your enterprise could survive without an effective sales function. You or a participant can serve as secretary at the chalkboard or easel pad to record conclusions agreed upon.

Learning Exercise No. 2   *Chapter 1*

Part A

Sales work is a form of service that contributes to bettering society as a whole. Inventory all the ways you can think of in which the products or services you sell promote the common good. Make note of the obvious immediate benefits of your wares to your customers. But also let your imagination roam beyond those specifics. What greater good does what you sell create for others? For example, a better mousetrap rids its user of pesty rodents more rapidly, but in a broader sense it also helps eradicate disease. See how long a list you can compile of the big-perspective benefits of whatever you sell. This can provide new insight into the real worth of your work.

Retain your list; some of those "blue sky" benefits are likely to slip into your sales talks later with good results.

Part B

Make assignments similar to Part A. Lists can be compiled individually for review by the group, or ideas can be volunteered freely during guided discussion. A secretary can record the most meaningful ideas brought out. Much mirth may be generated because some suggestions invariably seem far-fetched. Nevertheless, sober reflection usually brings out previously overlooked broad-gauge benefits that can be used to reinforce traditional selling points.

Learning Exercise No. 3   *Chapter 2*

Part A

Select several principal products or services that you sell. 1. List separately for each all the *features* you consider to be important selling points. Condense your description of each feature into a clear statement that concisely but fully explains its nature. 2. For each feature, list all the ways it *benefits* your customers. Express each benefit statement in a way that emphasizes the aspects most meaningful to a customer. 3. Practice linking features and corresponding benefits into usable selling statements by employing connector phrases like "this means for you" or "that's because." Also, try coming up with other connector phrases that you can use smoothly.

Part B

Assign the above exercise to each participant in your group as homework prior to the session. Preferably, two or more persons should concentrate on each product. During the group discussion, a secretary can record all suggested features and corresponding benefits for reference. Feature-benefits statements offered can be refined by the group during guided open discussion. Those agreed upon as being accurate and effective can then be compiled for distribution to all sales people who can make good use of them.

As an option, you can also conduct role-playing sessions in which each participant in turn verbalizes various feature-benefits statements developed by the group. This kind of practice is rigorous but very effective.

Learning Exercise No. 4   *Chapter 2*

Part A

Develop a feature-benefits inventory for the products or services you sell, including the feature-benefits you developed for Exercise No. 3. Adopt a format you conclude will be easiest for you to maintain for reference. Because this is likely to become a long-range project, schedule a regular period of time for it each week. Concentrate first on the products or services that occupy most of your selling time. Try out each new set of feature-benefits combinations soon after creating them. Also make notes on new feature-benefits ideas that occur to you while selling that merit inclusion in your inventory. Update the inventory as often as new or better feature-benefits ideas evolve from your selling experience.

Systematic maintenance of a feature-benefits inventory will have a notably positive impact on your overall selling effectiveness.

Part B

You may want to assign Part A as an exercise for all members of a sales force as a long-range project. Various products or services can be assigned for study to different teams of sales people at suitable intervals. Group discussion sessions can be conducted periodically to compare ideas as well as to exchange feature-benefits inventories on specific products as they are worked out. Every member of the sales force would thereby obtain a feature-benefits inventory covering all products, over a period of time.

Learning Exercise No. 5   *Chapter 2*

Part A

Catalog the disadvantages of competitive product characteristics that are offset or eliminated by selected feature-benefits of the comparable product you sell. Concentrate on the competitive products you find it most difficult to sell against. Study their characteristics carefully — especially those for which you can identify customer disadvantages contrasting with advantages of specific feature-benefits of your product. Record these data using the format suggested in Chapter 2 or originating a pattern better suited to your special needs.

This provides a systematic basis for analyzing competitive products in a search for questionable characteristics on which to focus effective counterselling tactics. How valuable it may be to create and maintain a *continuing* catalog of competitive product disadvantages depends on the severity of your competitive sales problems.

Part B

Assign Part A to a group of sales people facing serious problems in selling against a competitive product. Follow with creative brainstorming sessions conducted with the group to evolve new, more effective ways of outselling the competitor. Try to identify competitive disadvantages that can be offset by dramatic, new emphasis on advantages of your product that may have been discounted or not promoted forcefully enough before.

Learning Exercise No. 6   *Chapter 2*

Part A

Create a list of customer services that your company regularly provides or can make available that you can exploit whenever this will give you a selling advantage. Also, make notes on how each service can be used effectively — including any limitations or restraints to be observed. If your company has not previously employed customer services as a strategic selling tool, this project may require exploratory discussions with your superiors and associates in order to establish what services can properly be utilized to help you sell.

After compiling particulars of the sales services available, practice using them to gain advantage in difficult selling situations. Occasionally all that is needed is to focus customer attention on the valuable services he already receives but is overlooking. Employ service systematically to help you sell more.

Part B

Make an assignment similar to Part A as preparation for group discussion of the pros and cons of, and tactics appropriate for, using each approved customer service identified. You can also use this opportunity to point out all limitations that should be observed as well as the advantages to be gained from proper use of service in selling. Conclusions reached can be recorded, refined, and circulated for the benefit of all company personnel involved.

Learning Exercise No. 7   *Chapter 3*

Part A

Chapter 3 explores only the more common barriers to good sales communication and several means of penetrating each. To learn more:

1. Jot down other variations of each sales communication barrier cited that occur to you.
2. Jot down all additional barriers you can think of that are not examined in this chapter—especially any commonly encountered in your particular sales field.
3. Jot down favorable ideas for tactfully overcoming each additional communication barrier occurring to you—techniques that have worked for you or that common sense tells you should work.

The payoff comes from putting into practice the ideas about better sales communication gleaned from this book and augmented by continued study of this vital subject.

Part B

Give preparation assignments similar to Part A to each participant, preferably in advance. Then conduct group discussion of ideas for better sales communication as offered by each participant. A secretary can record promising new ideas agreed upon for better ways to penetrate the sales communication barriers faced most frequently in your selling field. The new ideas generated can be reproduced and circulated for the benefit of others in your organization.

Learning Exercise No. 8   *Chapter 4*

Part A

Reinforce your understanding of the idea-selling concept by thinking through and writing out the key selling ideas for each principal product or service in your line. If you were given the opportunity to make *only* one brief statement to a sales prospect covering reasons he should buy your product, what would you say? For most products it isn't possible to cover all the features and benefits in one or two sentences. So this mental exercise forces you to select the *key selling ideas* you consider to be most important and most persuasive. These ideas become the central theme around which to develop a complete sales presentation.

Keep your notes; you can use them for subsequent learning exercises. You can also use them in selling.

Part B

Assign variations of Part A, perhaps by giving different products to each participant. With your guidance, members of the group can then critique the various selling ideas developed. Lead the group in refining each key selling idea into one or two statements about each product that all can agree upon as being *most* arresting and persuasive to a sales prospect.

As a constructive option, you can collect the best selling ideas developed and have them reproduced for distribution to all members of the sales force.

Learning Exercise No. 9   *Chapter 4*

Part A

You can master the skills of idea selling *only* by practicing them. Begin by writing out *Step 1 introductions* for idea-selling presentations covering selected products or services you sell. Experiment with variations in introductions according to product, prospect, and particulars of the selling situation. Give special attention to the justifying and qualifying requirements of Step 1. Include assurance that you are familiar with a prospect problem or need that warrants the sales proposal you're about to make. Employ language expected to stimulate your prospect's interest.

You're likely to find that some statements or phrases can be used in several Step 1 introductions with little modification. This helps you fix them in mind. This also makes it easier to customize sales presentations by drawing on your repertoire of selling ideas and adjusting them as needed to fit variations in selling situations.

Part B

Make assignments similar to Part A. For example, each participant can work on Step 1 introductions for different products or for different prospect types. The introductions prepared can then be reviewed and refined through evaluation by the group with your guidance. Similarities in phrasing that are certain to occur can help participants learn and retain idea-selling skills. But encourage personalized phrasing even though ideas expressed are essentially the same.

Learning Exercise No. 10 *Chapter 4*

Part A

Continue mastering the skills of idea selling by writing out *Step 2 proposal statements* for the same products or services for which you developed Step 1 introductions. Phase each proposal statement in language that conveys in concise terms your key selling ideas and the principal benefits they represent for your sales prospect. Keep in mind that each proposal statement should reflect your prime selling objective for the specific sales effort being planned. Thus your proposal statement embodies the *key idea* that the balance of your sales presentation will be designed to sell.

Part B

Assign Part A to your group. This involves preparing Step 2 proposal statements for the Step 1 introductions developed for, and evaluated during, group Exercise No. 9. Subsequent review and refinement of the various proposal statements by the group will enhance the participants' insight into idea-selling techniques.

Learning Exercise No. 11   *Chapter 4*

Part A

Now prepare idea-selling *Step 3 particulars* in writing for each sales presentation you've been working on for products or services you sell. Step 3 is the body of your sales talk, in which you articulate for your prospect in suitable detail all relevant reasons why he should buy. Spell out point by point the features and benefits, concentrating on the latter, that are most likely to persuade him to buy. Give only those feature-benefits combinations that contribute to satisfying an identifiable prospect problem or need. This may require variations in Step 3 particulars for different types of customers.

Part B

Assign Part A to your group, allowing participants time to prepare for this exercise as prior homework; putting together a good Step 3 for an effective sales presentation requires quiet concentration and clear thinking. As before, reviewing and refining each participant's selling-idea contributions through guided group discussion will benefit every member of the group.

Learning Exercise No. 12   *Chapter 4*

Part A

Your next step in practicing the skills of idea selling is to develop a written *Step 4 summary* for each of the sales presentations you've been creating for products or services you sell. Step 4 should draw together and highlight for your prospect the most notable benefits of your proposal — including special emphasis on the *results* he can expect. Reassure him confidently but concisely that your product and proposal have merit, that you are personally dependable, that your company is competent and reputable, and that your entire proposition will work out to his advantage. Idea-selling Step 4 summaries also may need to be varied somewhat according to the type of sales prospect involved.

Part B

Assign Part A modified in any way you consider appropriate for your particular group. After the assignment is completed, conduct open group discussion and evaluation of the Step 4 summaries of each participant. This contributes to the continued growth of understanding and skill of every member of the group.

Learning Exercise No. 13   *Chapter 4*

Part A

Conclude your practice with idea-selling techniques by setting down in writing alternative ways of asking for the order — or asking for a favorable decision — as the *Step 5 close* for each of the sales presentations you've been developing for your own products or services. Alter your phrasing to incorporate several different approaches to asking for the order. Devise your own variations by modifying the closing techniques suggested in Chapter 4.

Part B

Assign Part A to your group. Then conduct open discussion of the relative merits of each Step 5 close developed, as a means of refining its effectiveness.

An interesting and effective variation is to suggest that participants respond to "ask for action" questions evasively while playing the role of sales prospects. The originator of each closing question is given opportunity, in turn, to improvise on-the-spot additional attempts to evoke a positive response from the "prospect."

This kind of practice can become amusing but shouldn't be viewed as farcical. Closing for the order with an actual customer can scarcely be any more difficult than role-playing a close before a group of one's peers. And the experience increases self-confidence.

Learning Exercise No. 14   *Chapter 4*

Part A

You have now prepared five-step idea-selling presentations for a number of your products or services. The next requirement is to practice them in preparation for actual use in selling. This does *not* mean to memorize them. But it does mean to fix them in mind well enough for conversational presentation during actual sales interviews. When you are interrupted by questions or objections, be prepared to resume your presentation at the right idea-selling step, but not necessarily in the same words.

Practice your presentations aloud in any suitable way — before an understanding listener, with a tape recorder, or before a video camera for playback, for example.

Part B

Conduct role-playing exercises in making sales presentations. One pattern is to assign each participant to prepare sales presentations based on the five-step idea-selling format covering selected products or services. Each participant practices his presentation aloud before the group. One or more participants can be designated to role-play sales prospects. The group then critiques the performance of each — *always* on a friendly, constructive basis.

Many variations of this learning exercise are possible. All can be quite effective when conducted sensitively by an empathetic, saleswise moderator.

Learning Exercise No. 15   Chapter 5

Part A

Reinforce the concepts presented for coping with sales resistance by experimenting with them. Create a series of brief "shaker upper" statements of key selling ideas relating to your own products or services. Carefully design each statement to arrest the prospect's attention and neutralize his natural tendency to resist new ideas. If you have a broad line, a shaker may be needed for each class of customer.

Startling product benefit statements are most effective during initial calls. Thus it is constructive to build them into introductions starting with: "I'm John Jones, representing . . ." or a similar expression, and going on from there. Write out your key shaker-uppers; work them over; rehearse them; even memorize them in order to strengthen your confidence and effectiveness during first calls on new prospects.

Part B

Assign exercises similar to Part A to each participant, perhaps as prior homework. Then conduct a series of role-playing exercises with participants taking turns trying out their introductory shakers on others selected to act as prospects. With your guidance, participants should exchange constructive critiques on their introductory statements. Then have participants try this technique on real sales prospects.

Learning Exercise No. 16   *Chapter 5*

Part A
Start developing an objection/answer reference file of your own. On the left-hand side of a sheet of paper, write the troublesome objections or questions you face most frequently. To the right of each objection, write the answer you now give the prospect. Is it effective? Can you improve on it? Have you a ready source for any additional information you need for improving the answer? Refine each answer until you are satisfied that it is the best response you can make to that particular objection.

Make this a continuing project. Adopt whatever record format proves to be most convenient for your use. As you work out answers for objections, fit them into that format. When you encounter a new objection, add it to your file with the answer you develop. Update the entire file occasionally. Refer to it regularly to improve your sales presentations.

Part B
Give each participant an assignment similar to Part A as advance homework, with variations by product, application, or customer type. During the discussion, have the group try to improve upon the objection answers contributed by each member. A summary of objections together with the corresponding best answers can then be prepared and distributed to all members of the sales force for reference. The net result can be a very constructive symposium on how to handle objections.

Learning Exercise No. 17   *Chapter 5*

Part A

We all learn best from experience. In Chapter 5 are listed seven different categories encompassing most customer complaints and claims. Review your handling of complaints within the past year. Regarding each complaint, jot down:

1. Which of the seven complaint categories applies? (Add new categories if needed.)
2. What principal decisions and actions most characterize your handling of each complaint?
3. Did the settlement retain your customer and his good will?
4. Do you now think the complaint might have been handled better? How?

Part B

Ask each participant to prepare suitable summaries similar to those asked for in Part A, covering disposition of recent complaints and claims. Make assignments in advance to allow adequate time for preparation. During the seminar, ask each participant to describe for the group one complaint and how he resolved it. Ask the group for comments on the following:

1. What was notably good in the way the complaint was handled?
2. How might the complaint have been handled better?

You may also wish to summarize for the group your own recommendations for complaint handling. This can be a very useful symposium on complaint handling.

Learning Exercise No. 18   *Chapter 6*

Part A

Plan a sales presentation involving display-and-explain tactics that employ visual sales aids such as samples and sales literature. Choose other visuals if samples or literature are unavailable or inappropriate for your sales line. Outline a sales talk based on the five-step idea-selling format. Mark or otherwise prepare the visuals to support key points of your talk. Decide *when* to display the visuals during your sales talk and *how* to display them to best advantage.

Rehearse your sales presentation to coordinate and perfect your display-and-explain tactics. It helps to enlist another person to role-play the buyer; or practice before a mirror and tape-record your talk for evaluation on replay.

Part B

Assign Part A to each participant as advance homework. For variation, have each use a different combination of suitable samples and/or visuals. During the ensuing group session, each participant can make his presentation before others serving as a panel of helpful critics or role-playing buyers. Videotaping the presentations for replay and review will benefit each learner even more, if such equipment is available.

This group session can also be used as a forum for reviewing *all* visual sales aids regularly available as well as for practicing how to employ them to best advantage in sales presentations.

Learning Exercise No. 19   *Chapter 6*

Part A

Select one product or service and plan a demonstration with the related sales talk explaining what takes place. Choose procedures that display key features and benefits meaningfully but as simply as possible. Add suitable touches of showmanship to accent important aspects of your sales message. For guidance, review the suggestions offered in Chapter 6; also review the demonstrations planner in Figure 6.

Rehearse your demonstration and sales discourse as much as is practical. Then carry it out as part of an actual selling effort when suitable opportunity and need arise. Refine demonstration procedures and sales commentary based on your actual experience and results. Repeat this exercise for other products and services as demonstration needs involving them arise.

Part B

Assign the planning portion of Part A as advance preparation, either to individual participants or to teams. Demonstration plans can then be presented during the group session for review and refinement. Plans chosen as most promising can be rehearsed to whatever extent proves practical. Schedule a follow-up group session if more time is needed.

You can then recommend for field sales use those demonstrations deemed most likely to be effective. Variations of this exercise can be carried out for other products or services as desired.

Learning Exercise No. 20   *Chapter 7*

Part A

Assume that a competitive product comparable to your _____ (identify product) is unexpectedly being offered at a slightly lowered price. Your best customer is seriously considering giving an order to the competitor. You cannot meet the lower price; besides, your product has a demonstrable edge on quality and other characteristics.

Put together a sales presentation marshaling selected features and benefits of your product, together with your superiorities in supplier services—all adding up to *value* that more than offsets the appeal of the lowered price. Use tactics suggested in Chapter 7. But avoid detracting overtly from your competitor or his product. Keep in mind that your objective is to *outsell* the lower competitive price *on product merit and service.*

If possible, rehearse with a colleague who role-plays the customer attracted by the lower competitive price. Or try using a tape recorder.

Part B

Assign Part A to the group for advance preparation. For variety, assign each participant a different product and define realistically the competitive situations faced. During the next group session, role-play each presentation for review and refinement by participants.

It can also be very constructive to conduct guided discussion of each topic in Chapter 7—bringing out how each relates to the real competitive selling problems commonly faced by members of the group.

Learning Exercise No. 21   *Chapter 7*

Part A

Good lay knowledge of the legal aspects of selling is essential for every sales person. Chapter 7 provides only a basic survey of this important subject. Therefore:

1. Review several current books that treat this subject more comprehensively. Give special attention to those legal provisions that impinge on your particular selling responsibilities. Make notes on pertinent material to aid your retention.

2. If possible, create an opportunity to augment your understanding through review with a lawyer qualified in this area. Also discuss critical topics with your sales supervisor for further clarification.

Part B

Assign Part A.1 to the group for advance preparation, varying assignments in any way that renders them most pertinent to the sales responsibilities of each participant.

If possible, conduct a seminar on this subject with a qualified lawyer present who can field questions and explain the application of the laws and statutes that relate specifically to the sales work of the group members.

As an alternative, devise a simulated sales case problem embodying a number of legal ramifications pertinent to your business. Guided group analysis and solution of the problem can then be very instructive — especially with a lawyer present to help explain complex situations.

Learning Exercise No. 22   *Chapter 8*

Part A
Analyze and organize your work by establishing or refining objectives to provide improved direction for your sales efforts.

1. Review objectives assigned to you or that you have set for yourself. Consider how well each focuses on your most promising sales opportunities. If your objectives do not cover all attractive market opportunities you can reasonably tackle, redefine them or add new ones.

2. If you have no objectives, develop a set by following the guidelines in Chapter 8. Write an objective covering each major sales opportunity; include an attainable goal for each.

Creating objectives consists largely of making a study of all market opportunities and setting realistic personal sales targets covering them. Review your objectives with your supervisor when opportune.

Part B
Make advance assignments adapted from Part A. Assignments can include devising objectives suitable for the whole group or for each participant. During the next session, have the group examine the merits of each set of objectives created. Use the best suggestions offered as a basis for improvements. This seminar can be employed to formulate objectives where none have been used previously or to improve techniques where selling by objectives is already well established.

Learning Exercise No. 23   *Chapter 8*

Part A

Write your own *case problem selling situation* for personal, step-by-step analysis, using the problem-solving process as it unfolds. Your problem can be hypothetical or can describe a situation you actually face. A combination of both real and fictitious factors is quite suitable. Be realistic, yet imaginative. Involve a product or service you sell. Incorporate facts, assumptions, and obstacles representative of a typical selling situation. Write your case problem as though explaining it to your supervisor in order to obtain his advice about how to handle it.

You'll be using your personal case problem for practice as we progress through the problem-solving process. Whether the solution you arrive at proves to be very practical is immaterial. Our purpose is to help you fix in mind the *reasoning processes* involved so you can begin applying them in your actual sales work.

Part B

Following the guidelines in Part A, work out a composite sales problem at the chalkboard or easel pad from ideas offered by participants during a group learning session. The case problem should be typical of situations regularly faced by the participants. As an alternative, devise a case problem in advance for group members to modify until they can agree that it is adequately realistic. This case problem will be "solved" by the group while working through the problem-solving process as it unfolds.

Learning Exercise No. 24   *Chapter 8*

Part A

Appraise the pertinent factors of the case problem you created for the prior learning exercise. Follow the outline provided in Figure 8 for thinking through problem-solving Step 1. First set down the primary sales objective you would hope to attain by solving your problem. Then let your thinking range over all meaningful factors in the sales situation that could influence the outcome. Jot down these factors; note each as fact or assumption. Then formulate from these factors the key subordinate problems that need to be solved in order to achieve your primary sales objective.

By making notes, you add a visual dimension to mental appraisal of your problem. This helps you avoid overlooking critical factors; it also contributes to learning how to think though a sales problem in order to devise the most promising solution.

Part B

Follow the format suggested in Part A. The group case problem evolved for Exercise No. 23 now provides the basis for practice in problem solving. Record on the chalkboard or easel pad the participants' conclusions on what factors are pertinent and whether each is fact or assumption. The key subordinate problems are then identified for solution. Subordinate problems agreed upon provide the basis for working through the next problem-solving learning exercise.

Learning Exercise No. 25   *Chapter 8*

Part A
Continue analyzing your personal case problem sales situation by following the outline in Figure 9 for thinking through problem-solving Step 2. Consider all key subordinate problems arrived at while appraising your problem situation in Exercise No. 24. Select the subordinate problems deemed most critical, and reformulate each into a meaningful *contributory objective.* Consider carefully *why* each contributory objective should be carried out; weigh the risks of *not* implementing each. This eliminates the less important contributory objectives (problems) so you can concentrate on those most consequential in terms of achieving your primary sales objective.

As before, make notes on the ideas that lead to your conclusions. This helps you visualize the reasoning processes involved and contributes to fixing them in mind for use during actual selling.

Part B
Follow the format described in Part A to guide participants' thinking through problem-solving Step 2. Subordinate problems agreed upon by the group during Exercise No. 24 are now reformulated into key contributory objectives. Guide participants into agreement on those objectives selected as being most critical in terms of helping to achieve the primary goal. Make notes on the contributory objectives agreed upon; they provide a starting base for the next exercise, covering problem-solving Step 3.

Learning Exercise No. 26   *Chapter 8*

Part A

For the preceding exercises, you formulated contributory objectives, each representing an important step toward achieving the primary goal established for your practice sales problem situation. Now examine several alternative ways of carrying out each contributory objective. Follow the outline for problem-solving Step 3 in Figure 10. Jot down the various courses of action open to you, with brief notes on the relative merits of each course.

To review: The purpose of problem-solving Step 3 is to identify and appraise all workable options for attaining each contributory objective. This prepares you for the next step, in which the potential results of each option are evaluated and a choice is made for sales action.

Part B

Using Part A as a guide, assign each participant to develop (separately) several alternatives for carrying out each contributory objective agreed upon during the previous exercise. (If time is limited, make participants select only one or two contributory objectives for this exercise.) Guiding the discussion, bring the group into consensus on (1) a single set of workable alternatives for reaching each contributory objective, and (2) the relative merits of each alternative agreed upon. The conclusions reached become the basis for choosing alternatives for sales action, which is the purpose of the next problem-solving exercise.

Learning Exercise No. 27   Chapter 8

Part A

Review your notes from Exercise No. 26 on the relative merits of various alternatives for carrying out each contributory objective. For this exercise, follow the outline for problem-solving Step 4 in Figure 11. Evaluate the results each alternative course could be expected to produce; weigh unfavorable as well as favorable possibilities. After deliberation, choose the alternative you consider most likely to succeed for carrying out each contributory objective. Make notes on your choice(s).

Apply this process of evaluating relative merits and probable results as a means of choosing the *best* alternative for *each* contributory objective leading toward your primary sales goal.

Part B

Assign each participant to carry out Part A for all alternatives for action agreed upon by the group for each contributory objective examined during Exercise No. 26. Then have the group review participants' individual evaluations of probable results of each alternative in order to formulate a consensus on the best course of action for attaining each contributory objective.

Make a record of choices agreed upon for alternative courses of action. They become the basis for sales planning—the subject of the next problem-solving step.

Learning Exercise No. 28   *Chapter 8*

Part A

Previous exercises have equipped you to prepare a sales plan, or combination of plans, for capitalizing on your practice sales case problem. Follow the outline for problem-solving Step 5 in Figure 12. First spell out the sales objective(s) to be achieved. Then set down answers to the questions of *what* sales actions will be taken and *why; who* will take each action; and *when, where,* and *how* each will be carried out. Together these answers describe what will happen to bring about the results (objectives) sought.

To review: A sales plan comprises decisions made on the best way to proceed based on appraising a sales problem situation and the alternatives available for solving it. A sales plan provides a checklist for making progress toward closing the sale.

Part B

Adapt Part A in assigning each participant to prepare separately a sales plan suitable for exploiting the sales problem situation the group has been analyzing. Then employ guided group discussion to reach a consensus on *one* sales plan agreed upon as most likely to achieve the *primary* sales goal by means of progressive accomplishment of selected contributory objectives.

Assiduous application of prior exercises may have produced voluminous data for sales planning. If time presses, curtail this exercise whenever the nature of the sales planning process has been adequately demonstrated.

Learning Exercise No. 29   *Chapter 9*

Part A

Whether or not you're new at selling, chances are you can benefit by devoting new attention to your system of *prospecting for new customers.*

1. Review your prospect file. Is it active? Is it concise, compact, readily portable and easy to use? If not, update it; or even remodel it completely by adapting any ideas in Chapter 9 that you find are applicable to your needs.

2. Evaluate your current sources for sales prospect leads. Are they productive? Adequate? If not, establish improved, dependable methods for obtaining fruitful data on promising sales prospects.

3. Reconsider the proportion of your time that you now devote to prospecting—including exploratory calls on new prospects. Is it adequate to ensure territory sales growth as well as to upgrade quality of your current customer establishment?

Part B

Give each participant prior preparation assignments similar to Part A. Then conduct a symposium on how to improve methods of sales prospecting, giving special consideration to ideas and techniques offered by the participants. This also gives you the opportunity to introduce and discuss any new sales prospecting methods you may want to recommend.

Learning Exercise No. 30 *Chapter 9*

Part A

Do you plan your work and work your plan? Are you a good territory manager? Only you can rate yourself fairly and improve any deficiencies. Here are more questions and suggestions to consider:

1. Do you have a master territory sales plan? If not, try working one out on paper.
2. Do you use a weekly sales call and travel plan? If not, try using one; you'll discover that it helps.
3. Do you prepare and follow a daily work schedule? If not, make this a habit; do first things first.
4. Do you often lack time for the important things? If so, keep a time log; reallocate your time.
5. Do you have an efficient customer record system? Ready reference cards for calls? If not, become better organized; try the ideas in Chapter 9.
6. Do you make appointments for sales calls? Use the telephone to good advantage? Prepare for every sales call? Conserve sales interview time? Limit waiting time? Restrict good will calls? Minimize travel time? Curtail other time leaks? Not always? Then make plans for self-improvement and apply self-discipline in large doses.

Part B

Conduct a symposium on improving sales territory management based on Part A and other pertinent items. This affords the opportunity to discuss other personal development topics since this may be the final seminar of the series. In closing, provide recognition of individual accomplishments where due, and a challenge for continued good sales performance.

BIBLIOGRAPHY

For additional reading on selling, consider the books listed below. Each differs in purpose, content, vantage point, and style. Selective review of all or parts of several books can further your understanding of the problems and skills of selling.

Carney, G. J. *Managing a Sales Territory.* New York: AMACOM, 1971.

Edlund, S. *There Is a Better Way to Sell.* New York: AMACOM, 1973.

Grief, E. C. *Personal Salesmanship.* Reston, Va: Reston Publishing, 1974.

Hanan, M., Cribbin, J., and Berrian, H. *Sales Negotiation Strategies,* New York: AMACOM, 1977.

Harrison, J. F. *Profitable Self Management for Salesmen.* Englewood Cliffs, N.J.: Prentice-Hall, 1972.

Kirkpatrick, C. A. *Salesmanship* (4th ed.). Cincinnati: Southwestern Publishing, 1966.

Ling, M. *How to Increase Sales and Put Yourself Across by Telephone.* Englewood Cliffs, N.J.: Prentice-Hall, 1963.

Marsh, U. *Salesmanship: Modern Principles and Practices.* Englewood Cliffs, N.J.: Prentice-Hall, 1972.

Micali, P. *Hot Button Salesmanship.* Homewood, Ill.: Dow Jones-Irwin, 1975.

Pederson, C. A., and Wright, M. D. *Selling Principles and Methods* (6th ed.). Homewood, Ill.: Richard D. Irwin, 1976.

Roth, C. B. *Secrets of Closing Sales* (4th ed.). Englewood Cliffs, N.J.: Prentice-Hall, 1976.

Smith, A. P. *Complete Guide to Selling Intangibles.* West Nyack, N.Y.: Parker Publishing, 1971.

Whiting, P. H. *The Five Great Rules of Selling.* New York: McGraw-Hill, 1957.

Whitney, R. A., Hubin, T., and Murphy, J. D. *The New Psychology of Persuasion.* Englewood Cliffs, N.J.: Prentice-Hall, 1975.

INDEX

acceptance, assuming of, 87
advertisements, selling and, 132–133
American economy, growth of, 5
American life, freedom of choice in, 6
antitrust laws, 162–164
Aristotle, 75
"asking for the order," 89–90

benefits
  coding of for customer appeal, 35
  in idea selling, 84–86
  inventory of, 218–219
  translation of features to, 28–30
  see also features and benefits
"blue sky" benefits, 217
business enterprise, "serving" function of, 12–13
buying, selling as related to, 72–73
buying motives, 71–74

card file, of objections, 121–122
career sales person, 14–15
chalkboards, in visual presentations, 135
charts and graphs, 134
claims
  coping with, 123–128
  technique for handling, 125–128
  see also complaints
Clayton Act, 163
college, financing of, 10
commercial transactions, laws governing, 160–162, 236
communication
  nature of, 48–50
  in professional selling, 17
communication barriers, 49–62
communication skills, 49–64
company history, as product knowledge, 39–40
competition
  attitudes toward, 147
  competing with, 147–167
  disparagement of, 150
  favorable differences in, 151

competition (*Continued*)
  genesis of selling function
      and, 148–149
  misrepresentation and, 162
  and need for selling, 149
  price, *see* price competition
  Uniform Commercial Code
      and, 160–162
competitive buying decisions,
      153–154
competitive products
  analysis of, 220
  knowledge of, 37–39
competitive selling
  advantages of, 150–152
  goodwill in, 152
  strategy and tactics in, 149–
      155
competitor, performance of,
      151–152
complaints, 94–108
  causes of, 124–125
  coping with, 123–128
  defined, 97
  handling of, 125–128
  investigation of, 126
  liability in, 125
  prompt action on, 125–126
  solution of, 127–128
computerized sales records, 206
consumer protection laws, 165
Cooper, Peter, 7
creative selling, 18–20
  acquiring skills in, 19
  see also professional selling
credit policies, administration
      of, 202
current customer needs, 12
customer, unburdening of, 125–
      126
  see also prospect

customer credit considerations,
      201–204
customer resistance, 94–108
  see also sales resistance
customer services, list of, 221

"deaf ear" barrier, 57–58
decisive action, asking for, 86–
      91
demonstrations
  advantages of, 138
  conducting of, 140
  preparation for, 139–140, 234
  reaping reward of, 140–141
  see also sales presentations
Dewey, John, 174
display-and-explain tactics, 233

economic growth, 5, 11–13
Edison, Thomas A., 6, 12–13
experience, learning through,
      232

fair deal, in professional selling,
      17
Fair Trade Acts, 163–164
features and benefits
  advantages in, 26
  cause-and-effect relationship
      in, 28–30
  commodities and, 36
  in product knowledge, 23–30
features and benefits inventory,
      33–35, 218–219
Federal Trade Commission Act,
      163
feedback, as communication
      tool, 56–57, 151

F.O.B. price, 157
Ford, Henry, 6
freedom of choice, 6
friendly persuasion, 66–67

General Motors Corp., 179
Golden Rule, sales resistance and, 101
guaranteed price, 158

idea selling, 74–91, 223–230
  "asking for decisive action" in, 86–91
  asking for order in, 89–90
  assuming acceptance in, 87–88
  benefits of proposal in, 84–86
  choice in, 88–89
  convincing prospect in, 81–84
  examples of, 69, 78–91
  origins of, 74–76
  practice in, 223
  prospect's interest in, 76–79
  sales proposal in, 80–81
  specifics of, 76–91
  steps in, 76–91
indifference and inertia, in sales resistance, 98–100
insincere objections, real reasons for, 106–109
  see also objections
interest, stimulation of, 76–79

Kettering, Charles, 179

learning exercises, 215–245
legal aspects, commercial code and, 160–162, 236

Lincoln, Abraham, 101
listening, objections and, 110–111
listening barrier, 52
list price, defined, 157

McCormick, Robert, 7
McGuire Fair Trade Act, 163–164
market economy, selling and, 13–14
masquerade barrier, 58–59
master planning, 208
misrepresentation, 162
moderator, preparation by, 3–4

net price, defined, 157
new customers, prospecting for, 198–199, 244

objection/answer reference file, 231
objections, 94–128, 231, 242
  A-B-C technique in, 117
  acknowledging of, 117–118
  agreement with, 114–115
  anticipating of, 120–122
  card file for, 121–122
  commitment and, 116–117
  coping with, 103–123
  counterbalancing of, 117–118
  defined, 104
  direct denial of, 119
  forestalling of, 120–121
  genuine, 105
  guidelines for handling of, 110–113
  insincere, 105–106

objections (*Continued*)
  listening to, 110–111
  meeting and handling of, 110–113
  motivations for, 107
  new ideas and, 114–115
  paraphrase of, 111–112
  postponing of response to, 118–119
  preparing for, 121
  price, *see* price objections
  rephrasing of, 111–113
  special techniques for, 113–120
  see also complaints
objectives, sales, 96–97, 172–177, 231, 237, 241
order, asking for, 89–90

peddlers, as salesmen, 8
personal development, 195–214
personality barriers, 53–54
persuasion, 65–93
  business-related buying motives and, 71–72
  customer buying and, 70–74
  sales presentations in, 91–92
  see also idea selling
planning
  master, 208
  productive, 205
  time for, 207
plans
  formulation of, 243–244
  types of, 206–207
  working, 204–208
postsale functions, 67–68
presentations, sales, *see* sales presentations
price
  types of, 156–158

vs. value, 153–154
price competition, coping with, 152–155
  see also competition
price objections
  coping with, 122–123
  prevention of, 154
  see also objections
pricing
  anatomy of, 155–166
  high, 154–155
  proficiency in, 158
primary goal, establishing of, 241
  see also objectives
primary sales objectives, sales results and, 191–192
private enterprise, primary functions of, 9–20
problem selling, 238–240
  alternative courses in, 184–186
  appraisal of sales situation in, 178–182
  complexity of, 177–178
  contributory sales objectives in, 182–183
  findings and plans in, 178
  four skills in, 169
  implementing of actions in, 188–191
  for new product, 180–181
  outline for, 183, 185, 187
  particulars in, 178–192
  primary sales objective in, 191–192
  reflective thinking and, 174
  relative merits and results of alternatives in, 186–188
  sales objectives and, 172–177
  sales plans in, 190–191
  as selling skill, 168–194

seven steps in, 193
"thinking through" process in, 177
problem-solving idea, selling of, 66–70
problem-solving process, origins of, 174–176
product development background, as product knowledge, 40
product knowledge
  advantages in, 26
  company history as, 39–40
  competitive position in, 41
  of competitive products, 37–39
  confidence and, 45
  customer wants and needs in, 27–28
  enthusiasm in, 45–46
  features and benefits in, 23–30
  information supportive to, 39–44
  kinds of, 22–26, 45–46
  prestige and personal satisfaction in, 48
  in professional selling, 16, 21–46
  product development as, 40
  "right things" in, 30–32
  sales supportive services in, 41–44
  sources of, 32–35
  summary of, 44–46
products, types of, 21–22
product samples, 131–132
professional selling
  basic concepts in, 15–17
  communication in, 17
  communication skills in, 49–64
  "fair exchange" in, 17
  features and benefits in, 17
  product knowledge in, 21–46
  service-oriented, 16
prospect
  finding of, 21
  stimulation of interest in, 76–79
  see also customer
prospect file, 199–200
prospecting information, sources of, 200

real estate selling, problem solving in, 69
recession, inflation and, 2
rehearsals, of sales presentations, 92–93
Robinson-Patman Act, 163
Royal Bank of Canada Monthly Letter, 12–13, 24

sales barriers, 224
sales communication, see communication; communication barriers; communication skills
sales complaints, see complaints
sales literature, in presentations, 135–136
sales manager, training responsibilities of, viii
salesmanship, fundamental principles of, viii
sales objections, see objections
sales objectives, 96–97, 171–177, 182–183, 191–192, 231, 237, 241
sales person
  as agent, 159–160

sales person (*Continued*)
  as credit representative, 202–204
  as manager, 170–171
sales plan, 243
  master territory, 245
  see also planning; plans
sales presentations
  appeal of, 129–146
  display and explanation in, 130–131
  demonstrations in, 137–141
  planner for, 145–146
  planning of, 234–235
  rehearsals of, 92–93
  reinforcing of appeal in, 129–146
  showmanship in, 141–146
sales problems
  external, 171–172
  internal, 171
  multifaceted, 173–174
  nature of, 171–172
  "thinking through" in, 177
  see also problem solving
sales proposal, in idea selling, 80
  see also sales presentations
sales records, computerized, 206
sales resistance, 95–97
  coping with, 97, 103
  friendship and trust in, 101–102
  Golden Rule and, 101
  inertia and indifference in, 98–100
  reinforcing of, 100–101
  self-identity and, 102–103
  see also customer resistance
sales talks
  practice in, 234
  product samples and, 131–132

visual props for, 131–136
sales territory
  improvement of, 245
  management of, 196–198, 245
sales training program
  cost effectiveness and, vii
  group participation in, 2–4
  moderator's role in, 3
  sales manager and, viii
self-development, continuation of, 212–214
selling
  antitrust laws on, 162–165
  buying motives in, 70–74
  changing image of, 7–8
  competitive, *see* competitive selling
  creative, *see* creative selling
  of ideas, *see* idea selling
  as key social and economic function, 8–9
  legal aspects of, 159–166, 236
  market economy and, 13–14
  nature of, 5–20
  persuasion in, 65–93
  phases in, 65–68
  postsale functions in, 67–68
  preparation in, 66
  professional, *see* professional selling
  self-development and, 1–2
  as sustaining force of private enterprise, 10–11
  as trigger for economic growth, 11–13
selling skills
  improvement in, 213–214
  product knowledge and, 21–46
semantic barriers, 54–57
service, professional selling and, 16

Sherman Antitrust Act, 163
showmanship, 141–146
   applied, 143–144
   defined, 141–142
   imagination and, 142
   precautions relating to, 144–146
situation barriers, 50–53
success, "freedom of choice" in, 195–196

telephone, as selling tool, 211–212
territory management, 194–214
   defined, 196
   functions of, 197–198
territory plan, 245
testimonials, in sales presentations, 134–135
test reports, in sales presentations, 134–135
time, in planning, 207
time leaks, remedies for, 210–211

time management, 208–212
"too busy" syndrome, 209
training, see sales training program

unethical buyer, 166–167
Unfair Trade Practices Acts, 163
Uniform Commercial Code, 160–162

vendible products, 21
visual sales aids, 132–136

Westinghouse, George, 6
Wheeler-Lea Act, 163
work, planning for, 204–208
writing
   as barrier or opportunity, 59–62
   goals in, 60–61

zone price, 158